The Super Radiance effect
A new technology for national invincibility and international peace

Jeremy Old
Natural Health Research Trust

The Super Radiance effect

Copyright© Jeremy Old

All rights reserved. No part of this publication may be reproduced, stored in a retrieval system, or transmitted, in any form or by any means, electronic, mechanical, photocopying, recording or otherwise, without the prior permission of the publisher.

Published by Team Business Development Ltd
**On behalf of Natural Health Research Trust and the
World Peace Group**
UK charity registration number 1024407

40 Wimborne St Giles, Near Wimborne,
Dorset, BH21 5NF
V2
www.worldpeacegroup.org

Published September 2015, revised April 2017

SBN 978-0-9929104-2-6

The Super Radiance effect

Contents

Preface		13
Introduction		17
1.	The origins of Super Radiance	17
2.	The role of meditation in creating world peace	21
3.	Why politicians, government officials, and the media have yet to recognise the potential of Super Radiance	27
4.	World peace is now within our grasp	37
Chapter 1: Field-research summaries		41
Summary 1.	Improved quality of city life through the Transcendental Meditation program: Decreased crime rate.	41
Summary 2.	Influence of the Transcendental Meditation Programme on crime rate in suburban Cleveland.	46
Summary 3.	The growth of coherence in society through the Maharishi Effect: Reduced rates of suicides and auto accidents.	48
Summary 4.	The Transcendental Meditation Programme and crime rate change in a sample of forty-eight cities.	53
Summary 5.	The Transcendental Meditation Programme and a compound probability model as predictors of crime rate change.	55
Summary 6.	The Transcendental Meditation Programme and crime rate change: A causal analysis.	57
Summary 7.	Maharishi's Global Ideal Society Campaign: Improved quality of life in Rhode Island through the Transcendental Meditation and TM-Sidhi program.	59

Summary 8.	An experimental analysis of the application of the Maharishi Technology of the Unified Field in major world trouble spots: Increased harmony in international affairs.	63
Summary 9.	The Maharishi Technology of the Unified Field and improved quality of life in the United States: A study of the First World Peace Assembly, Amherst, Massachusetts, 1979.	71
Summary 10.	Effect of coherent collective consciousness on the weather.	73
Summary 11.	Sociological effects of the group dynamics of consciousness: Decrease of crime and traffic accidents in Holland.	75
Summary 12.	The effect of the group dynamics of consciousness on society: Reduced crime in the Union Territory of Delhi, India.	79
Summary 13.	A time series analysis of the effect of the Maharishi Technology of the Unified Field: Reduction of traffic fatalities in the United States.	81
Summary 14.	Reduction in homicide in Washington DC through the Maharishi Technology of the Unified Field, 1980-83: A time series analysis.	84
Summary 15.	The effect of the Maharishi Technology of the Unified Field on stock prices of Washington, DC area based corporations, 1980-83: A time series analysis.	86
Summary 16.	The group dynamics of consciousness and the U.K. stock market.	88
Summary 17.	The Maharishi Technology of the Unified Field and reduction of armed conflict: A comparative, longitudinal study of Lebanese villages.	89
Summary 18.	The long-term effects of the Maharishi Technology of the Unified Field on the quality of life in the United States (1960 to 1983).	92

Summary 19.	International peace project in the Middle East: The effect of the Maharishi Technology of the Unified Field.	96
Summary 20.	A time series analysis of the relationship between the group practice of the Transcendental Meditation and TM-Sidhi Programme and crime rate change in Puerto Rico.	99
Summary 21.	The effect of the Maharishi Technology of the Unified Field on the war in Lebanon: A time series analysis of the influence of international and national coherence creating assemblies.	100
Summary 22.	The effect of the 'Taste of Utopia' Assembly on the world index of international stock prices.	102
Summary 23.	The influence of the Maharishi Technology of the Unified Field on world events and global social indicators: The effects of the 'Taste of Utopia' Assembly.	104
Summary 24.	A comparative study of dimensions of healthy functioning between families practising the TM programme for five years or for less than a year.	112
Summary 25.	Consciousness as a field: the Transcendental Meditation and TM-Sidhi Programme and changes in social indicators.	113
Summary 26.	Test of a field model of consciousness and social change: the Transcendental Meditation and TM-Sidhi Programme and decreased urban crime.	116
Summary 27.	Time series analysis of U.S. and Canadian inflation and unemployment: a test of a field-theoretic hypothesis.	118
Summary 28.	Simultaneous transfer function analysis of Okun's misery index: improvements in the economic quality of life through Maharishi's Vedic Science and technology of consciousness.	120
Summary 29.	A multiple-input transfer function model of Okun's misery index: an empirical test of the Maharishi Effect.	123

Summary 30.	Consciousness and the quality of economic life: empirical research on the macroeconomic effects of the collective practice of Maharishi's Transcendental Meditation and TM-Sidhi program.	125
Summary 31.	Test of a field theory of consciousness and social change: time series analysis of participation in the TM-Sidhi Programme and reduction of violent deaths in the USA.	126
Summary 32.	Change in the quality of life in Canada: intervention studies of the effect of the Transcendental Meditation and TM-Sidhi program.	129
Summary 33.	Creating world peace through the collective practice of the Maharishi Technology of the Unified Field: improved U.S.-Soviet relations.	133
Summary 34.	Alleviating political violence through enhancing coherence in collective consciousness: impact assessment analysis of the Lebanon war.	134
Summary 35.	Time series impact assessment analysis of reduced international conflict and terrorism: Effects of large assemblies of participants in the Transcendental Meditation and TM-Sidhi program.	137
Summary 36.	Time series analysis of improved quality of life in Canada: Social change, collective consciousness, and the TM-Sidhi program.	140
Summary 37.	The dynamics of US-Soviet relations, 1979-1986: Effects of reducing social stress through the Transcendental Meditation and TM-Sidhi program.	141
Summary 38.	The effects of the Maharishi Technology of the Unified Field: Reply to a methodological critique.	143
Summary 39.	Improved quality of life in Iowa through the Maharishi Effect.	144
Summary 40.	The Maharishi Effect (Super Radiance effect): A model for social improvement: Time series analysis of a phase	145

	transition to reduce crime in Merseyside metropolitan area.	
Summary 41.	Results of the national demonstration project to reduce violent crime and improve governmental effectiveness in Washington, D.C.	149
Summary 42.	The Peace and Well Being of Nations: An Analysis of Improved Quality of Life and Enhanced Economic Performance Through the Maharishi Effect in New Zealand, Norway. A Longitudinal, Cross-Country, Panel-Regression Analysis of the IMD Index of National Competitive Advantage.	154
Summary 43.	Case study on the impact on the quality of life in Cambodia due to the Maharishi effect.	158
Summary 44.	Mozambique transformation case study.	161
Summary 45.	Preventing terrorism and international conflict: Effects of large assemblies of participants in the Transcendental Meditation and TM-Sidhi programs.	168
Summary 46.	Alleviating political violence through reducing collective tension: Impact assessment analyses of the Lebanon war.	174
Summary 47.	Societal Violence and Collective Consciousness: Reduction of U.S. Homicide and Urban Violent Crime Rates	176
Summary 48	The Contribution of Proposed Field Effects of Consciousness to the Prevention of US Accidental Fatalities: Theory and Empirical Tests	186
Summary 49	Group practice of the Transcendental Meditation and TM-Sidhi program and reductions in infant mortality and drug-related death: A quasi-experimental analysis	190

Chapter 2: Laboratory research 195

Summary 50.	Can time series analysis of serotonin turnover test the theory that consciousness is a field?	195

Summary 51.	Inter-subject EEG coherence: Is consciousness a field?	196
Summary 52.	Field model of consciousness: EEG coherence changes as indicators of field effects.	198
Summary 53.	Effect of group practice of the Transcendental Meditation program on biochemical indicators of stress in non-meditators: A prospective time series study.	199

Chapter 3: Is the research reliable?   201

Chapter 4: Published Super Radiance research   209

Chapter 5: What is Transcendental Meditation?   217

Chapter 6: Contrast in meditation techniques   221

The Super Radiance effect

The Super Radiance effect

Preface

A worldwide group of loosely affiliated individuals and organisations are quietly creating the ground conditions for world peace through a natural phenomenon called the **'Super Radiance'** effect.

The term Super Radiance denotes the positive and immediate impact that small groups of specially trained meditators, known as TM-Sidhas have on open warfare, terrorism, political violence, crime levels and other symptoms of social disorder.

In this book I summarise, in more or less chronological order, the course of fifty-three studies into Super Radiance undertaken over about thirty years in a variety of countries across all continents. Together these studies prove beyond a shadow of doubt the practical potential for the Super Radiance effect to establish national security for any nation and international peace

Highlights from different research projects include:

- A reduction in global terrorist activity of 72% during three different peace projects

- A drop in war deaths of 81% during the Rhodesian (now Zimbabwe) civil war and a 71% drop in war deaths during the civil war in the Lebanon

- Increased international cooperation by 352% during a brief global peace project according to 'Conflict and Peace Data Bank' statistics (COPDAB)

- Cessation of open warfare in Nicaragua, Mozambique and the Lebanon during different Super Radiance projects

- 24% comparative drop in crime trends in a five-year study of 48 US cities

- 4% improvement in a composite Quality of Life (QOL) index composed of eight variable factors including crime rate, mortality rate, unemployment, and auto accidents over a three-month study period

- Transformation of economic progress in six different countries including the elimination of hyper-inflation, the reversal of stagflation, liquidation of national debt and a significant reduction in unemployment

I have written the summaries for the layperson, so as to enable access to a wider readership. Otherwise, for those readers who are intent on a deeper study, you will find that much of the research that follows has been published in peer-reviewed journals or presented to academic conferences (See chapter-six for a schedule of published works). For this purpose, I have headed each research summary with the original author's research title and also included the author's name. If the study has been published in an academic journal, I have listed the name of the publication.

You will see that nearly all of the studies are available in the *'Collected Papers of the Scientific Research on Maharishi's Transcendental Meditation and TM-Sidhi Program volumes 1 – 6'*. As indicated by the title, the Collected Papers comprise research studies carried out since the 1960s on Transcendental Meditation and its more advanced version, the TM-Sidhi meditation programme.

The studies on Super Radiance form only a small portion of the work in these volumes of collected papers on meditation. But even so collectively they add up to more than 430,000 words. The remaining 550 or more studies in these volumes are focussed on the physiological, psychological and neurological influence of this particular meditation technique.

The Super Radiance effect

The Super Radiance effect

Introduction

1. The origins of Super Radiance

2. The role of meditation in creating world peace

3. Why politicians, government officials, and the media have not yet recognised the potential of Super Radiance

4. World peace is now within our grasp

1. The origins of Super Radiance

"I had one thing in mind, that I know something which is useful to every man" His Holiness Maharishi Mahesh Yogi

Despite the innumerable and intractable problems confronting humanity to day, the fact is that the world has been transformed in just over half a century. Looking at our immediate troubles such as global terrorism, the conflicts in the Middle East and Afghanistan or the recent economic downturn, it is difficult to remember that back in the nineteen-fifties, the whole of mankind was facing a looming disaster that dwarfs the scale of our current predicament.

The first half of the 20th century had already seen two unprecedented and catastrophic world wars. Hundreds of millions of lives had been violently terminated in a bloodletting unparalleled in history. Far from seeing the end of war and tyranny as hoped, the post Second World War period saw much of humanity further embroiled in ruthless cold war rivalry between colossal super powers. At the same time a billion or more people lay crushed under the grinding yoke of tyrannical ideologies both in the Soviet empire and in communist China.

But that was not all, the combination of mass-produced weaponry at an incomparable scale and the proliferation of powerful new technologies threatened to wreak imminent obliteration upon the whole planet. People everywhere lived on a knife-edge. There was a real prospect that nuclear annihilation was literally only minutes away.

Very quietly and almost unseen this dire state of circumstances has mercifully slipped away from us. Undoubtedly there are still many problems too numerous to mention here. But today's problems are hardly on the same scale or at the same level of urgency or intensity as in the immediate post Second World War era. So, what has happened to precipitate this change?

At that darkest of times, what was badly needed was a new evolutionary force, a big new organising principle to counter the negative balance of the seemingly overwhelming tendencies threatening the very life of our planet. Through the medium of some fascinating scientific research projects, this report tells the story of how this new organising principle emerged and is still now transforming mankind's destiny from darkness and chaos to one of light and order.

A new organising principle emerges

Aham Brahmasmi – I am the totality

"The collective consciousness of the whole universe is in one's own single awareness"

Maharishi Mahesh Yogi.

In 1958, the need of the time brought His Holiness Maharishi Mahesh Yogi[1] out from his silent retreat in the Himalayas. From the very start Maharishi's mission was to bring about a planetary transformation from chaos, oppression and destruction to peace and prosperity.

Maharishi's chosen method to achieve this end was to initiate a worldwide spiritual regeneration. He set out to raise the consciousness of humanity to a level where it would be impossible for people

---

[1] In India the title 'Rishi' is bestowed upon a person who sees the truth about creation. A 'Maharishi' (literally - Great Rishi) is recognised as one of those rare beings who not only sees the truth but also enlivens it in everyone else. In the ancient Vedic tradition of India they see a Maharishi as a sage who has the special ability to teach others to rise to his own level of experience of the unity of creation and of a life of perpetual heaven on earth. Heaven on earth in this context means all good to everyone and non-good to no one.

to even think of hating, harming and fighting one another.

But unlike other spiritual teachers who from time to time have emerged from the East, Maharishi wasn't just delivering a message of inner peace and enlightenment to a few mystically inclined individuals. Instead what he proposed was an easy and practical method for everyone to achieve his or her full potential, attain real happiness and experience deep fulfilment.

Within every human being is an unlimited reservoir of energy, intelligence, and happiness

Maharishi emphasised that within every human being is an unlimited reservoir of energy, intelligence, and happiness. He explained that spiritual enlightenment entailed the effortless ability to spontaneously access this potential to the benefit of not just the enlightened one but also the wider community.

Maharishi even went so far as to declare that the desire to achieve higher states of consciousness (enlightenment) represented the most practical option available for anyone wanting to live a useful and happy life.

Again, in contrast to many other spiritual masters from the East, he saw that achieving enlightenment was compatible with the day-to-day living of the ordinary householder. Effectively, Maharishi offered us the unique reassurance that, with this knowledge, a life in enlightenment was available to anybody with a human nervous system.

Maharishi's consistent message for fifty years was that when enough people had taken up this life, then heaven would reign on earth.

"If you want a green forest you must grow green trees".

In essence Maharishi revived the ancient understanding of Vedic Science[2] that the infinite potential of the mind can be nourished and developed with

---

[2] Vedic Science is literally the science of Veda. Veda is an ancient Sanskrit term that means pure knowledge. Pure knowledge means the knowledge of the unmanifest, all-powerful, self-referral, immortal, infinitely dynamic field of pure consciousness. This knowledge is pure because it is uncontaminated from anything from outside itself. Essentially pure knowledge or Veda is knowledge or comprehension of the infinite. But this knowledge is

the naturalness of what he originally called deep meditation. It was through this fundamentally practical route that benefits would accrue not just to the individual but to the rest of society as well.

His principle here was that we could only have a peaceful society if the individuals within society were peaceful themselves. As he liked to put it 'if you want a green forest you must grow green trees'.

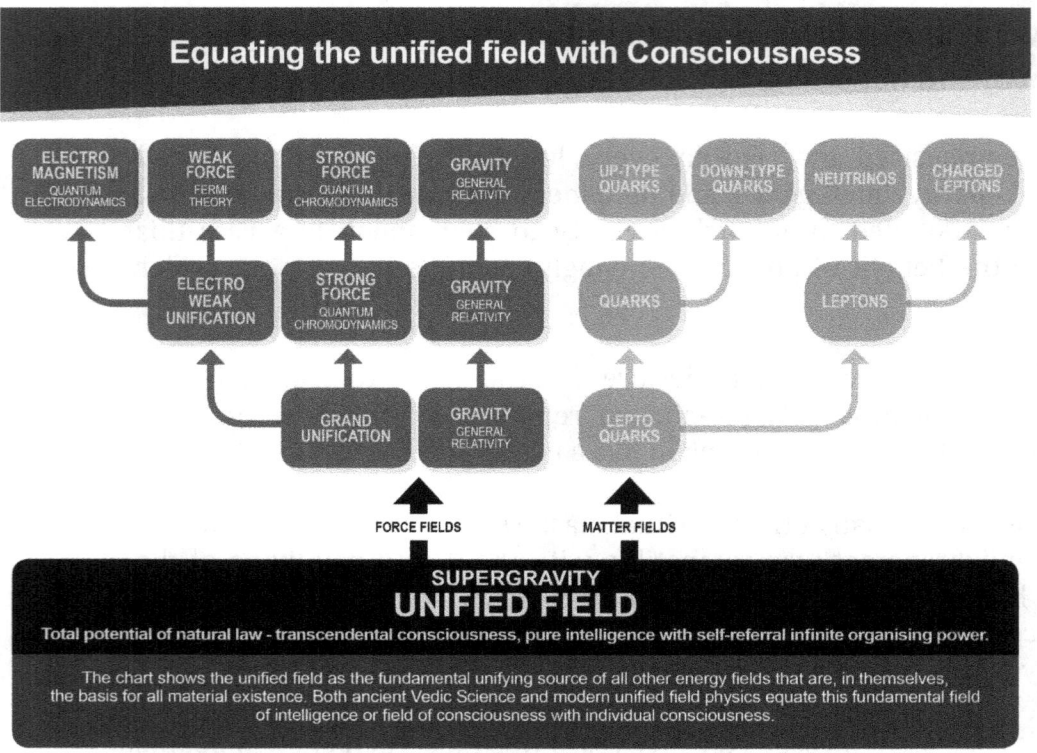

A key understanding of Vedic Science is that there is a reciprocal relationship between a person's consciousness and the collective consciousness of that same person's host group. Both interact fluidly with each other just as drops of water interact to form an ocean. As such, consciousness or our awareness is not just a product of our human nervous

---

not just an abstract intellectual construct. The supreme practical value of this knowledge is the understanding that human awareness can identify itself with this most basic, self-referral value of consciousness in the state of Samadhi, or transcendental consciousness. This state of consciousness is easily attained and enjoyed entirely naturally through the pleasant practice of regular daily Transcendental Meditation (See chapter 5 and 6).

system but is an integral part of an all-embracing fundamental field of intelligence.

Maharishi's Vedic science sees the un-manifest, unbounded, all pervading field of pure intelligence as the root cause of all the expressions of nature including the human physiology and of course the human nervous system. Incidentally, this view is increasingly supported by unified field theories in modern physics. Such theories recognise that the unified field, being a field of infinite intelligence is the most basic level of both individual and collective life (See chart above).

2. The role of meditation in creating world peace

This is why meditation has such an important role to play in creating a more peaceful society.

During deep meditation, the meditator experiences profound and blissful states of consciousness and as such taps into or integrates more clearly with this universal field of pure intelligence. When this integration happens, the profound inner peace experienced by the meditator is naturally transmitted spontaneously to the outer environment as well. This intimate connection between the individual and the host group is why Maharishi emphasised that the peace of the individual is the prerequisite of world peace.

But his global mission to create world peace confronted Maharishi with a serious challenge. How was he going to teach millions of people to meditate?

For generations previously, the technique of deep meditation had only been passed down from master to disciple on a one to one basis. Initiation into the mystery of meditation was given only after the disciple had showed deservedness after years of work, devotion and service to the master. Maharishi's novel solution not only enabled him to teach millions of people to meditate but also laid the foundation for systematic scientific research.

Meditation that is practical, consistent, measurable and predictable

In line with his core principle that a spiritual life is the most practical life, Maharishi began developing a systemised method of teaching deep meditation from very early on after his arrival in the West. This systemisation enabled him to train teachers so that meditation could be taught to others on a massive scale previously undreamt of.

The outcome of this development was the technique of **Transcendental Meditation** or TM as it is usually shortened to. Essentially, TM not only retains the advantages of the ancient Vedic system of deep meditation cherished by the spiritual masters, recluses and hermits of the Himalayas but also enables the practitioner to integrate this sublime practice into their daily life of work, career, family responsibilities and community activity.

Maharishi's rigorous focus on what we might now call 'quality control' meant that the teaching and practice of TM became essentially practical, reliable and replicable. These three qualities led to two other radical departures from tradition.

Firstly, the replicable nature of TM teaching opened up the possibility of thousands of highly trained professional teachers being able to teach whole swathes of society to meditate. So far over six million people have learned TM worldwide and more are learning everyday.

Secondly, the consistency of the TM method, its susceptibility to exact measurement and the predictability of results laid the foundations for a unique body of scientific study into the mechanics and benefits of meditation. The replicable nature of TM teaching also enhanced this research opportunity. As teaching activity expanded initially in America and then across the globe, so millions of new meditators provided large-scale samples for the study of a wide range of benefits using a variety of study methods. Not the least part of this future research was to be the extensive study of the collective effect of TM and later on research into the more advanced form of meditation known as the TM-Sidhi programme.

The 1% effect – A new dimension to the benefits of meditation

As early as 1960, after successful teaching initiatives especially in the USA, Maharishi was able to announce a profound new dimension to the understanding of the benefits of meditation. He made the prediction that when 1% of a given population had taken up the practise of Transcendental Meditation there would be a substantial improvement to the quality of life in that whole society.

Amazing though it seemed at the time, Maharishi's prediction appeared to be validated when, in 1974, research scientists discovered that 1% of the population in several towns in the USA had learned the TM technique. And sure enough in those same towns the crime rate, often seen as an indicator of social wellbeing, seemed to be dropping.

This first research study indicated pretty clearly that the 1% effect claim was valid.

Briefly, what seemed to be happening was that as soon as 1% of a town's population started to practice TM then that community experienced a sudden sea change in the trend of social behaviour from negativity to positivity. This change was quite easily identified by publicly available measures that showed reductions in crime and violence. In later studies, researchers observed excellent results from a range of other social indicators monitoring both positive and negative collective behaviour.

The initial crime research project inspired a stream of other studies, as more and more opportunities arose to explore and further reinforce the exciting theory that here was an easy and quick formula to create a more orderly and peaceful society.

From that time on, the 1% effect became known as the 'Maharishi effect'. This name of course was in deference to Maharishi himself who, had not only predicted the phenomenon fourteen years before, but had worked for so long and so tirelessly to achieve it.

The square root of 1% effect

But even more incredible news was yet to come.

As though the 1% effect wasn't incredible enough, Maharishi made another prediction in the mid 1970s when he introduced his meditators to the more advanced TM-Sidhi meditation programme. This time he asserted that the power of this new programme was such that when a group of this type of meditators (known as TM-Sidhas) meditate together at the same time, they only need enough participants equivalent to the _square root of 1%_ of a given population in order to create the same effect as the Maharishi effect or 1% effect. This new capability became known as the 'Extended Maharishi effect' or 'Super Radiance' effect. The term 'Super Radiance' is used due to the analogous effect of coherent light waves in lasers.

Maharishi explains that, at the precise point that a group of TM-Sidhas achieve Super Radiance, the enhanced individual brainwave coherence they experience during their group meditations begin to influence the brainwave coherence of the entire non-meditating population. This meditating influence is transmitted through the underlying field of consciousness, the unified field, and has the effect of reducing stress in the collective consciousness of a society. As stress is reduced in the collective consciousness so stressed driven thinking, stress driven decision-making and stress driven behaviour begins to evaporate among the local inhabitants.

This means that whenever a TM-Sidha group reaches the square root of 1% of a given population there is an immediate (The effect starts to happen within 24 hours.) and dramatic reduction of hostility and violence within the host community. At the same time the community experiences a boost in creative activity and positivity. In other words just a tiny few highly coherent brains help create a more coherent society. When a society is coherent it enables the many diverse and complex social systems to operate together in an integrated way that is conducive to the positive evolution of all of them.

As with the Maharishi effect, the sudden and sometimes dramatic change in a society is easily monitored in publicly available statistics. You will see from the research summaries in this book that studies record reduced armed conflict, reduced terrorism, reduced war deaths, decreased crime rates, less emergency calls, less suicides and fatal accidents even less alcohol and cigarette consumption. In the economic arena, whenever Super Radiance occurs, there are suddenly more patent applications, improved stock indices (share prices), and this feeds through to higher employment rates, higher economic growth rates, lower inflation and so on.

One important feature of the Super Radiance effect is that the larger the group the more disproportionate the impact. The larger the group of TM-Sidhas, the wider the effect stretches. This key factor has huge implications for the creation of a more orderly and peaceful international society. So for instance to produce the Super Radiance effect, for a country the size of the UK with a population of 62 million all that is needed is about 790 TM-Sidhas meditating together in one place all at the same time. To create Super Radiance for the USA with a population nearly five times bigger than the UK we need just over twice as many TM-Sidhas. In fact the US needs roughly 1,770 TM-Sidhas.

8,400 trained meditators can create permanent peace on earth

And for the whole world of seven billion people we only require a group of about 8,400 TM-Sidhas. A permanent group of this number will bring about an immediate and sustained cessation of warfare, terrorism, and political and criminal violence across the entire globe. In other words although the world's population is 112 times bigger than the UK's we only need to bring a group together that is eleven times bigger than required for UK Super Radiance. And although the world's population is 22 times larger than the USA, we only need attract a group that is just over four and a half times bigger than that required for USA Super Radiance. This simple maths demonstrates the awe-inspiring opportunity within our grasp.

The most cost effective means to create world peace

The disproportionate impact that a Super Radiance group achieves as it grows larger means that the creation and maintenance of global Super Radiance is easily within the resources of any one of the developed nations both in terms of money and numbers of trained TM-Sidhas.

Compare the annual defence budget of the worlds leading spenders on national defence with the amount estimated to support and maintain a global Super Radiance group of 8,400 TM-Sidhas (See the chart - Which makes the world safer?). As you can see, the contrast in costs is staggering. Yet repeated research shows that only the Super Radiance group can actually guarantee the safety of any of these nations. But in addition, a global group of TM-Sidhas is capable of securing the peace and safety of all the other nations as well.

Super Radiance Comparison table

The larger the group the more disproportionate the impact

Number of Sidhas in group	Super Radiance impact (size of population effected)	Research examples (Where to look)
1	100	
2	400	
4	1,600	
10	10,000	Baskinta Village; reduction in war deaths, summary 17 (This study looked at the effect that 100 TM meditators had in a village of 10,000 people - The 1% effect rather than the $\sqrt{1}$ % effect)
100	1,000,000	Rhode Island study; summary 7
120	1,440,000	Merseyside crime rate; summary 40
245	6,000,000	New Delhi crime rate; summary 12
400	16,000,000	Holland traffic and crime study; summary 11
1,000	10,000,000	Cambodia case study; summary 43
1,800	324,000,000	USA - various studies relating to crime, traffic fatalities, violent fatalities, QOL and economic prosperity; summaries 9, 13, 27, 28, 29, 31, 47, 48, 49.
8,367	7,000,000,000	Whole world; summaries 22, 23, 35 plus summary 34 on the impact of global groups on conflicts in the Middle East

With Super Radiance nobody loses, everybody wins.

What is required, to achieve peace on earth once and for all, is for a sufficient number of people to be aware of this immense possibility and then take the personal responsibility to help make it happen. And herein lies the immediate problem.

3. Why politicians, government officials, and the media have yet to recognise the potential of Super Radiance

In addition to corroborative results from forty-seven field studies, we now have laboratory experiments that demonstrate precisely how TM-Sidhas impact the serotonin and cortisol levels of nearby non-meditators. The researchers can actually observe and measure how a group of TM-Sidhas drives down non-meditators' stress levels and precipitate a more natural and happy brain state in them. And as though this extensive research isn't enough, modern quantum physics underpins these findings by creating a coherent scientific framework that goes a long way to explain the theoretical concept of Super Radiance.

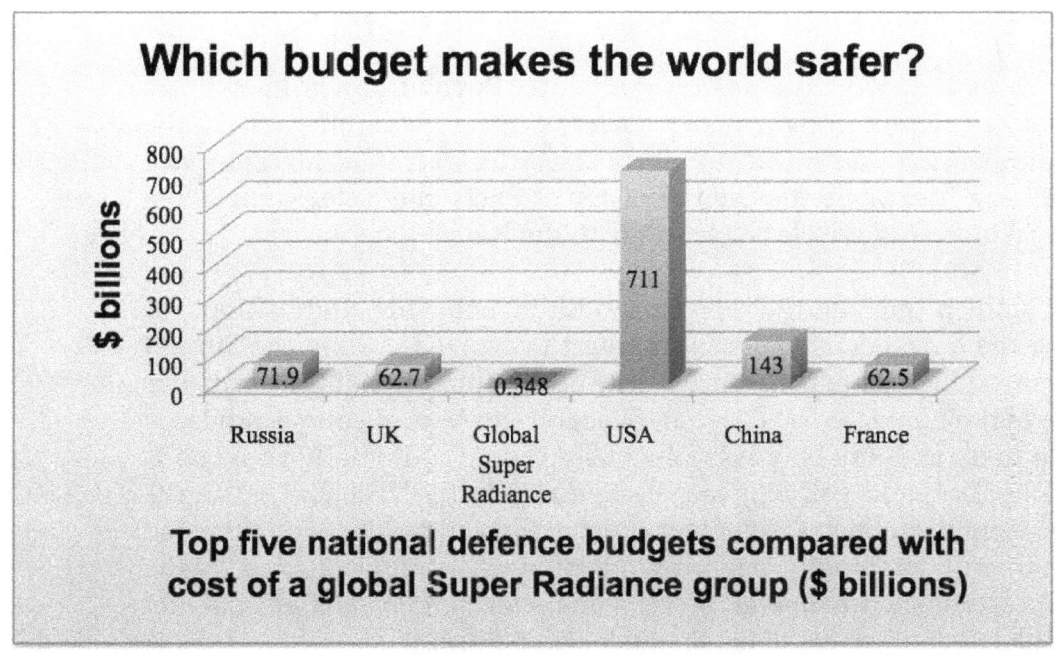

Even so, after twenty-years of this type of research being carried out, much of it published in peer reviewed academic journals and after thirty-five years of trying to get the message across about Super Radiance, governments, at least in the G20 nations, have resolutely refused to hear the message and respond constructively. The media have remained deaf to reason, as have the politicians, NGOs, think tanks, academia and government officials.

You might well think that with such an impressive track record, Super Radiance would be a household name. Anything capable of reducing terrorism must be highly sought after in the much-vaunted global war against terrorism. Surely politicians of every persuasion should be clamouring for this technology to help control the international conflagration in the Middle East and provide a fertile environment to rebuild their economies after the recent recession?

In a supposedly scientific age, this indifference or derision seems incongruous with our society's alleged values and 'rational' understanding. Scientific studies backing up the claims for Super Radiance are extensive and irrefutable, so why do politicians, governments, the media, think-tanks and most of academia stubbornly refuse to even acknowledge the research let alone do something useful to assist its introduction into society?

History tells us that we have been here before. Revolutions in knowledge take time to be accepted by a wider society. In the meantime getting the ideas a fair hearing can be an uphill task. As an example, Marconi was written off as a lunatic by the then Minister of Posts and Telegraphs when he first introduced his 'wireless telegraph' to the Italian government.

Similarly, Galileo got into a spot of bother with the Inquisition for advocating the outrageous idea that the earth revolved around the Sun. At the time most educated people were firmly of the opinion that the earth was the centre of the universe. Traditional 'Geocentrism' was of course validated by Biblical texts and any way was obviously correct. All you have to do is watch the horizon and you will see the Sun rise in the East and set in the West. The common senses reinforced the theory that the Sun revolved around the earth. Eventually science vindicated Galileo and showed up the rest of the established order as being somewhat simple minded, but not before he had spent the rest of his life under house arrest.

Well, now we have another revolution in thinking, one that once again upturns common sense perceptions that the world around us is purely material. As a technology Super Radiance offers mankind a giant leap forward in social cohesion and progress and, as is usual in these circumstances, people who really ought to know better and who are incidentally paid quite well to look after our interests are avoiding the whole issue. An inestimable technology to alleviate human suffering is being left redundant.

Why is this? Why do people reject new ideas so swiftly, even though they offer an invaluable way forward?

Fortunately modern neuroscience can come to our assistance here. The answer to this perennial puzzle can be found from new understanding about the way the human brain handles our beliefs and assimilates new information. Neuroscience now reveals why pre-existing beliefs can be a huge obstacle to the adoption of radical or counterintuitive ideas. In fact this new understanding tells us why our beliefs can also block the learning of anything significant, prevent successful problem solving, and subvert effective planning and decision-making.

How premature cognitive commitment obstructs the learning process

The obstacle to radically new ideas arises because whenever our senses pick up new evidence that conflicts with our pre-existing beliefs, a particular facet of the brain filters out this evidence before it even reaches our conscious perception. In this sense, the brain is hard-wired in a way so that we literally can't see what we don't already believe in. When this deception occurs, we make, what the psychologists term, a '**premature cognitive commitment**'. In other words we jump to a conclusion based, not on available new evidence, but on our pre-existing belief about the situation. In this context, I use the term 'belief' not in the religious sense but generically to include any pre-existing supposition, assumption, preconception, self-belief, ideology, hypothesis, theory, premise, attachments or the emotional memory of some past associated event or situation. All these sub-categories of belief are fully capable of getting in the way of us seeing the facts.

Cognitive dissonance and confirmation bias

As you can see, whenever we may be experiencing premature cognitive commitment our beliefs become seriously self-limiting. The brain seems programmed to use beliefs to help us make sense of customary situations quickly. But, sometimes this rough and ready measure is at the expense of really learning what is going on, especially when the environment we are looking at is changing. The obstruction to learning occurs because we are by nature creatures of habit, and so are comfortable with our beliefs, whereas the process of changing them or being confronted with their inadequacy can be acutely uncomfortable to us. Typically our beliefs are very dear to us, and even form part of our identity. So, new information that contradicts our existing beliefs essentially threatens our sense of meaning and even our sense of security, or of knowing whom we are (or more accurately threatening our belief as to who we are). The key factor here is that, like any other threat to our emotional needs, these acutely intimate threats to both our sense of meaning and our identity, trigger a powerful stress response.

In other words, at the point of conflict between our pre-existing belief and the contradictory facts, we become emotionally aroused, our higher rational faculties are hijacked and we slip quickly into our primeval flight or fight mode. This type of mental stress response is known as **'cognitive dissonance'**.

The relevance of cognitive dissonance to the assimilation of new information is important. In a situation where the apparent facts or evidence seem to contradict entrenched beliefs, cognitive dissonance compels us to remove the threat and reduce the pain of the dissonance. To achieve this immediate aim we do one of two things. Either we change our belief to match the revealed facts, or we try and preserve our belief by conducting what has been termed **'confirmation bias'** (sometimes known as 'myside bias'). Typically where we have been caught unawares or where we are not accustomed to having our settled worldview challenged or where we have deep-rooted attachments to our beliefs, we tend to adopt the second approach. As mentioned above, we are essentially creatures of habit, so at the moment of stress arousal, we take the easy route and go for some sort of confirmation bias.

In effect, when given the choice of either doing what is right or doing what is easy, we tend to choose the easy option. What comes easy to people is a range of less than useful learning tactics. These can include a stubborn resistance to change; a wilful misinterpretation of the facts; the denigration of evidence that contradicts our beliefs; the demonization of opposing views; the obsessive hunt for any possible evidence (however weak) to back-up our beliefs; a trancelike or oblivious denial of the situation, hysterical opposition to the alternative idea and solution; an evangelical crusade to persuade others to follow our beliefs; and the persistent advocacy of anachronistic and otherwise highly inappropriate solutions that tend to perpetuate the problems not ease them; all this as a ruse to escape the pain of adapting to new ideas and new evidence.

What is missing in the heat of this emotional reaction is the cool, calm and objective assimilation of the new ideas by our higher faculties. As at any other time when we experience stress, the stress response shuts down our higher faculties and so prevents a balanced evaluation of the facts and the development of rational judgement.

The confirmation bias process

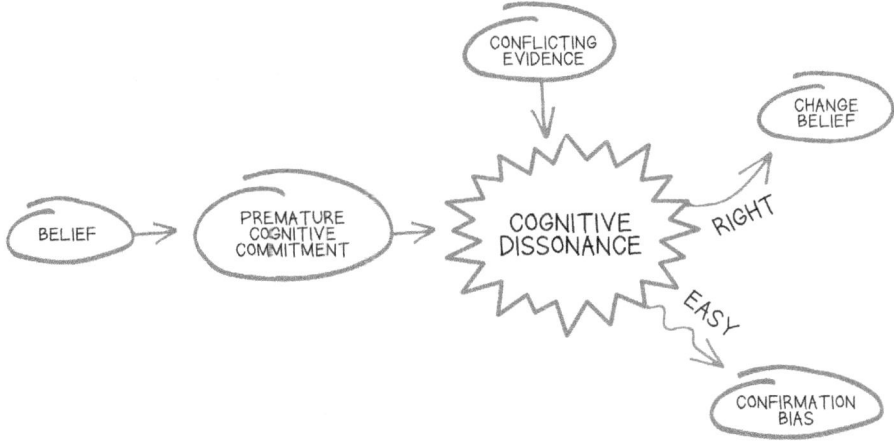

The three unwise monkeys of premature cognitive commitment, cognitive dissonance and confirmation bias are responsible for a lot of harm in society, especially in organisational and political life. In an organisational setting, this new understanding of the brain's filtering system explains why bad news moves slowly up the organisational hierarchy and is often met with disbelief by senior managers. It also explains why, senior managers often find it difficult to accept negative feedback that disrupts their settled worldview of how they are running things. Instead of working with the new information to improve the business they tend to chastise those who offer differing opinions or who expose the facts and brand them as 'whistle blowers'.

Similarly, this phenomenon accounts for the common experience of scientists, politicians and others dismissing or disregarding factual evidence when it does not meet the criteria laid down by their pre-existing beliefs, ideologies, theories and understanding.

Cognitive dissonance is the main obstacle to world peace

The significance of this phenomenon in the context of Super Radiance and world peace is therefore obvious. Most of us have been brought up with the ingrained view that the universe is a purely material phenomenon. Despite Albert Einstein and others challenging the concept of the material nature of the universe some one hundred years ago, essentially the common belief, reinforced of course on a daily basis by our common senses, is still that the universe exists within a linear time frame and is made up of bits and pieces of matter separated by vast tracts of intergalactic space. In essence the common and habitual belief is that I am in here and everything else is out there. Our intellect takes the cue from our common senses and sees us as separate to the rest of the world. Whereas the fact is that the universe is a playground of self-interacting energy and intelligence and every one of us is an integral part of it. Unfortunately, those who still hang on to their old beliefs are literally physically blocked from recognising the actuality that the widespread view of the material universe is largely an illusion of the common senses.

Propositions that contradict the established worldview are deeply threatening to people's sense of meaning, which explains the rigid resistance or simple denial to the idea of Super Radiance.

Psychology recognises that 'meaning', is an important motivational human need. Those of us who have now got used to the idea about Super Radiance have to accept that the research around it violates an important sense of meaning for many people and this of course includes scientists, academics, journalists, politicians and officials in senior positions. Violating an emotional need can quickly trigger a powerful stress response. In other words the sort of cognitive dissonance provoked by this type of situation, where the evidence conflicts directly with both the subject's belief and sense of meaning, is extremely uncomfortable. You can see that the experiencer is faced with evidence that seems to undermine the very purpose of their work, their careers, their belief in their own competence (a feeling of competence also being an emotional need) and perhaps even the fundamental validity of their organisation. As a result, the reptilian survival mechanism kicks in and it becomes far easier, quicker and simpler to ignore the evidence, carry on as usual and try and persuade everybody that everything is OK the way things are. This is by way of an explanation not an excuse.

Our supreme challenge is not so much trying to create world peace but getting enough people to believe that we can.

So, premature cognitive commitment to an essentially materialistic view of existence is predominantly the reason why the exciting research on Super Radiance has been largely ignored by governments, international agencies such as the UN, and also the media. The people who inhabit such organisations literally cannot see the evidence placed before them. As a consequence, Super Radiance is mostly unheard of among the wider public.

So how do we remove premature cognitive commitment?

Ironically the most powerful way to reduce our natural tendency for premature cognitive commitment is to practice Transcendental Meditation (TM). Learning how to meditate and then regularly experiencing the universal field of lively consciousness (the Transcendent) promotes self-awareness. As you become increasingly familiar with the transcendent you become increasingly aware that you are not your beliefs, anymore than you are your thoughts, or your bodily sensations. Gradually, greater self-awareness loosens the attachment to personal beliefs and diminishes the tendency to identify so closely with them. Furthermore, practising TM regularly sees a steady erosion of stress in the nervous system that allows you to relax into being more <u>who you are</u> rather than <u>who you think</u> you are or <u>who you think you should be</u> or for that matter <u>who other people think you should be</u>. In a more relaxed state of 'being' it is much easier to discern between your true self and your beliefs.

This separation of self and beliefs is important because it allows you to feel less threatened when you suddenly discover that your beliefs are being challenged by some awful 'new' reality. The reduced 'threat' means less stress arousal, which means that you are a lot less prone to cognitive dissonance and so are more amenable to making the 'right' decision rather than opting for the 'easy' one.

When, from personal daily experience, you recognise the deeper reality that all the diverse strands of life in the universe coexist and interact in a universal field of lively consciousness, then the apparent magical effect of people sitting in a room in silence with their eyes shut and having a direct impact on millions of others, thousands of miles away suddenly becomes a plausible possibility.

But here we have the problem. If people have a premature cognitive commitment to the materialistic view of existence they are probably not going to learn to meditate are they? The various TM teaching organisations throughout the world are already doing their level best to teach as many people as possible to meditate; but first people have to want to learn, and if they don't we are stuck where we are today with a priceless technology for world peace languishing in wasteful redundancy.

What to do?

Fortunately, there are other ways to deconstruct premature cognitive commitment to particular ideas. From my own experience of leading team-planning workshops I have learned that the twin pressures of a cascade of corroborative information in addition to gentle peer pressure can help most people handle evidence, that conflicts with their beliefs, in a rational and grown-up way.

When I work with organisations to develop performance improvements, the first step in my team planning process is the extraction of 'bottom-up' feedback from all the stakeholders; most importantly this includes feedback from subordinate staff. As you may imagine when people are asked to submit anonymous feedback on the state of the organisation they work for very often this precipitates a torrent of data about the defects in the organisation. The volume of the data and the fact that it is put in writing tends to swamp management's own beliefs and complacency about how the system is working and their own self-belief about how well they are running it. Similarly, in this type of planning workshop setting, peer pressure tends to prevent executives get away with ignoring new evidence that contradicts their personal preconceptions or beliefs. In other words, executives are less able to slip into denial about overwhelming evidence when they know that everyone else in the group knows about it.

We are by nature highly collaborative group problem-solving animals and derive a sense of security where the group is striving jointly to overcome some problem. An emergent group consensus as to what the problems are and how to solve them tends to override the individual's own fear that their personal cherished beliefs are being destroyed. In other words, working together as a group with shared information tends to overwhelm the defensive mechanisms of the participant's personal belief systems. The natural process of gently deconstructing premature cognitive commitment by providing group security underlines the importance of a secure, non-judgemental and supportive atmosphere. If peer pressure is hostile and critical it is likely to have the opposite effect and get the various antagonists to dig their heals in.

The implications for the promotion of Super Radiance, as a viable mechanism to create world peace, are that we need to tell more people about it – a lot more people and a lot more often than we have done in the past. In addition there is nothing to be gained by criticising those who have not got the message yet. Generally we can accept that people in positions of power and influence are genuinely trying to do there best. They may be screwing up big time but that is only because they are still locked into their pre-existing beliefs. It is the responsibility of everyone who understands the concept of Super Radiance to get this message across about the awesome and proven potential of it to transform the destiny of mankind. The more that people in power know about it and the more they talk with colleagues and associates, the more familiar the whole concept becomes. It is this familiarity that makes the concept of Super Radiance the less unreal, less intangible and less threatening.

> **The need for tough-minded thinking**
>
> "Let us consider first the need for a tough mind, characterized by incisive thinking, realistic appraisal, and decisive judgment. The tough mind is sharp and penetrating, breaking through the crust of legends and myths and sifting the true from the false. The tough-minded individual is astute and discerning. He has a strong, austere quality that makes for firmness of purpose and solidness of commitment. Who doubts that this toughness of mind is one of man's greatest needs? Rarely do we find men who willingly engage in hard, solid thinking. There is an almost universal quest for easy answers and half-baked solutions. *Nothing pains some people more than having to think.*" – Martin Luther King

In practical terms this means transmitting relentlessly the research findings to government ministers, MPs, Congressmen, civil servants, think tanks, the media, social media and so on. In this sense, running petitions, like the recent World Peace Group's call to the three world leaders helps to generate further peer pressure. The more people that sign, the more individuals feel they are part of some supportive group process. Everyone wants to be on the side of history. Ultimately, an unremitting wave of advocacy for Super Radiance will gradually untie the knots of cognitive dissonance in some group of individuals who will then feel confident to back the idea. We only need one government or large institution to take the plunge, for Super Radiance to suddenly become a practical reality in our day-to-day lives.

The main aim of this report on 'The Super Radiance effect' is to help more people break through the fallacy of their common senses and social conditioning and so become aware of what our generation can achieve if we are alert enough to grasp the responsibility. Read the research summaries for yourself and you will see that the facts are unequivocal; the evidence is beyond doubt. We now have a practical and reliable technology to release our societies from the grip of warfare, terrorism, violence and crime.

Whether or not we take advantage of this opportunity is entirely up to us.

4. World peace is now within our grasp

There are already several large groups of TM-Sidhas established at different locations around the world. And these are quietly creating a powerful Super Radiance effect for their nearby populations. The longest-term group is in Iowa with roughly 1,500 TM-Sidhas covering the USA[3]. There are also groups of traditional pandits trained in the TM-Sidhi meditation programme in India. Thousands of students and school children have been taught the TM-Sidhi meditation programme in South America. Smaller groups of a few hundred or more TM-Sidhas are dotted across the world in various countries including the UK, Holland and Cambodia.

But what is still missing is a group of the size required for global Super Radiance. We live in volatile and turbulent times and just as much as ever we need to establish a group of 9,300[4] TM-Sidhas gathered together in one place to create a permanent and stable base for world peace.

The goal of the World Peace Group

Perhaps the quickest and easiest way to achieve this overriding goal is to attract existing TM-Sidhas to come together to live and work in one area. There are still in existence some tens of thousands of individual TM-Sidhas, already trained and fully established in this advanced meditation programme.

Unfortunately, these experts in consciousness-based peacekeeping are dispersed across numerous countries doing their daily programme of deep

---

[3] Although the Super Radiance threshold is from time to time being reached in the USA, account must be taken of the role that the US plays as a world leader in the international community. The reciprocal relationship US collective consciousness has with world consciousness will dilute the impact a purely national Super Radiance group has on the country. For further explanation read research summaries 14 and 41. Despite this dilution, violent crime in the USA almost halved between 1991 and 2012 from 758.1 crimes per 100,000 people pa to 386.3 per 100,000. Total crimes have reduced by 44% over the same period.

[4] The actual square root of 1% of the world's population is about 8,400. However, for the purposes of establishing a full-time Super Radiance group, account has to be taken of natural absences from the group due to holidays, sickness, family visits and other commitments hence the use here of the higher number.

meditation in their own homes. The problem for world consciousness is that fitting in several hours of meditation a day with family and work responsibilities is often difficult and always time consuming. As a result, over the last two decades, many have dropped the practice. Perhaps the supreme responsibility of our time is to draw enough of these experts together in one place so that they can take up their group meditation practice again and make world peace an immediate and permanent reality.

As the name indicates, the ultimate aim of the World Peace Group is to create world peace. We can achieve this aim by finding the means to pay for a sufficient number of TM-Sidhas to meditate together on a full-time professional basis. By paying these experts a proper salary, we will free them up from having to pursue other means to earn a living. This will enable them to fulfil the more valuable task of ensuring a more peaceful and prosperous society.

Although raising the necessary funds may be a daunting task for private individuals, the overall cost of a global Super Radiance group is insignificant for any Western government. To put this in context, the annual cost of maintaining a global group of TM-Sidhas will be about half the procurement costs of one single solitary Stealth bomber.

If, having read the research summaries in this book, you can see for yourself the immense opportunity that is opening up for us, please give serious consideration to helping us achieve our aim. If you know of anyone or any organisation including government and international agencies and not-for-profit organisations that you think may be interested to help us raise the necessary funds, please pass on the good news to them also.

Only with your help will we achieve our goal of peace on earth for all.

The Super Radiance effect

The Super Radiance effect

Chapter 1: Field research summaries

Research Summary 1

Improved quality of city life through the Transcendental Meditation program: Decreased crime rate

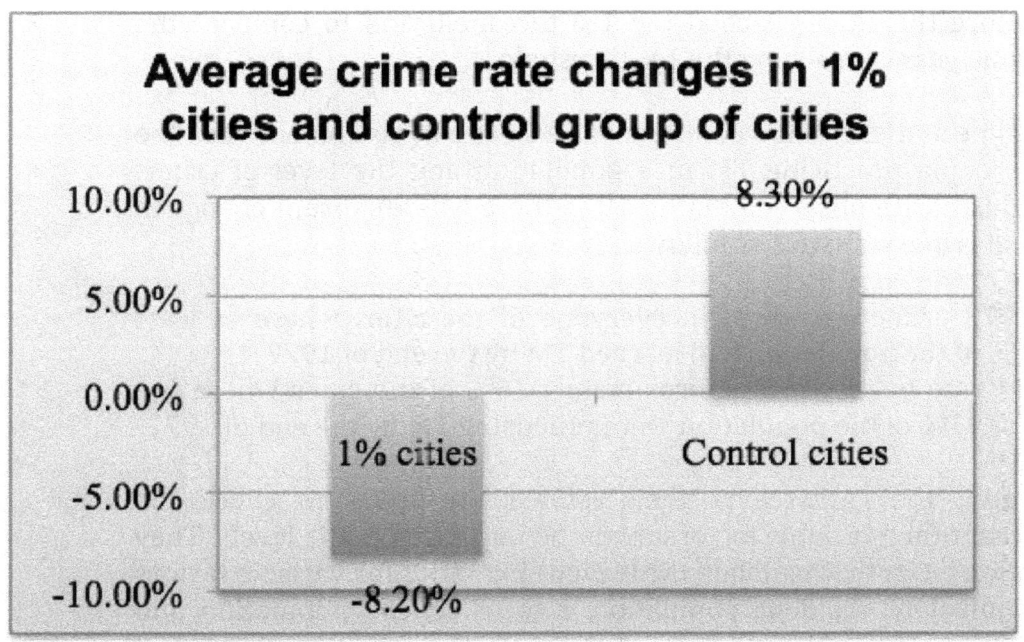

Maharishi Mahesh Yogi predicted in 1960 that just 1% of a given population practising Transcendental Meditation (TM) was enough to rejuvenate society and reverse the negative trends of crime and social disorder.

Although this was certainly an astounding prediction at the time, nevertheless by 1974 it seemed to be coming true. After a wave of extensive TM teaching in America, four Mid-Western cities actually reached this seemingly magical 1% threshold of meditators. Sure enough, it was apparent that in these four cities crime had started to buck the inexorable upward trend and was instead on the decline. This exciting revelation inspired this first research study into the collective effect of TM. The researchers, Borland and Landrith carried out two parallel studies.

First study; the researchers trawled through data for 101 US cities that fell into the FBI Uniform Crime Rate statistics category of a population between 25,000 and 50,000 people. Of these 101 cities, they discovered that 11 had achieved more than 0.97% of their populations practicing the TM technique by the end of 1972.

They then obtained crime figures from the FBI Uniform Crime Reports or directly from the relevant city authorities. Where possible they ran this analysis across the years 1967 to 1973. The idea was to demonstrate the situation before the cities reached the 1% threshold and to compare the effect after one year of reaching the 1% threshold.

The 1973 crime statistics showed there was a clear correlation between the number of people practicing TM in a population and the level of crime. Borland and Landrith observed that in 1973 there was an abrupt change in the pattern of crime statistics as follows:

1. In 1973 crime *decreased* in everyone of the cities where at least 0.97% of the population had learned TM by the end of 1972
2. Crime rate *increased* in approximately 76% of the cities where *less* than 0.97% of the population were practising TM by the end of 1972.

Second study; the researchers then refined the study to check the possibility that other variable factors might be impacting crime levels. They selected eleven cities that matched the eleven '1%' cities for variable factors including equivalent resident population, size of college population and geographic region. They then compared the relative crime rate changes of the control cities with the '1%' cities.

1% cities reverse trend in crime

The results showed that the eleven 1% cities achieved an average decrease in crime for 1973 of 8.2%. On the other hand the control group of eleven matching cities showed an average increase of 8.3%. (Three control cities showed small decreases, two control cities on the other hand experienced a jump of over 20% and three other control cities experienced increased crime of over 11%). See charts below for further details.

Table of percentage changes in crime rates

One-percent cities			Controls – Non 1% cities		
	City name	% change		City name	% change
1	Chapel Hill, NC	-9.3	1	Rocky Mount, NC	+20.2
2	Ithaca, NY	-0.6	2	Poughkeepsie, NY	+14.4
3	Lawrence, KS	-18.4	3	Lafayette, IN	+11.1
4	Bloomington, IN	-4.5	4	Columbia, MO	+11.2
5	Carbondale, IL	-9.9	5	Marshalltown, IA	+5.0
6	Iowa City, IA	-2.5	6	Oshkosh, WI	+8.3
7	Ames, IA	-3.6	7	Norman, OK	+20.8
8	Boulder, CO	-9.1	8	Fort Collins, CO	-3.2
9	Santa Cruz, CA	-7.9	9	Monterey, CA	+8.5
10	Santa Barbara, CA	-8.8	10	Costa Mesa, CA	-3.9
11	Davis, CA	-15.2	11	Pleasant Hill, CA	-1.2
	Mean change	**-8.2%**		**Mean change**	**+8.3%**

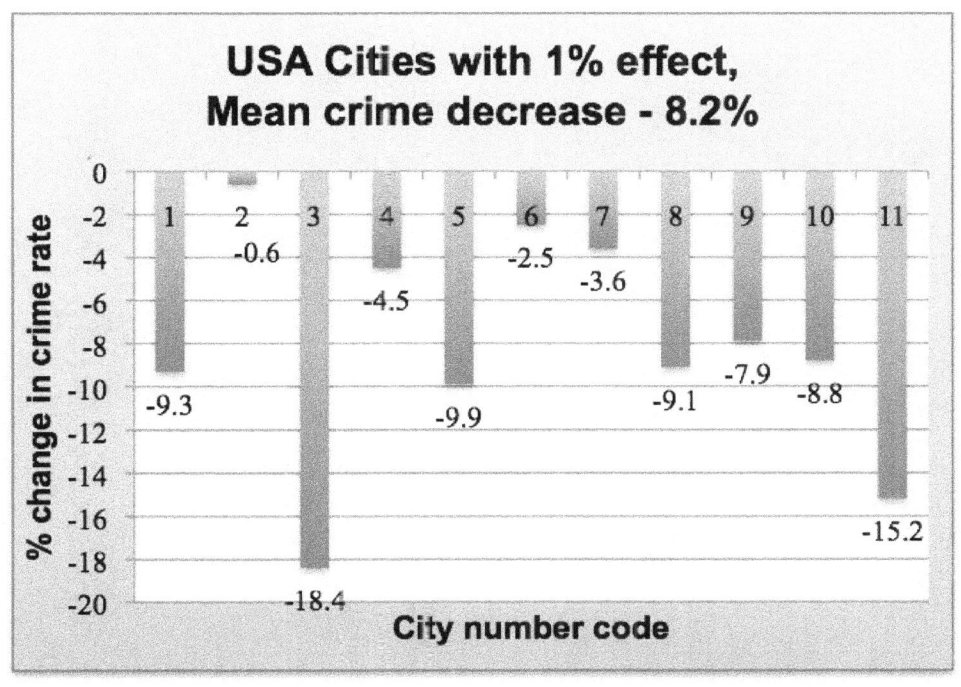

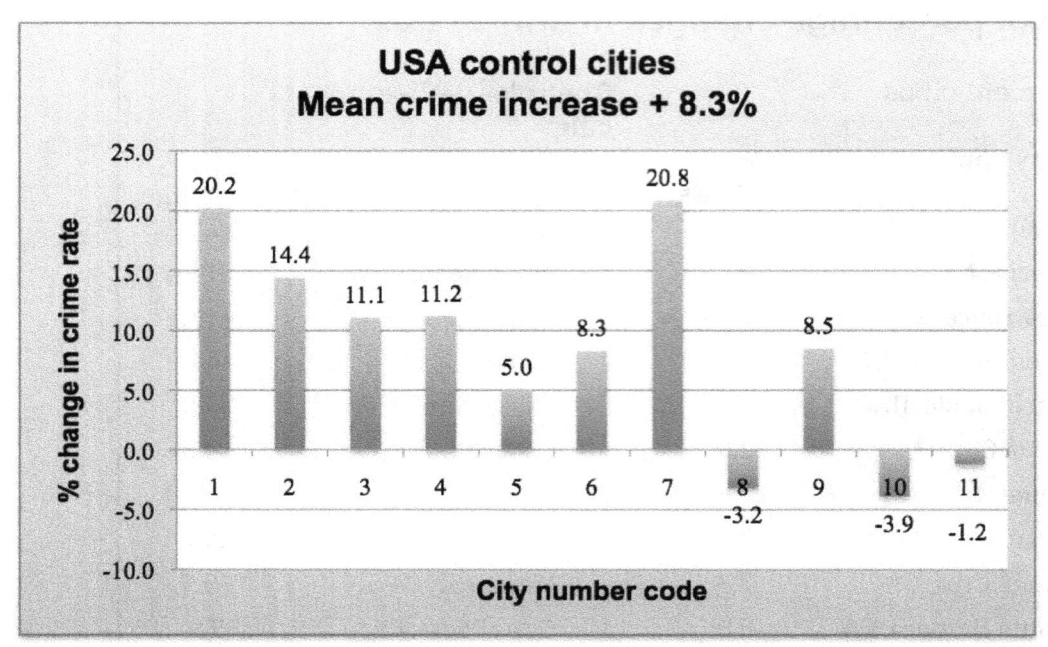
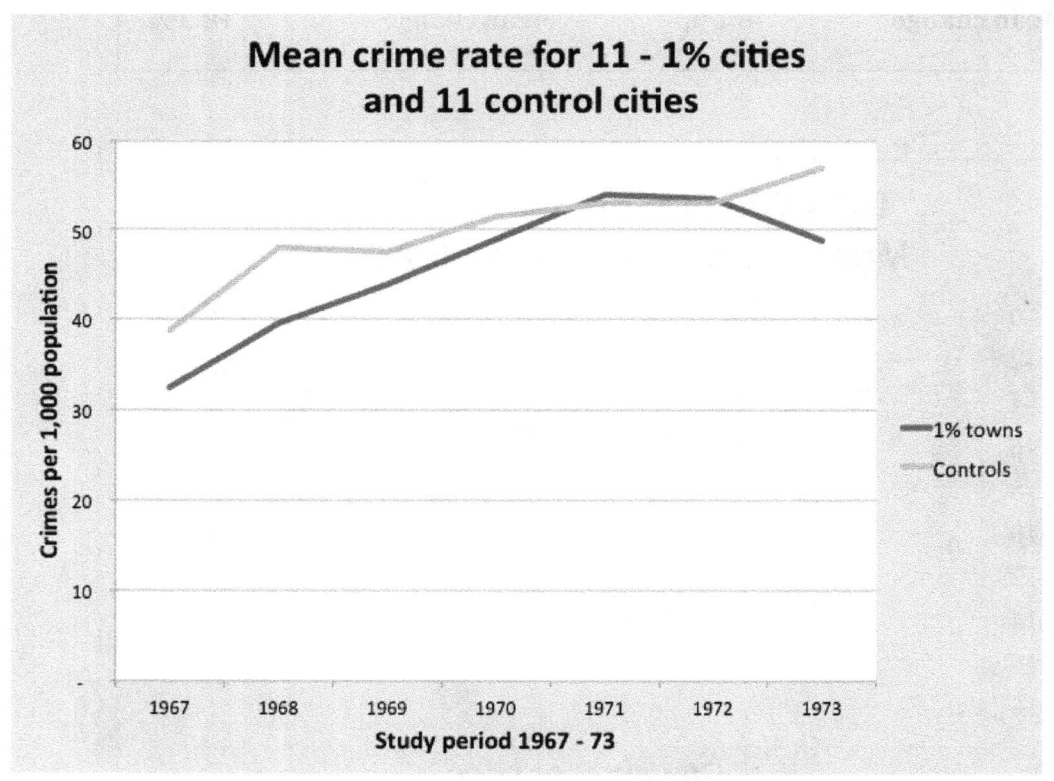

Significantly, in the years leading up to 1973, the researchers observed that both the experimental group of eleven cities and the matching control group had more or less followed a parallel growth in crime rate (See chart above).

Clear divergent trend

Looking at the last chart, you can see clearly that a sharp divergence in crime trends occurs during the year when each of the experimental cities achieved the threshold of 1% of their population learning the Transcendental Meditation technique. The 1% effect reverses the rising trend in crime in every case.

Research authors:

Borland C, and Landrith III GS; Department of Educational Psychology, Maharishi European Research University, Switzerland, and Department of Psychology, Maharishi University of Management, Fairfield, Iowa, USA, 1976.

Collected Papers v1.98[5]

---

[5] 'Collected Papers' depicted at the bottom of most summaries refers to the Collected Papers of the Scientific Research on Maharishi's Transcendental Meditation and TM-Sidhi Program volumes 1 – 6 published by Maharishi European Research University and Maharishi International University.

Research Summary 2

Influence of the Transcendental Meditation Programme on crime rate in suburban Cleveland

This study extends the previous work carried out by Borland and Landrith. The researcher, Guy Hatchard, tested the idea that just a few people learning to meditate would also have some impact on the level of orderliness and harmony of the surrounding society, even before the 1% threshold was reached.

In the early 1970's crime in the USA continued an inexorable rise

As a backdrop to this study it must be pointed out that in the early 1970s the USA was experiencing a prolonged growth in crime. Observers in the media and social studies couldn't help but expect this increase to continue on into the eighties. Despite massive government sums being spent on crime prevention methods of one sort or another, neither the causes of crime nor the means to reduce it seemed clear.

The inevitability of a continued increase in lawlessness was becoming accepted with more or less passive resignation. What was lacking at the time in academic circles was any understanding of the potential to intervene on the level of consciousness to reduce antisocial behaviour.

This Cleveland study was another step in the opening up of our understanding that even a small number of meditators within a population can start to have a significant impact on the lives and wellbeing of everyone else in society.

The study sample consisted of forty suburbs within the Greater Cleveland area of the USA with populations of over 5,000 people. This gave a total sample of 966,000 people. Crime rate figures and the numbers of people meditating were correlated for consecutive periods 1973 to 1975 and 1976. Other variable factors including family income and numbers of police were also looked at for correlation. The results of the first period under study showed that the correlation between very low percentage levels of meditators and crime levels is insignificant. This low correlation indicated that very small numbers of TM practitioners do not have any measurable impact on society at large.

However as the number of TM practitioners grew over the next few months so an impact began to emerge. In the 1974 to 1975 study period, ten suburbs out of 40 had reached percentages of TM practitioners above 0.39% of their host population. These areas showed significant positive changes in crime trends compared with the rest of the sample.

Five of the areas actually recorded a drop in crime despite an overall increase in crime being recorded elsewhere in Cleveland. Collectively the ten TM-prevalent areas showed a marginal increase in crime of less than 1%, whereas elsewhere in Cleveland crime continued to increase at the record rates of the time and often in double-digit percentage figures.

Suburbs with 1% of TM meditators showed a drop in crime

By 1976 Shaker Heights and a cluster of four small suburbs headed by Moreland Hills had breached the 1% threshold. These areas recorded crime drops of 3.65% and 1.81% respectively. Two other suburbs had achieved a percentage of TM practitioners just below 1%. Cleveland Heights had 0.86% and University Heights had 0.83%. Crime in these two areas had reduced by 2.39% and 1.23% respectively.

It was observed that a number of these suburbs were areas of fairly high median income. However, it was also noticed that none of the other wealthier areas where the TM population had not risen experienced a commensurate reversal in the crime trend. Similarly there seemed to be no correlation between police activity and protection and the reversal in crime trends.

Hatchard G; Cleveland World Plan Center, Cleveland, Ohio, USA, 1977.

Collected Papers v2.166

Research Summary 3

The growth of coherence in society through the Maharishi Effect: Reduced rates of suicides and auto accidents

This was the second study designed to test the theory that when 1% of a given population practices the Transcendental Meditation technique then there will be an immediate, significant and positive shift in the general quality of life. To achieve their aim, the researchers selected 21 US cities each with a population larger than 10,000 people and that had reached the 1% threshold in time for the experimental date of 1972.

An independent researcher formulated a control group of 21 cities where there was less than 0.7% meditating and that were otherwise matched for population, college population and geographic region. Care was taken to avoid monitoring cities where major changes occurred during the experimental period or where no suitable matching control could be identified. The control also avoided cities that were an integral part of a larger metropolitan area, as these larger areas might influence the result.

The full experimental period covered the ten-year from 1967 – 1977. The 'baseline period' extended from 1967 – 1972. The 'intervention period', defined as the period when the 1% threshold was reached for each of the experimental cities, ran between 1972 and 1977.

For this study, instead of crime, the researchers monitored statistical changes to suicide rates and auto accident rates. These two factors were and still are of major concern as they are seen to have a major negative impact on the quality of life in the USA. Suicide rates among adolescents had doubled between 1961 and 1975 and auto accident injuries had become a major health problem with an economic impact second only to cancer. The problem of suicide has been particularly intractable with no effective community prevention programmes being apparent, especially among the young.

The results

Impact of 1% effect on suicides in 21 US cities

1% cities	Suicide rate change	Control cities	Suicide rate change
Davis Ca	-5.23	Pleasant Hill Ca	-4.14
Los Altos Ca	-14.39	El Cerrito Ca	0.34
Mill Valley Ca	-6.65	Ukiah Ca	-4.48
Boulder Co	-5.7	Fort Collins Co	-1.62
Ames Ia	-4.26	Norman Ok	1.18
Iowa City Ia	-5.13	Oshkosh Wi	-1.43
Chico Ca	-3.92	Redding Ca	9.30
Moscow Id	-7.79	Centralia Wa	-6.56
Carbondale Il	-4.56	De Kalb Il	-2.93
Bloomington In	-4.86	Columbia Mo	1.90
Lawrence Ks	-5.74	Lafayette In	3.97
Concord Ma	-0.97	Bedford Ma	-4.49
Princeton NJ	-9.16	South Orange NJ	0.70
Ithaca NY	-3.30	Oswego NY	-2.27
Pullman Wa	-7.61	Walla Walla Wa	4.48
Falls Church Va	-7.83	Radford Va	-1.59
Burlington Vt	-4.02	Poughkeepsie NY	0.79
Bellingham Wa	-2.29	Vancouver Wa	1.26
Chapel Hill NC	-1.09	Rocky Mount NC	1.72
E Lansing Mi	-6.33	Ypsilanti Mi	2.84
Santa Cruz Ca	-9.01	Monterey Ca	5.12
Average rate change	**-5.71**		**0.19**

Changes are raw scores adjusted for covariates and expressed relative to expected value for no participation in the TM programme. The control cities should have a mean of approximately zero according to this measure (as is the case).

The study showed four unequivocal findings:

1. Suicides (average reduction -5.7%) and auto accidents (average reduction – 7.05%) decreased in every single town that reached the 1% threshold of meditators.

2. On the other hand, there was a small average increase in suicides (0.19%) in the 21 control cities and no change in the rate of auto accidents.
3. These changes were independent of changes in other major demographic variables.
4. In direct contrast, during the baseline period, (i.e., the period prior to the 1% threshold being reached) there were no significant divergent trends observed between the experimental cities and the control cities ($p<.001$).

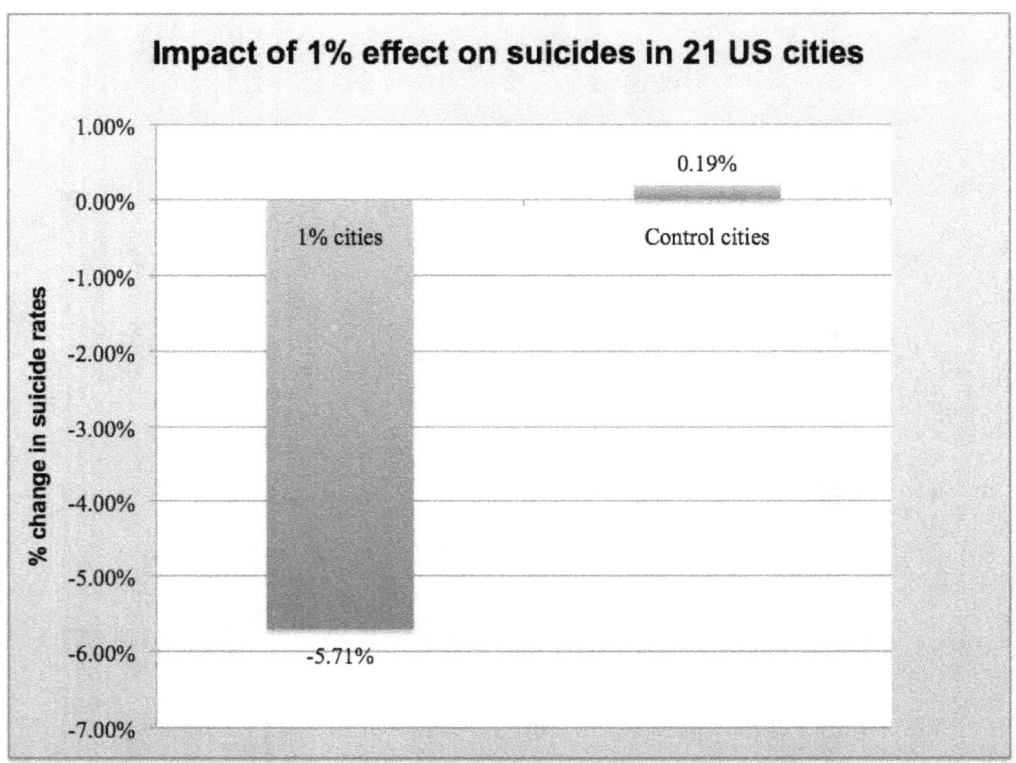

The study implies that there is a new factor influencing group cognitive and perceptual-motor functioning. The findings reinforce the researchers' understanding that this new factor is consciousness, which they hypothesize is a basic determinant of individual human behaviour.

The small number of meditators required to create a significant shift (only 1%) obviously precludes the possibility that the positive shift in auto accidents and suicides is due to any social or physical interaction by the meditators with the rest of the community. This fact lends further weight to the argument that the spontaneous shift in community quality of life is due to a field effect arising from increased coherence in the collective consciousness of the communities involved.

Impact of 1% effect on car accidents in 21 US cities

1% cities	Car accident rate change	Control cities (non 1%)	Car accident rate change
Davis Ca	-5.35	Pleasant Hill Ca	-0.72
Los Altos Ca	-7.65	El Cerrito Ca	-2.00
Mill Valley Ca	-6.63	Ukiah Ca	2.35
Boulder Co	-15.55	Fort Collins Co	3.42
Ames Ia	-6.63	Norman Ok	-1.79
Iowa City Ia	-6.35	Oshkosh Wi	3.50
Chico Ca	-3.62	Redding Ca	4.47
Moscow Id	-7.24	Centralia Wa	-4.84
Carbondale Il	-7.07	De Kalb Il	6.73
Bloomington In	-8.64	Columbia Mo	0.45
Lawrence Ks	-3.96	Lafayette In	-3.45
Concord Ma	-6.93	Bedford Ma	-0.13
Princeton NJ	-5.81	South Orange NJ	-2.12
Ithaca NY	-8.32	Oswego NY	-4.73
Pullman Wa	-7.32	Walla Walla Wa	2.43
Falls Church Va	-14.62	Radford Va	3.15
Burlington Vt	-8.39	Poughkeepsie NY	-4.53
Bellingham Wa	-0.97	Vancouver Wa	2.72
Chapel Hill NC	-4.32	Rocky Mount NC	0.17
E Lansing Mi	-7.45	Ypsilanti Mi	0.52
Santa Cruz Ca	-5.32	Monterey Ca	-5.68
Average rate change	**-7.05**		**-0.00**

Changes are raw scores adjusted for covariates and expressed relative to expected value for no participation in the TM programme. The control cities should have a mean of approximately zero according to this measure (as is the case).

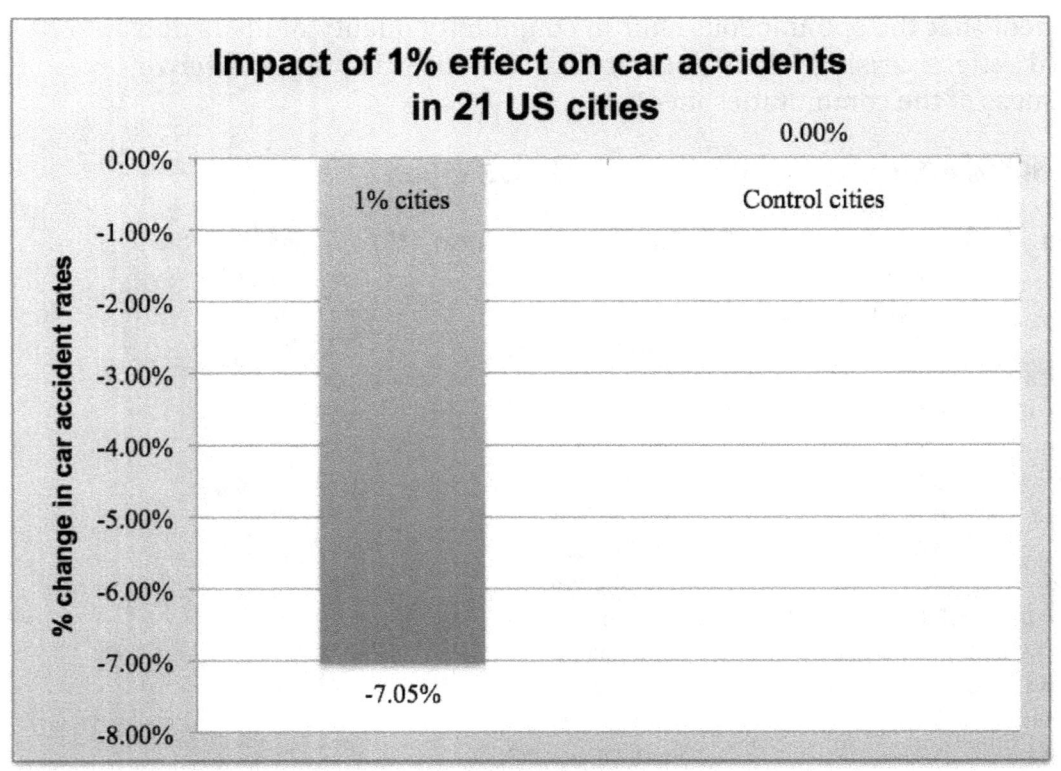

Landrith III GS; and Dillbeck MC; Maharishi University of Management, Fairfield, Iowa, USA, 1983.

Collected Papers v4.317.

Research Summary 4

The Transcendental Meditation Programme and crime rate change in a sample of forty-eight cities

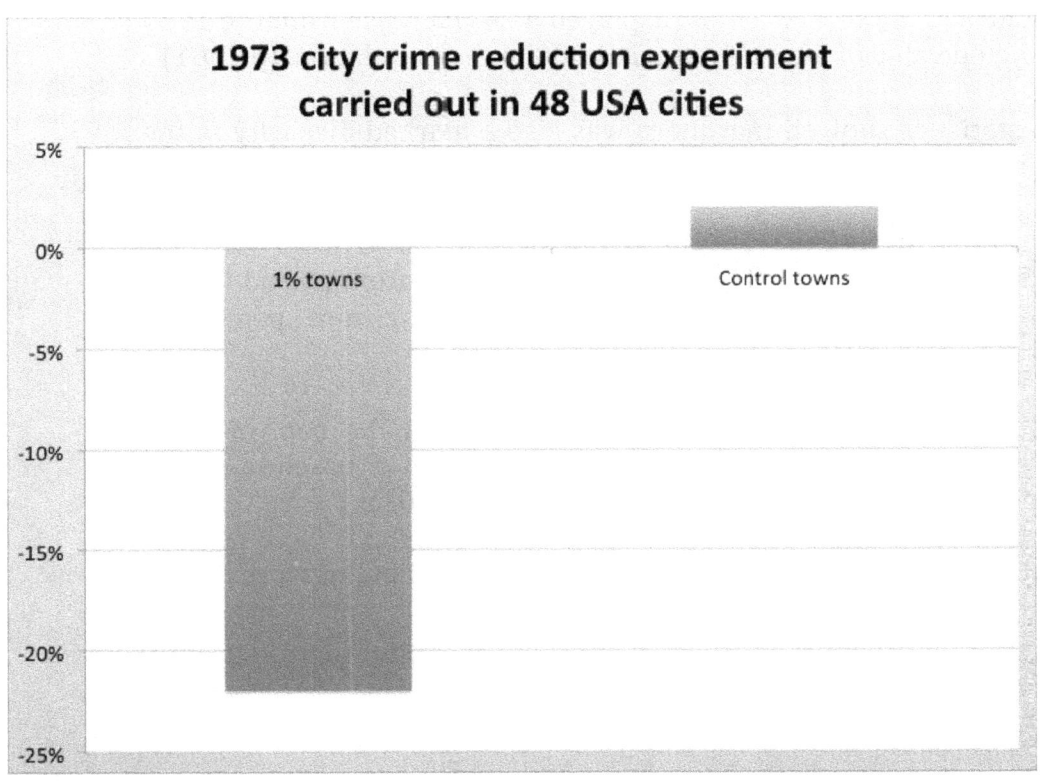

This study covered a period of five and a half years in an attempt to identify the cause of relative crime rate changes in 48 cities in the USA.

The methodology involved comparing 24 'experimental cities' (where one percentage of the population practised the Transcendental Meditation technique) with 24 'control cities' where few people had learned to meditate.

To try and ensure a fair comparison, the researchers carefully matched the control cities for geographic region, population size, college population and changes in reporting methods.

Findings summarised:

- The experimental cities with 1% of the population meditating displayed a decrease of 22% from the 1973 predicted value of 65.2 crimes per 1,000 of the population.

- In contrast, the control cities displayed a 2% increase from the 1973 predicted value of 58.0 crimes per 1,000 of the population. ($p<.001$)

- The statistics showed that there was also a marked disparity in the *trend of crime rate* between the two groups:

- The trend of crime rate in the experimental cities (with 1% meditating) decreased 89.3% during the intervention period from a 1967 – 72 baseline yearly increase of 4.30 crimes per 1,000 population.

- On the other hand, the trend of crime rate in the control cities increased 53.9% during the same period, from a baseline yearly increase of 2.32 crimes per 1,000 population ($p<.01$).

Dillbeck MC; Landrith III GS; and Orme-Johnson DW; Findings previously published in *Journal of Crime and Justice 4: 25-45, 1981.*

Collected Papers v4.318.

Research Summary 5

The Transcendental Meditation Programme and a compound probability model as predictors of crime rate change

The fifth research study built on the earlier TM research findings that indicated that when 1% of a given population practised the Transcendental Meditation technique (TM) then there is a commensurate improvement in social order as manifested by a decrease in crime levels. The study was specifically designed to test the theory that the '1% effect' was a reliable predictor of crime decrease in a population.

The study carried out during the early to mid 1970s was split into three parts. The first two parts were designed to test the reliability of predicting crime levels in society using different variable factors that are sometimes considered by social scientists to influence the crime rate. These variables included:

- Density of population,
- Percentage of unemployed,
- Per capita income,
- Percentage of the population living below the poverty level,
- Percentage of the residents living in the same residence after five years,
- Percentage of the population over the age of 65 and
- Median years of education

The third part looked at the prevalence of TM in a community as a means to predict crime levels.

To carryout the investigation into the influence of TM on crime rates, the researcher, Michael Dillbeck selected a sample of twenty-three towns in the Kansas City metropolitan area. These towns comprised at least 4,000 people and each was within a 20-mile radius of Kansas City Missouri. Either permanently or temporarily, during the period covered by the study, four of these towns (Fairway-Westwood, Leawood, Mission Hills, Prairie Village) reached the 1% threshold whereby at least 1% of the local population were meditating using the TM technique.

The research monitored 'Part 1' crimes per one thousand members of the population over different periods. 'Part 1' crimes include murder, manslaughter, rape, robbery, assault, burglary, larceny, and motor vehicle theft. These types of crimes are considered useful indicators of the level of social order and disorder.

On review, the statistics showed that where the TM 1% threshold had been achieved in each city there was a universal and significant reduction in Part 1 crimes. On the other hand most of the control sample towns experienced an increase in crime.

The larger the number of meditators above the 1% threshold the higher the drop in crime seemed to be. (In Mission Hills where 2.92% of the population was meditating there was a drop in crime of 30.03% recorded during one of the periods under study.)

In one period of study, the difference between the mean averages of the two groups (1% threshold towns and non 1%) was approximately 30% points ($p<.001$) in a later period the difference between the two groups was still 14% points.

None of the other variables tested, proved to be a viable alternative hypothesis for crime rate changes compared with the 1% TM threshold effect. Dillbeck concluded that compared with other models, the TM probability model based on Maharishi Mahesh Yogi's principles of the collective consciousness, appeared to be a useful tool to empirically predict the existing level of crime rate, crime rate growth and crime rate decrease.

Dillbeck MC; Maharishi University of Management, Fairfield, Iowa, USA, 1978.

Collected Papers v4.319.

Research Summary 6

The Transcendental Meditation Programme and crime rate change: A causal analysis

From the early 1970s the number of people being taught Transcendental Meditation (TM) in the USA was growing fast. By 1976 the number of TM practitioners had reached an average of 0.45% in cities (over 25,000 population) and 0.33% in the larger metropolitan areas (over 200,000 population).

This large randomly dispersed group of individuals gave researchers the opportunity to carryout twin studies using large-scale random samples of both cities and metropolitan areas. The idea was to confirm that TM was a causal factor in the reduction of crime in US urban areas.

The researchers wanted to build on the earlier studies into TM and crime reduction and eliminate the possibility that the cause of the reducing crime rate was due to alternative unmeasured variable factors. To achieve this they adopted the statistical method of 'crossed lagged panel correlation' (CLPC), as this was considered the best means to determine whether the relationship between TM and crime was either causal or spurious.

The study period extended from 1964 to 1978 and covered 40 randomly picked cities and 80 standard metropolitan statistical areas (SMSAs). FBI Uniform Crime Index figures were used to track the crime rates. Multiple regression analysis was used to assess the contribution other social variable factors had on crime trends. These other factors included education attainment levels, unemployment rates, per capita income, and poverty levels.

Adopting this more systematic approach still showed that there was a statistically significant relationship between TM participation and crime rate change. It must be pointed out that unlike other studies the samples were not selected for high TM participation. This meant that the size of the correlations were lower than seen in other studies. However the random samples were both large and diverse lending further weight to the hypotheses that TM is a causal factor in urban crime reduction (probability factors varied in different years and ranged from $p<.05$ to $p<.01$).

Dillbeck MC; Landrith III GS; Polanzi C; and Baker SR; Department of Psychology, Maharishi University of Management, Fairfield, Iowa, USA; Center for the Study of Crime, Delinquency, and Corrections, Southern Illinois University, Carbondale, Illinois, USA; and Department of Educational Psychology, West Virginia University, Morgantown, West Virginia, USA, 1982.

Collected Papers v4.320.

Research Summary 7

Maharishi's Global Ideal Society Campaign: Improved quality of life in Rhode Island through the Transcendental Meditation and TM-Sidhi program

The first prospective study on the collective effect of TM and the TM-Sidhi programme

Up until the time of this study, research carried out into the Maharishi effect had been retrospective. In the previous studies scientists had chosen for study those towns where the 1% threshold had already been achieved organically as more and more people had learned to meditate in those areas. The researchers had never been in a position to predict the results beforehand they had only observed what had already happened.

An important test for a scientific theory is to replicate an experiment and predict the result before the experiment commences. So, in this instance, the research team considered it was time to intervene proactively and teach enough people to meditate in an area so as to achieve the 1% effect. Just as importantly they wanted to predict the results publicly beforehand.

QOL research across a whole state

The researchers also felt it would be useful to broaden the scope of the study both in terms of size of sample and range of quality of life benefits. They therefore decided to monitor the results across a state level as well as across a range of quality of life factors, not just crime, suicides and accident levels.

The team chose Rhode Island for the case study, as it is the smallest state in the USA. With a population of one million people it was felt that achieving a 1% level of meditators in the state was within the capacity of the TM teaching organisation. This was still an ambitious objective as it meant having to teach 10,000 people the TM technique before the QOL could be significantly improved for study purposes.

Public prediction of anticipated results

Before the commencement of the project, the team made a public prediction that they were intending to create a significant improvement in the Quality of Life (QOL) Index in Rhode Island by instigating the 1% effect. To this end a team of 300 TM teachers travelled from all parts of the USA and arrived in Rhode Island in June 1978, remaining there for three months.

In the event the team was only able to teach 5,045 people to meditate during the time available. However, each and every one of the newly arrived teachers was also a TM-Sidha. This meant that although the massive teaching initiative was unable to meet the 1% threshold, the teachers themselves were still making a powerful contribution to the Super Radiance ($\sqrt{1}$ %) effect with their own daily programme of meditation.

During the study period, the teachers were scattered across the state engaged in teaching activities. But none-the-less these teachers still managed to meditate in a variety of group sizes ranging in number from two individuals to forty-six. The combination of these scattered groups of 300 TM-Sidhas with the 5,045 new meditators was enough for Rhode Island to reach the Super Radiance threshold for that entire period.

Data studies using time series analysis

After the intervention phase of the experiment was concluded the researchers compared data during the three-month experiment with similar monthly data available for a seven-year period between 1974 and 1980. To improve the efficacy of the findings the researchers also analysed data using time series analysis.

The results confirmed exactly what the research team had predicted at the start of the project. Statistics showed that the experimental period displayed a significant improvement in a composite QOL index composed of eight variable factors.

- Total crime rate – FBI statistics
- Mortality rate – US Bureau of Census
- Motor vehicle fatality rate – Departments of Transportation RI (Rhode Island) and Delaware
- Auto accident rate – Departments of Transportation RI and Delaware

- Unemployment rate – Department of Employment Security, RI; Department of Labor, Delaware
- Pollution (particulates) – Department of Environmental Management, RI; Department of Natural Resources and Environmental Control, Delaware
- Beer consumption rate – United States Brewers Association
- Cigarette consumption rate – Tobacco Tax Council, Richmond Virginia

As can be seen in the chart, a significant but less pronounced improvement on the baseline period in composite QOL scores was seen in the post intervention period when the 300 TM-Sidhas had departed. Even after the TM teachers had left there were still a sizeable number of new meditators dispersed across the community. And as we saw from the Hatchard study (Summary 2), once a town has about 0.39% of its population practicing Transcendental Meditation new meditators start having a noticeable impact on their surroundings.

In the chart an increase shows an improvement in the combined index of all the variables.

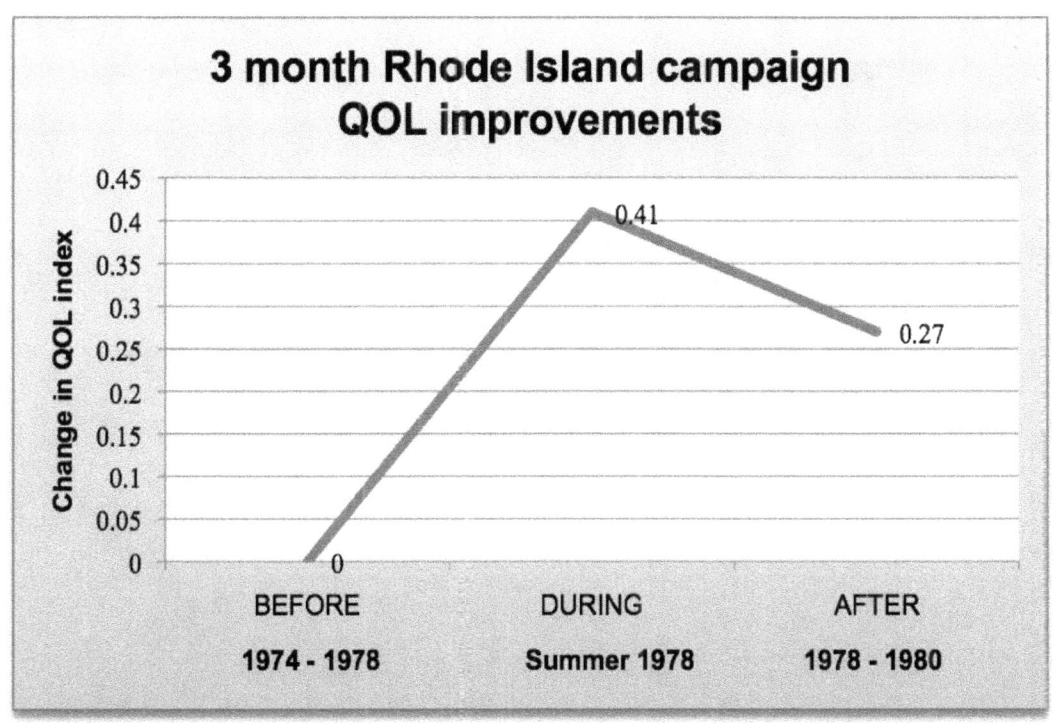

Impressive 'before and after' effect

The uniqueness of the 'before and after' event clearly indicates a causal relationship between the combination of new meditators and TM-Sidhas participating in the project and improvement in the quality of life in the state.

To check that the improvements in QOL were not part of some local or regional trend, the researchers carried out a similar analysis in the nearby state of Delaware over the same period. They found that the significant improvements seen in Rhode Island were in no way matched by the social indicators for Delaware.

Dillbeck MC; Foss APO; and Zimmermann W J Maharishi University of Management, Fairfield, Iowa, USA, and MERU Research Institute, Mentmore, Buckinghamshire, England, 1983. Consciousness as a field: The Transcendental Meditation and TM-Sidhi programme and changes in social indicators, *The Journal of Mind and Behavior* **8:** *67-103, 1987.*

Collected Papers v4.321.

Research Summary 8

An experimental analysis of the application of the Maharishi Technology of the Unified Field in major world trouble spots: Increased harmony in international affairs

Introduction

The confirmation of the Super Radiance effect during the Rhode Island research project (See research summary 7 above) inspired a more ambitious experiment - the World Peace Project.

Basically the objective was to explore the practicalities of using groups of TM-Sidhas to quieten down areas of serious conflict in the world. In the event, this World Peace Project set the pattern for a number of future peace projects. Typically during these projects we see the following trends occur:

1. Conflict, chaos and open warfare immediately stop with the arrival of the required number of TM-Sidhas that meet the Super Radiance threshold for the area (the square root of 1% of the host population).
2. This pacification only continues for so long as the necessary numbers of TM-Sidhas are in place. When they leave the conflict zone, or when the number of TM-Sidhas drops below the Super Radiance threshold the violence gradually erupts again.
3. A temporary Super Radiance group of TM-Sidhas does not substitute or replace traditional means of long-term peace making such as mediation, diplomatic negotiations and the formation of workable constitutional structures. The increased coherence in the collective consciousness simply creates sympathetic ground conditions in which conventional peace making efforts can prosper.
4. Unless diplomatic and political efforts come to fruition whilst the coherence group is in place, the violence tends to break out again soon after the departure of the TM-Sidhas.

In essence what we now know is that temporary coherence creating groups create a window of opportunity for governments and other agencies to come to terms with one another and make practical peace agreements.

Five sub-projects

During a ten-week period in 1978, Maharishi despatched groups of volunteers who, were trained in the TM-Sidhi meditation techniques, to five principle trouble spots around the world. At the time, these were:

- Nicaragua
- Lebanon
- Iran
- Thailand and Kampuchea (now Cambodia)
- Rhodesia (now Zimbabwe)

Unfortunately for the residents of these countries, they had become the focal points of collective global stress, as they lay on the fault lines between the two rival super powers the USA and USSR. Each of the countries suffered from political violence of some sort. In essence these countries had become surrogate, fighting grounds in Cold War geopolitical manoeuvrings.

The objective of the World Peace Project was to show that introducing coherence in these areas using the group practise of the TM-Sidhi programme would not only create progress towards peace in these specific areas but would also improve peaceful cooperation at a global level.

Between October and December 1978 approximately 1,400 TM-Sidhas in separate groups visited strategically selected locations to precipitate the desired local Super Radiance effect.

- 121 TM-Sidhas went to Rhodesia and neighbouring Zambia
- 140 TM-Sidhas went to Nicaragua with a further 160 sent to the surrounding countries of Honduras, Costa Rica, Guatemala, and El Salvador
- 206 TM-Sidhas went to Iran
- Lebanon benefited from 100 TM-Sidhas in Syria and Cyprus, and 400 trainee TM-Sidhas in Northern Israel
- 260 meditators and TM-Sidhas went to Thailand to bring coherence to that local region with the specific intention of preventing the violence and genocide spreading across the border from communist Kampuchea.

Zero social, political or diplomatic interaction by peace project participants

It is important to note that the TM-Sidhas made no attempt to influence the situation through social, diplomatic or political interaction. Their influence spread directly from the enlivenment of collective consciousness precipitated by their daily meditation programmes.

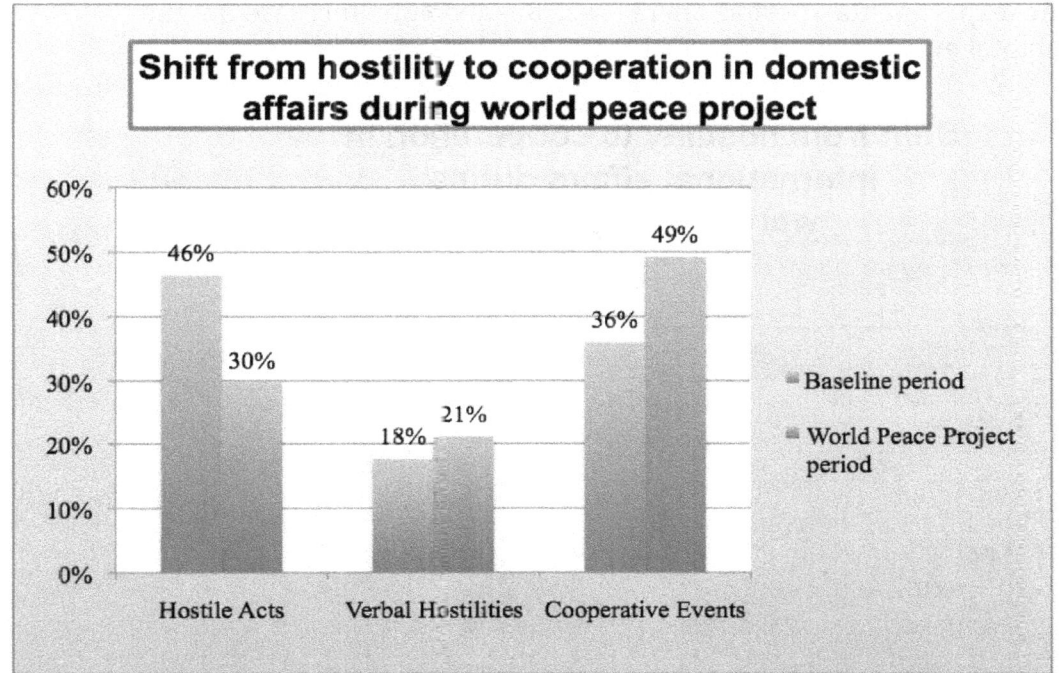

The impact of the TM-Sidha groups on the trouble spots was gauged through analysis of data drawn from COPDAB (The Conflict and Peace Data Bank), the largest independent daily data bank in the world recording conflict in international affairs.

The data categorised events into a Conflict Scale of 15 subheadings broadly under the three main categories of:

1. Cooperative Events: These were measured in scale from voluntary unification into one nation at the top end and the creation of alliances to verbal support by minor officials at the minimum end of the scale
2. Verbal Hostilities

3. Hostile Acts ranging in scale from hostile diplomatic actions such as troop mobilisations and withdrawal of ambassadors to full-scale war.
4. The results showed a significant shift in international relations and domestic affairs towards proportionally fewer hostile acts and more cooperative Events ($p=.0001$).

During the experimental period there was an absolute increase in the number of total events recorded by COPDAB.

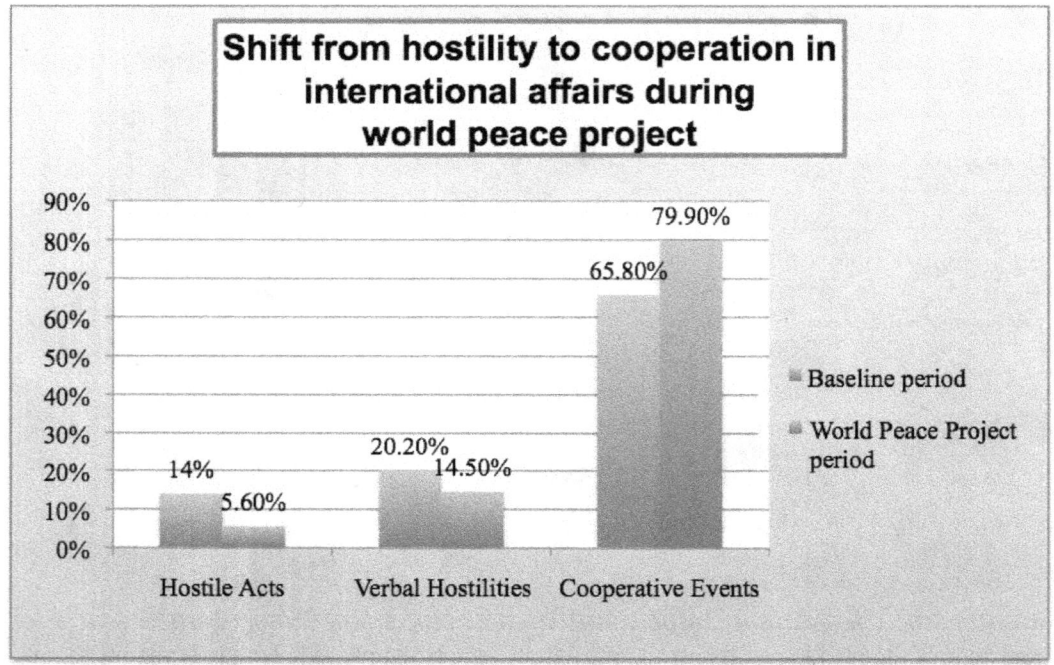

Thus in terms of absolute frequencies the greatest change in domestic affairs was in the number of cooperative events. These increased from 90 during the baseline period to 194 during the experimental period, an increase of 115.6%.

In terms of absolute frequencies the greatest change in international affairs was observed in the number of cooperative events.

These cooperative events increased from 610 during the baseline period to 2,758 during the experimental period. In other words there was an increase in international cooperation of 352% during the brief period the World Peace Project was underway.

Specific results by country

Rhodesia – 81% drop in war deaths

War deaths in September 1978 had actually been as high as 1,000 people or 33 people per day. However the researchers took their baseline from the October/ November period just prior to the project.

The result showed war deaths dropping from an average of 16.1 per day during the baseline period to 3.0 per day during the main experiment period. This equates to a reduction of 81% in war deaths as compared with the lower baseline period. ($p<.05$).

Nicaragua – Open warfare stopped

During one month in September 1978 1,200 people had been killed in the country's civil war. From October 11th groups of TM-Sidhas started arriving in Nicaragua itself and also neighbouring countries including Costa Rica, Honduras, Guatemala, and El Salvador. Soon afterwards the violence in Nicaragua eased.

A second group of TM-Sidhas was quickly despatched to Nicaragua in November to calm the situation when it was heard from the US embassy that an escalation of violence was anticipated.

Again, towards the end of November, Maharishi sent more TM-Sidhas to the capital Managua when negotiations between the rival factions broke down and turbulence started erupting. Following the arrival of the latest group, violence and tension subsided to an extent that President Somoza was able to suspend military rule, granted an unconditional amnesty to political prisoners and exiles and removed censorship. Uncharacteristically he also agreed to set-up a plebiscite on his own rule.

However when in December, the TM-Sidha group left the country, progress reversed. Somoza rejected his own plebiscite, negotiations between the rival parties broke down and violence sparked off once again.

Iran – Return to normality

The first groups of TM-Sidhas arrived in the capital Teheran on 17th October. The country was in the midst of a constitutional crisis with strikes and civil resistance growing against the Shah's dictatorial regime. Demonstrations and strikes were paralysing the country and the conflict was rapidly becoming more heated and violent.

The arrival of the TM-Sidhas coincided with the BBC noting that the demonstrations had suddenly become more peaceful. Further political turbulence arose from 1st November but this was also stabilised when additional TM-Sidhas arrived. November 28th Newsweek commented that Iran was 'calm but not quiet'. During November and early December, oil strikers returned to work, the colleges opened and 477 political prisoners were released.

In Mid December the TM-Sidhas started leaving as visas began expiring. The problem being that the Shah's government felt they could no longer guarantee the safety of foreigners and asked them to leave. Tragically, the government had no idea what Super Radiance was and the effect it had been having on its own country. When the TM-Sidhas finally left disorder and chaos quickly ensued. By mid January The Shah had left the country and two weeks later Ayatollah Khomeini returned to a stupendous welcome. After several weeks of armed street fighting the Royal regime finally collapsed and was replaced by the Islamic Republic.

Lebanon – Two months of peace

Throughout the summer of 1978 Lebanon suffered from almost ceaseless civil warfare interspersed with a few ceasefires that typically lasted only a day or two. Observers were forecasting that total economic collapse was imminent and business people were leaving the country.

The first group of TM-Sidhas arrived in the area on 23rd October with other groups following shortly after. From this point onward, the country enjoyed a period of almost continuous calm interspersed by sporadic, but relatively minor incidents.

This ceasefire lasted until late December with refugees beginning to return to Beirut, a new security plan was being developed and reconstruction was getting underway.

At the end of December, when the TM-Sidhas left, heavy fighting erupted once again in what was described as the "worst onslaught since October" (Lebanon News February 1979).

Kampuchea/ Thailand – Invasion averted

In November 1978 there was a well-documented, fear among political and diplomatic observers that the barbaric conflict and genocide in neighbouring communist run Kampuchea would escalate into Thailand. The government had a serious apprehension that Thailand might be invaded. During the experimental period, the feared escalation failed to materialise and Thailand remained free from invasion.

Improved international relations

Although the size of the TM-Sidha groups was relatively small and nowhere near the size needed for Global Super Radiance, nonetheless they intervened in the world's focal points of stress. The result was a rise of peace throughout the world that was not predicted by prior events and was not typical for that time of year.

Both analysts and politicians noted improvements in international relations during the experimental period. According to a report in the International Herald Tribune 18th November, President Carter stated; "I think that in recent weeks there has been an alleviation of tension between us (USSR and the USA) and I would like to see it continue." Poignantly he continued, "I can't say why there has been an improvement in US-Soviet relations."

COPDAB recorded 4.9% fewer Hostile Acts during this period despite an increase of 43.4% events worldwide being recorded in the file. There was a massive 352% change in the Cooperative Events category.

A Mid West paper the Des Moines Register noted " …No nations are actively engaged in open warfare at the moment – a historic rarity" (30th November 1978)

Group coherence enhances communication

The absolute increase in the number of total events recorded by COPDAB and especially the total number of positive events reinforces the understanding about stress and communication. Negativity and stress in the collective consciousness mirrors the impact stress has on the individual. Just as stress in the individual tends to damage and block communication, reduce fruitful interaction and arouse hostility, so the same outcomes tend to arise when a nation becomes stressed. On the other hand, the more coherent atmosphere where there is increased positivity in the collective consciousness due to a Super Radiance effect, tends to encourage the flow of communication, increase the number of human interactions and produce proportionally more cooperation between people and institutions.

The World Peace Project proved the power of Super Radiance to dampen down hostility and violence, but also showed the limitations of temporary groups. Perhaps the main lesson learned from this project was the overall imperative of securing a permanent world peace group and permanent national peace groups.

Orme-Johnson DW; Dillbeck MC; Bousquet JG; and Alexander CN; Department of Psychology, Maharishi University of Management, Fairfield, Iowa, USA, 1979.

Collected Papers v4.322.

Research Summary 9

The Maharishi Technology of the Unified Field and improved quality of life in the United States: A study of the First World Peace Assembly, Amherst, Massachusetts, 1979

In 1979 an extended educational course on Vedic Science drew 2,500 TM-Sidhas to Amherst Massachusetts USA for a six-week period. For the duration of the course, these TM-Sidhas were able to meditate together and as a result comfortably achieved the Super Radiance effect for the USA.

Researchers took the opportunity to measure the impact of this temporary group by analysing a range of quality of life indicators (QOL) for the United States as a whole. They achieved a valid comparison by matching QOL indicators for the study period with US trends for the years between 1973 and 1981.

As the researchers predicted, they found significant improvements in all QOL variables during the six-week study period. Although these improvements took place across the whole of the USA the research team observed more accentuated improvements in Massachusetts where the group was located.

Recorded improvements included:

- 3.4% decrease in violent crime across the USA ($p<.02$).

- 6.5% decrease in motor vehicle fatalities across the USA ($p<.0001$)

- 4% mean reduction across 14 major independent categories in the number of fatal accidents from (e.g. from fire, poisoning etc) and from homicides and suicides ($p.005$).

- 20.8% decrease in air traffic fatal accidents across the USA ($p<.05$).

- Increased confidence, optimism, and economic prosperity was indicated with a rise of 5.2 points in the Standard and Poor's Composite 500 stock market index, a leading economic indicator, and a rise of 40.3 points in the Dow Jones industrial index ($p<.04$).

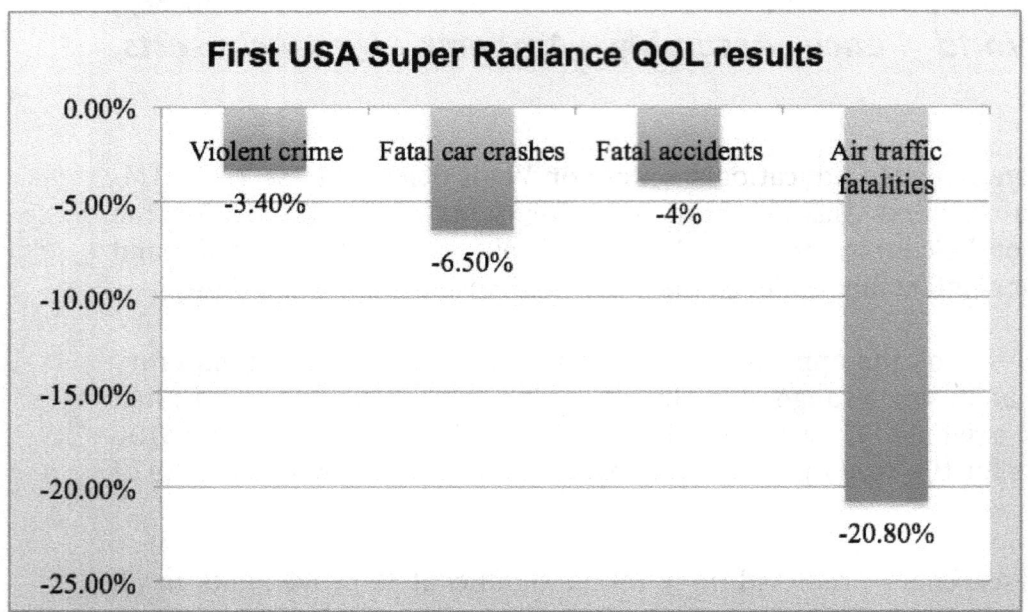

Significantly improved QOL factors for Massachusetts included:

- 18.9% reduction in motor vehicle fatalities ($p<.05$).
- 10.1% reduction in violent crime ($p<.00001$).
- 83.3% decrease in air traffic fatal accidents for the New England region ($p<.001$).

Davies JL; and Alexander CN; Macquarie University, North Ryde, New South Wales, Australia, and Harvard University, Cambridge, Massachusetts, USA, 1983.

Collected Papers v4.323.

Research Summary 10

Effect of coherent collective consciousness on the weather

In 1979, the need of the time drove the TM organisation in the USA to try and establish a permanent Super Radiance group for the whole nation. The cold war was seen to be heating up and it was felt that America's unique and pivotal position in global politics made a national coherence group an imperative.

The urgency of the situation meant there was an immediate need to build two large meditating facilities capable of holding at least 2,000 TM-Sidhas; 2,000 being just over the square root of 1% of the USA population. The location for the group was to be the Maharishi International University (MIU) in Fairfield, Iowa.

Unfortunately the decision to go ahead with the construction project coincided with the onset of winter. And winter in the Mid West of the USA is so bitterly cold as to prevent building construction. The specific problem that had to be overcome was that builders are unable to mix and pour concrete below about 30 degrees Fahrenheit.

Never one to be put off by mundane practicalities such as impossible weather conditions, Maharishi Mahesh Yogi intervened directly. He insisted the construction should go ahead straight away regardless of the weather conditions. His response to the protests of the building contractors was to suggest to the group of 1,200 TM-Sidhas at the university that they put their collective attention on the need for milder weather on the critical days when concrete was due to be mixed and poured on site. This they duly did.

The construction project's tight schedule required concrete pouring on eight specific days at different times during the course of the whole programme. In the event each time, one of these crucial days arrived, the weather became mild enough to allow the concrete pouring to go ahead. As a result the construction schedule continued unimpeded.

Subsequently, researchers used data from the National Weather Service to compare the temperature of these eight experimental days with 84 other days during the three-month construction period both in Fairfield and the seven nearest cities.

The findings showed that the eight experimental (concrete pouring days) days displayed higher temperatures of 3.5 – 4.5 degrees Fahrenheit over the control period of 84 days across the whole region ($p=.01$). The entire period under study was seen to be warmer than average by one standard deviation (40-year baseline).

"The findings support the view that (coherent) collective consciousness can interact directly with macroscopic systems through the medium of desire or attention, and that the field of consciousness is intimately related to the physical world." (Editors of Vol 4 of the Collected Papers).

Rabinoff RA; Dillbeck MC; and Deissler R; Departments of Physics and Psychology, Maharishi University of Management Fairfield Iowa USA, 1981.

Collected Papers v4.324.

Research Summary 11

Sociological effects of the group dynamics of consciousness: Decrease of crime and traffic accidents in Holland

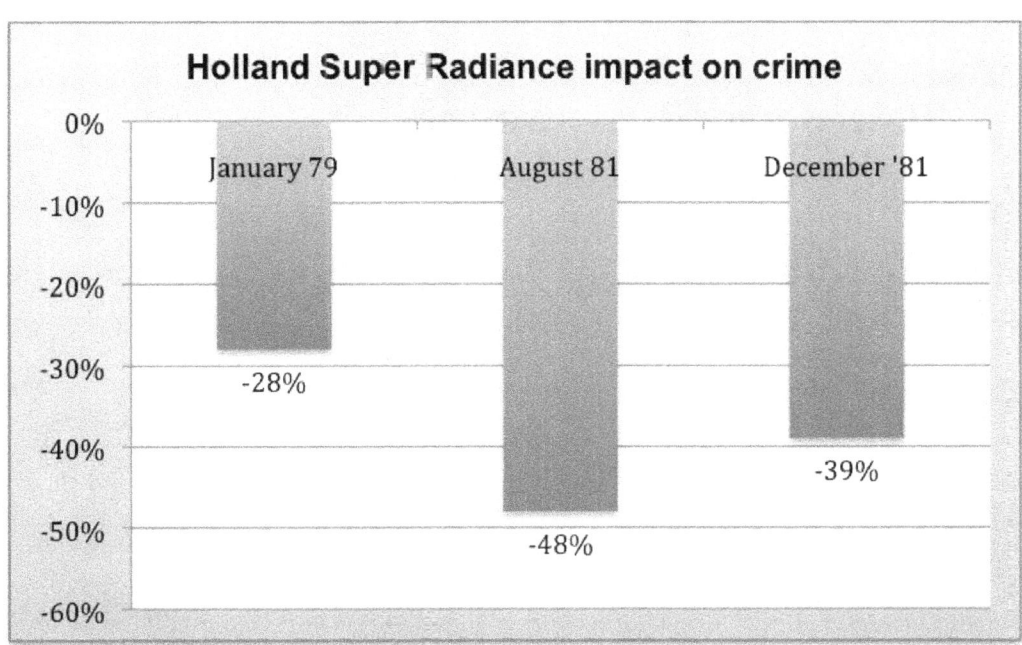

During two periods in 1979 and 1981, The Dutch TM organisation managed to attract sufficient numbers of TM-Sidhas to meditate together in one place to carry out a Super Radiance study. On both occasions they achieved or exceeded the square root of 1% of the national population (376 TM-Sidhas). On a third occasion, a TM-Sidha group meeting in Germany achieved the Super Radiance effect for a large part of Northern Europe and this extended area included providing Super Radiance for Holland as well.

Researchers decided to carry out a retrospective study to test the hypothesis that during these three experimental periods both crime and road traffic accidents with injury would have decreased across the whole of Holland.

The researchers collected monthly data for a ten-year period between 1971 and 1981 from the Dutch Central Office for Statistics and compared these statistics with events occurring during the three experimental periods.

Here it is interesting to note that even though the data used by the researchers was for full monthly periods and the coherence groups were only of the right size for a proportion of those months, the results obtained are still very significant.

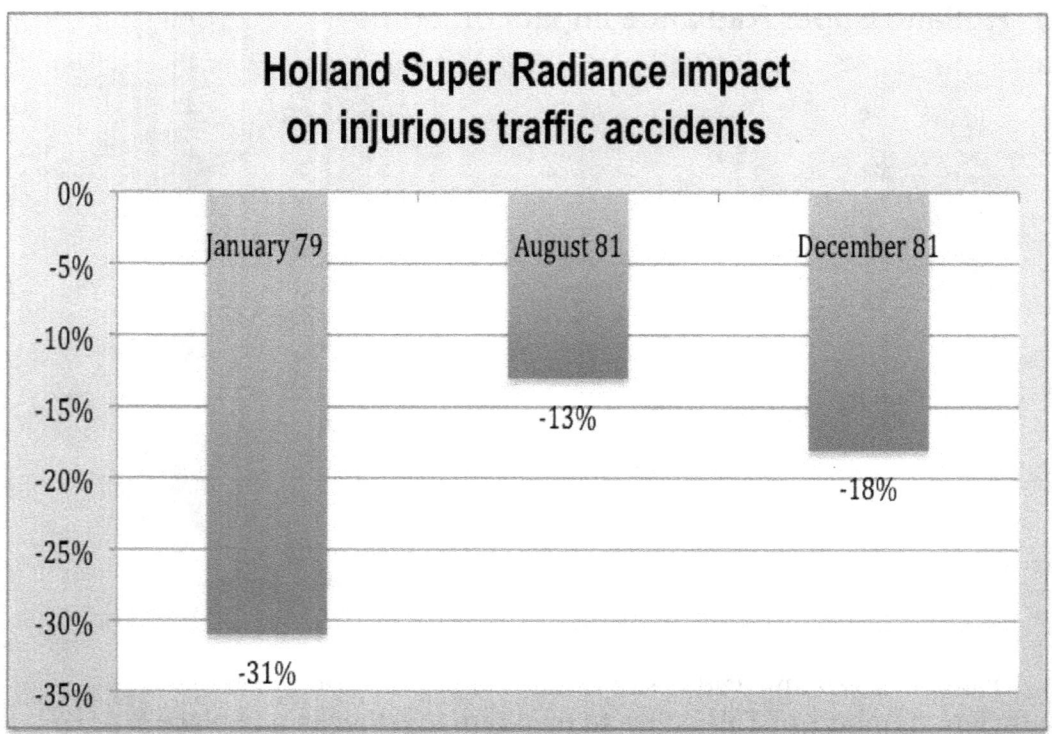

Crime reduction figures:

- January 1979 group: 28% drop in crime ($p = .02$).
- August 1981 group: 48% drop in crime ($p = .04$).
- December 1981 group: 39% drop in crime ($p = .03$).

Combined p value is $p = .004$

Traffic accidents with injury reduction figures:

- January 1979 group: 31% drop in traffic accidents ($p = .002$).
- August 1981 group: 13% drop in traffic accidents ($p = .08$).
- December 1981 group: 18% drop traffic accidents ($p = .02$).

To check on the probability that such improvements might occur at random, the researchers investigated how often such substantial shifts in traffic accidents occurred under normal conditions.

They found that on only one occasion during the previous ten years had there been an unexpected drop in traffic accidents outside the three experimental periods. The drop of only 10% occurred in June 1971 ($p<.005$).

Burgmans WHPM; Burgt AT Van Der; Langenkamp FPT; and Verstegen JH
Maharishi College of Natural Law, Rotterdam, the Netherlands, 1982.

Collected Papers v4.325.

Research Summary 12

The effect of the group dynamics of consciousness on society: Reduced crime in the Union Territory of Delhi, India

In November 1980 Maharishi held a residential educational course on Vedic Science, in New Delhi and this drew a large number of TM-Sidhas to India's capital city. The course initially attracted 3,000 course participants and lasted five-months, starting on 6th November 1980 and lasted until March 30th 1981. During the course this figure gradually dwindled to about 250 participants during the last few weeks.

Despite the attrition in numbers, this large number of TM-Sidhas gathering together to meditate in the same place at the same time everyday still provided a rare opportunity for another Super Radiance study. The Union Territory of Delhi had at the time a population of 6,000,000, of which the square root of 1% is just 245. In other words throughout the duration of the course the citizens of Delhi all benefited from the enhanced brain wave coherence emitted by the Super Radiance effect.

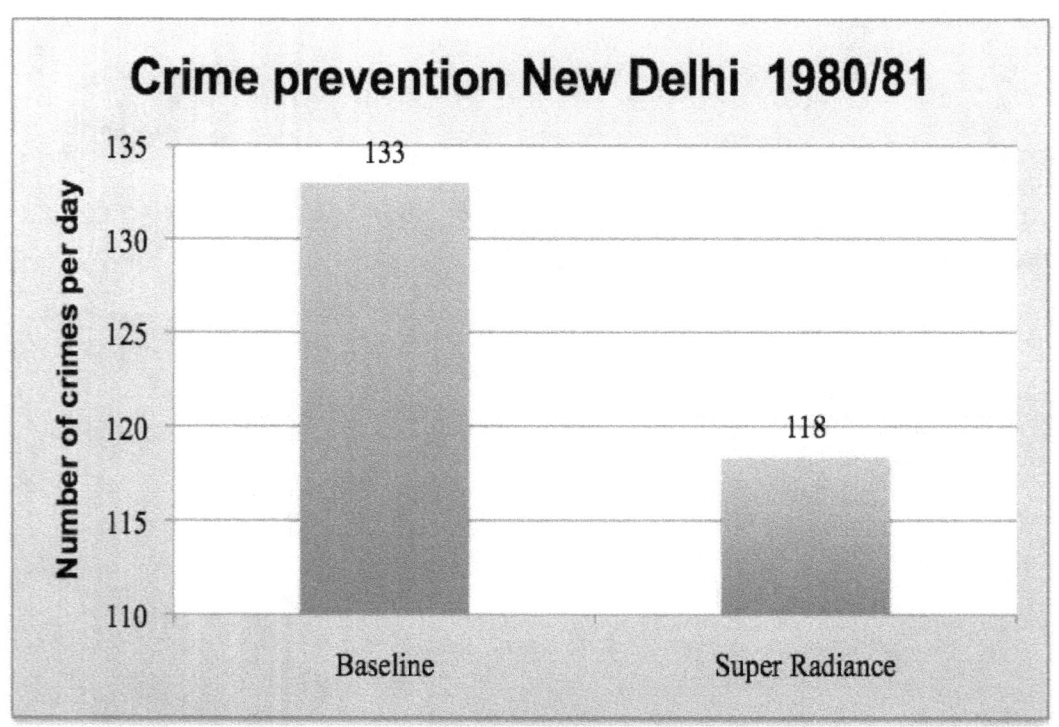

To carry out the study, daily totals of IPC (Indian Penal Code) crimes were obtained from the Delhi Police Headquarters for a period extending from June 1980 through to March 1981. IPC crimes comprise a number of categories including: murder, robbery, riot, dacoity (dacoity is a category of crime fairly unique to India and involves violent crimes committed by roving bands of criminals), burglary, snatching, injury, motor vehicle theft, cycle theft, miscellaneous theft and other miscellaneous non-grievous injuries.

The results showed a highly significant drop in crimes of 11% or 14.65 crimes per day for the duration of the experimental period ($p<.0001$) as compared with the pre-intervention period.

Subsequent research by a senior Indian police official could identify no changes in local police policy, no special 'drives' on crime, no systematic transfer of staff and no apparent changes in the number of criminals through 'externment' or court clearance. Similarly there were no causal seasonal variations.

There was one potential objection to the Super Radiance effect being the causal factor to the drop in crime. However after deeper analysis this factor was also discounted. In October 1980, just prior to the arrival of the TM-Sidhas, the government issued a National Security Ordinance enabling the detention of habitual criminals in certain circumstances. This it was felt may have cleared habitual criminals from the area resulting in a consequent drop in crime. However, further analysis showed that this ordinance still did not account for the magnitude in crime decrease, as violent crimes including dacoity (usually involving habitual criminals) was seen to rise to former levels at the end of the Vedic Science course. In other words after the departure of the last TM-Sidhas, the National Security Ordinance was still in effect and crime rose back to its usual levels.

The researchers also checked to see what variations in crime occurred under normal conditions. They found that average crime totals for the periods July – October and November – January between 1976 and 1980 varied by less than 1%. This meant that the 11% drop in crime during the project was truly a positive and somewhat dramatic deviation from the normal trend of crime.

Dillbeck MC; Cavanaugh KL; and Berg WP Van Den; Maharishi University of Management, Fairfield, Iowa, USA; University of Washington, Seattle, Washington, USA; and Maharishi European Research University, Seelisberg, Switzerland, 1983.

Collected Papers v4.326.

Research Summary 13

A time series analysis of the effect of the Maharishi Technology of the Unified Field: Reduction of traffic fatalities in the United States

This 1982 study examined the impact that a national Super Radiance group of TM-Sidhas had on road traffic fatalities across the USA. During that year this permanent group experienced a number of occasions when they managed to increase their number by about 60 to 70 individuals. As a result, each time the group achieved these temporary increases in attendance it achieved the square root of 1% or Super Radiance threshold for the whole of the USA (1,520 TM-Sidhas in 1982).

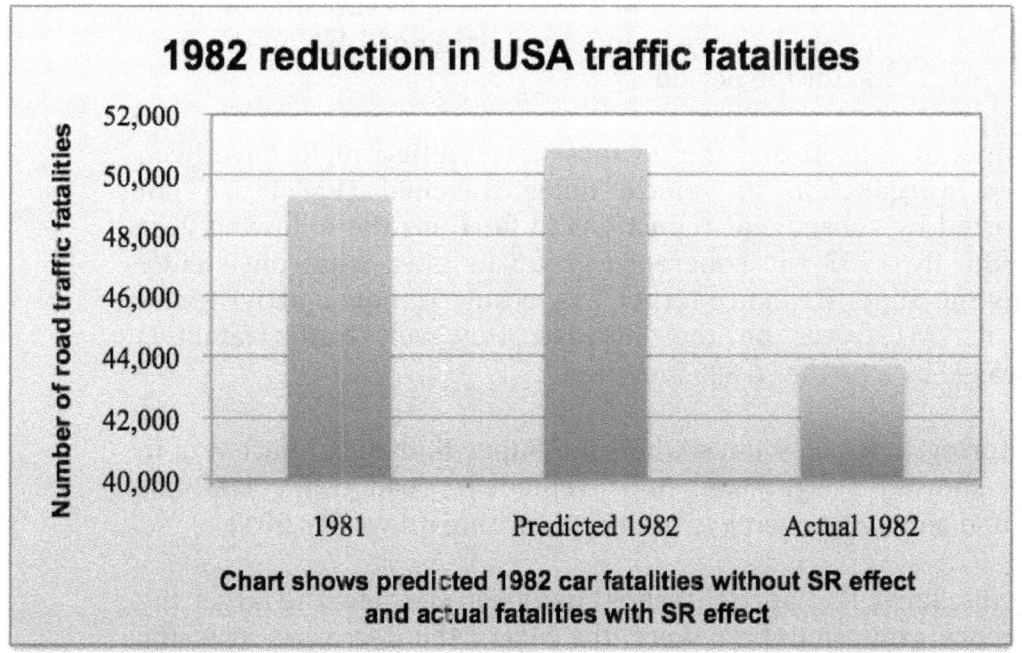

It should be noted that the group size fluctuated inconsistently during the year and only reached the Super Radiance threshold on 17 separate occasions.

The length of these occasions varied from 1 day to 37 consecutive days and in all totalled 125 days out of the 365 days in the year.

Interrupted time series analysis was used to compare 1982, the experimental year, with the previous seven years to predict what the average daily level of traffic fatalities would be without the all important Super Radiance intervention. Points of interest from the research include:

- The multiple times the national group reached Super Radiance in the year and the variations in lengths of time it was maintained reinforces the evidence that Super Radiance is having a beneficial impact on the level of traffic fatalities. This irregularity and frequency of occurrence effectively means that, the Super Radiance conditions under test, benefited from multiple replications within the one study.

- Even though the Super Radiance effect was only achieved for about a third of the year, the overall road fatalities for the whole year fell from 49,301 in 1981 to 43,721 in 1982. This is a reduction of 5,580 or 11.3% on the previous year and a reduction of 14% on the time series prediction for the period.

- Attempts to explain that the decrease in fatalities might have been due to a reduction in vehicle miles travelled (VMT) are not supported by subsequent reductions in fatalities the following year in 1983. By 1983 the coherence group in Iowa was consistently hitting the Super Radiance target, as a result economic activity, and with it VMT, were on the increase. However, traffic fatalities decreased by a further 6.3% that year.

- Monitoring those 125 days when the Super Radiance effect was in place, showed a significant improvement in road traffic fatalities over and above the averages predicted for those days ($p<.001$).

- Once the Super Radiance threshold had been reached, the larger the coherence group numbers were, the bigger the decreases in traffic fatalities. The decrease in fatalities, on days when there were sudden increases in the number of TM-Sidhas by over 100 people, could be five times as great as the average daily decrease for the year.

- Decreases in traffic fatalities were seen to be greater in states roughly closer to the coherence group in Iowa.

- Evidence that reduced drunken driving, increased use of safety restraints and other direct improvements to driving conditions helped create the reduction in fatalities is congruent with the Super Radiance theory. Super Radiance is predicted to produce measurable improvements in thinking, decision-making, emotions and behaviour among the subject populace. It is to be expected that these improvements will translate into more responsible driving, less alcohol consumption, improved alertness and so on. The Super Radiance effect is not independent or exclusive of other mechanisms for improving quality of life factors such as reduced traffic fatalities or crime.

Dillbeck MC; Larimore WE; and Wallace RK; Maharishi University of Management, Fairfield, Iowa, USA, and Scientific Systems, Inc., Cambridge, Massachusetts, USA, 1984.

Collected Papers v4.327.

Research Summary 14

Reduction in homicide in Washington DC through the Maharishi Technology of the Unified Field, 1980-83: A time series analysis

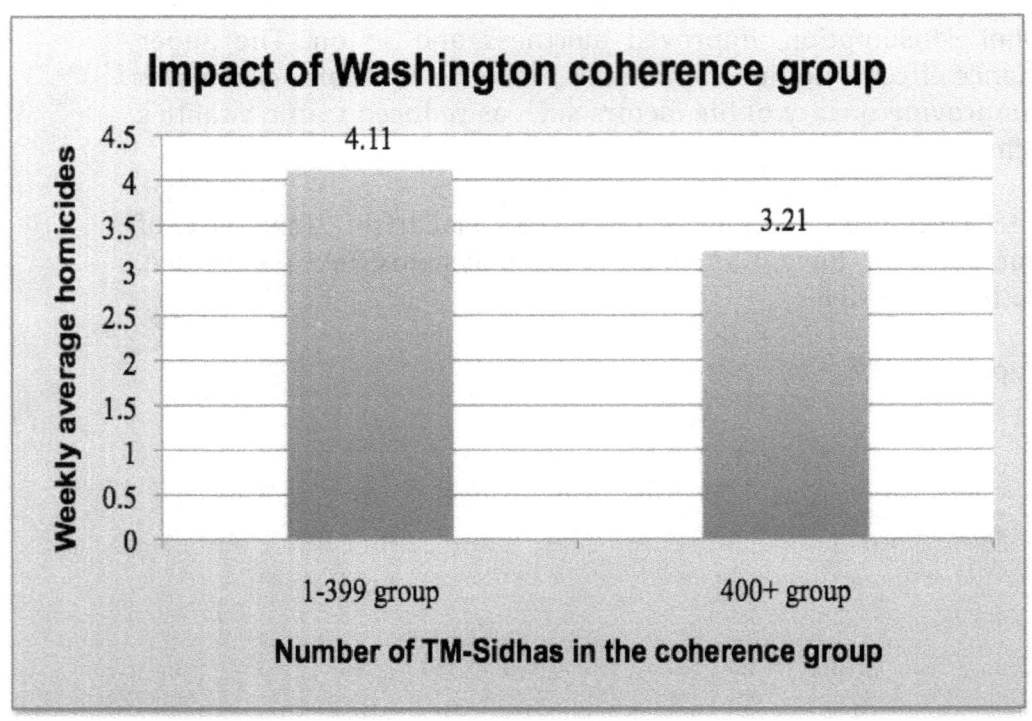

In 1982 the FBI's Uniform Crime Reporting System estimated that there were 21,012 homicides in the USA. This is equivalent to 9.1 murders per 100,000 inhabitants. The same year Washington DC had a murder rate of 30.74 per 100,000 population. This means Washington DC had a murder rate 3.38 times higher than the national average.

Washington clearly had a serious crime problem. Fortunately at the time a growing number of TM-Sidhas were moving to the area to work in a local TM academy. So, it was decided to set-up a coherence group to help the situation. This newly formed group provided another useful opportunity to study the impact of the Super Radiance effect over a longer term than just a few weeks.

In the study, researchers monitored the Super Radiance impact of the group over a 173-week period from August 1980 through to November 1983. During this time the coherence group achieved the crucial $\sqrt{1}$ % (square root of 1%) of the population (173 TM-Sidhas) for the District of Columbia for most of the study period.

However, in this instance Maharishi Mahesh Yogi, who was guiding the setting-up of the study, intervened to change the parameters of the study. He pointed out that Washington has a unique position as the national capital of the world's number one super power. The collective consciousness of Washington is not isolated but interacts intimately with influences in global and national consciousness. As a result this global capital city had become the focal point of a large amount of collective stress both nationally and internationally. He saw that this concentration of collective stress was the root cause of the high rate of homicides in the area.

As a consequence, Maharishi considered that the number of TM-Sidhas required to create the same effect as the usual $\sqrt{1}$ % factor would be 400. In the event this figure of 400 TM-Sidhas was achieved for 38 weeks during the study period.

22% drop in Washington homicides

Comparison between the 135 weeks, when the group reached $\sqrt{1}$ % for the District of Columbia but was still too small for the national capital, and the 38 weeks when the group achieved the special Super Radiance effect, showed an average drop of 22% in homicides. ($p<.02$)

Researchers considered other possible causes including, seasonal variations, changes in police coverage and neighbourhood watch programmes, population changes and the weather. None of these other factors were seen to have any influence on the pattern of homicides.

Lanford AG; Maharishi University of Management, Fairfield, Iowa, USA, 1984.

Collected Papers v4.328.

Research Summary 15

The effect of the Maharishi Technology of the Unified Field on stock prices of Washington, DC area based corporations, 1980-83: A time series analysis

The 1980 – 1983 coherence group in Washington (see research summary 14 above) also offered the opportunity to study the influence of the Super Radiance effect on economic prosperity.

The researchers took as the study period roughly the same time period as for the homicide study namely from January 1980 through until September 1983. It was during this time that Washington DC benefited from a growing number of TM-Sidhas who had moved to the area to live. Thus by October 1981 Washington first achieved the Super Radiance threshold with 173 TM-Sidhas meditating together in the City (173 TM-Sidhas being approximately the square root of 1% of the local population). The city achieved this threshold a further four times during the next eight weeks. At which point the threshold was maintained for the rest of the study period.

However as we have seen in summary 14, another and higher threshold was also adopted for this study due to the unique circumstances of Washington DC being the national capital of the world's number one super power. It was understood that the US government's national responsibilities and international activities would make it a focal point of collective stress from a much larger catchment area than just the District of Columbia. The chosen threshold of 400 TM-Sidhas meditating together first occurred in June 1982 but was not sustained on a consistent basis until mid-May 1983.

The mode of assessing economic prosperity in this instance was the composite index of stock market prices for 30 corporations based in Washington DC. The reason for this choice was that average stock prices are often taken as a gauge of economic activity, productivity and confidence in a society. The statistical methodology used was impact assessment analysis or interrupted time series analysis.

The results show that, as anticipated, the impact of the lower threshold of 173 TM-Sidhas was hardly significant. On the other hand, after a short lag of a week there was always a statistically significant increase in stock prices whenever the coherence group achieved the 400-Super Radiance threshold. On average, stock prices increased $3.81 per week ($p<.001$) during the weeks, following weeks when the coherence group achieved the 400-threshold required for Washington.

The study also demonstrated the effect of the national coherence group in Fairfield Iowa. On the occasions when the national group reached the US Super Radiance level with a minimum of 1,530 TM-Sidhas meditating together there was a further improvement in the composite stock index.

Time series intervention analysis indicated that other factors such as interest rates, political statements, corporate profit etc., were unlikely to be the cause of these specific improvements to stock prices.

The synchronicity of random Super Radiance periods with matching stock price movements strongly support the hypothesis that collective coherence is a causal factor

An important supporting factor for the hypothesis is the random nature of the multiple Super Radiance thresholds' occurrences and the synchronised improvements to stock prices. The 400-Super Radiance threshold was reached for 30 out of 68 weeks for a total of six separate intervals, ranging from 1 to 20 weeks per interval.

Despite the haphazard nature of the occurrences, on each and every one of these six occasions there was a rise in stock prices.

Lanford AG; Maharishi University of Management, Fairfield, Iowa, USA, 1984

Collected Papers v4.329

Research Summary 16

The group dynamics of consciousness and the U.K. stock market

This Quality Of Life (QOL) research project looked at the impact that Super Radiance groups of TM-Sidhas might have on share price fluctuations. Although in this study the groups were too small to reach the Super Radiance threshold for the UK (about 750 TM-Sidhas), nevertheless a significant impact was observed every time there was an increase in the numbers of TM-Sidhas meditating together in a group.

As a means of measurement, fluctuations in the daily number of TM-Sidhas meditating together were compared with daily changes in the Financial Times Actuaries 'All Share' (FTA) Index. This index is a measure of the current market capitalization of the 750 largest public companies in the UK. Economists tend to view the All Share index as a barometer of optimism and confidence in the UK economy.

The researchers observed that whenever there was a significant spike in the number of TM-Sidhas meditating together in one place, then there was a commensurate lift in share prices in the FTA All share Index.

These increases in share prices, seen during the week during and immediately following the spike in TM-Sidha group meditation, were significantly higher than the mean daily increases in share prices seen over the remainder of the 17-month study period. ($t = 2.804$, $df = 352$, $p<.01$).

The increases in share prices were also significantly higher than the mean daily increase in the seven-day periods immediately before and after these experimental periods ($t = 2.325$, $df = 104$, $p<.05$). All that was required to precipitate a significant increase in share prices was about 250 TM-Sidhas.

Beresford MS; and Clements G; The group dynamics of consciousness and the UK stock market; MERU Research Institute, Mentmore, Buckinghamshire, England, 1983.

Collected Papers v4.330.

Research Summary 17

The Maharishi Technology of the Unified Field and reduction of armed conflict: A comparative, longitudinal study of Lebanese villages

The Lebanese war provided a valuable opportunity to carryout a prospective study of the Maharishi effect (1% effect) in an ongoing situation of hostility and warfare. The limited resources available at the time restricted the teaching of TM to only one town, but even so this was enough to demonstrate that a community could protect itself from harm by the simple expedient of getting a small fraction of the population to learn to meditate.

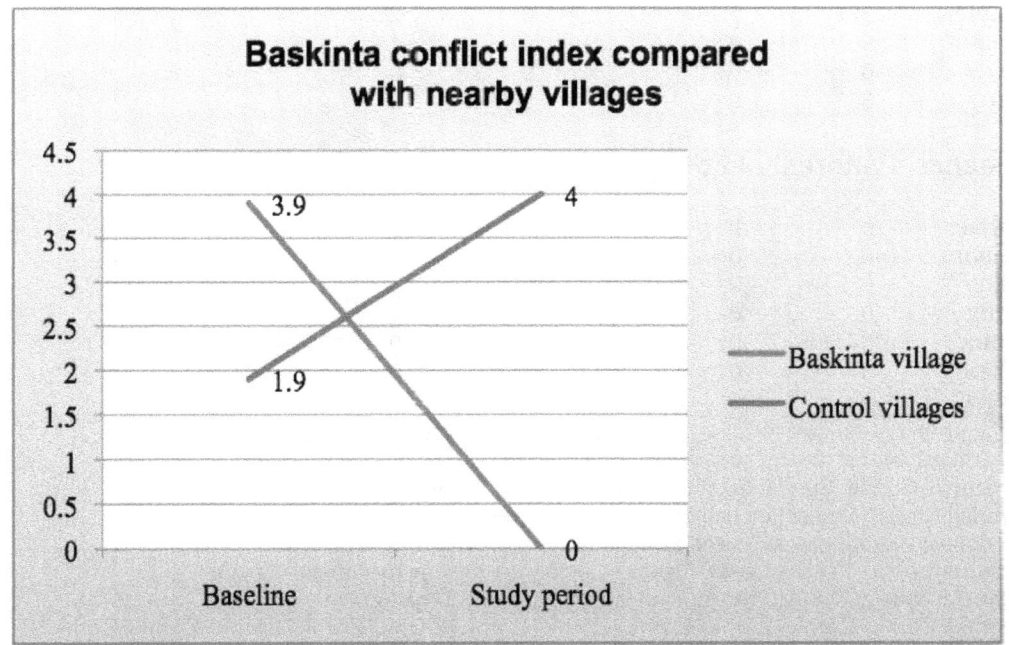

As a prelude to this study, in May 1981 two TM teachers began teaching the Transcendental Meditation technique to villagers in Baskinta, a village caught up in the focal region of the Lebanese conflict.

Baskinta is situated at the base of Sannine Mountain and has a population of

10,000 people. As such, the village occupies a strategic point in central Lebanon. This strategic position meant that the town had found itself in the middle of continuing battles between opposing 'leftist' and 'rightist' forces during the entire study period (1978-84).

Impact of 1% effect on Baskinta Village

		Shells	Wounded	Killed	Property damage[a]
1978	Autumn	134	0	1	1
1979	Winter[b]	0	0	0	0
	Spring	45	1	0	1
	Summer	30	4	0	1
	Autumn	35	2	0	1
1980	Winter[b]	0	0	0	0
	Spring	50	1	1	1
	Summer[c]	0	0	0	0
	Autumn	0	0	0	0
1981	Winter[b]	0	0	0	0
	Spring	1,705	2	1	2
	Summer	227	2	0	2
	Autumn[d]	50	0	0	1
1982	Winter[b]	0	0	0	0
	Spring	353	0	0	0

Baskinta reaches 1% threshold of TM meditators

	Summer	0	0	0	0
	Autumn	0	0	0	0
1983	Winter[b]	0	0	0	0
	Spring	0	0	0	0
	Summer	0	0	0	0
	Autumn	0	0	0	0
1984	Winter	0	0	0	0

a. Under the property damage heading 1 denotes damage and 2 denotes major damage, i.e., more than 2 houses destroyed or 4 seriously damaged.
b. Winter snow in Sannine Mountain prevented troop movements and therefore inhibited fighting. The exception being the winter of 1984, which was unusually warm. As a result heavy fighting experienced throughout Lebanon apart from Baskinta.
c. No fighting anywhere in Lebanon during the summer of 1980 due to national ceasefire
d. Following the Israeli invasion there is a lull in fighting across Lebanon

The town's main economic activity is agriculture, the residents are mostly Christian and during the length of the study the town remained in rightist hands.

By June 1982, the TM teachers had taught 100 people in the village to meditate. This meant that, as the village had a population of 10,000, from that time onward, the village had reached its Maharishi effect threshold with 1% of the population meditating.

As predicted by the researchers and in complete contrast to both its previous recent history and the continued experience of nearby villages, Baskinta experienced *an immediate and complete cessation of hostilities* as measured by:

- Incoming shells (p<.005)

- Property damage (p<.005)

- Casualties (p<.005)

As a research control, improvements in Baskinta were compared, over a period of five and a half years, to those of neighbouring villages of similar size and agricultural economic base. To do this the researchers adopted an index of conflict, using the measurement of 25 incoming shells per season for each point on the index.

The resulting index showed a drop for Baskinta from 3.9 to zero. At the same time worsening trends were observed in the surrounding control villages where there was an increase in the index mean for the control villages from 1.9 to 4.0 (p<.00001) (See chart above).

After the 1% effect had been achieved, Baskinta also experienced improvements in crop yields, increased social and sporting activities and accelerated municipal development despite the civil war going on in the rest of the country.

Abou Nader TM; Alexander CN; and Davies JL; American University of Beirut, Beirut, Lebanon. Harvard University, Cambridge, Massachusetts, U.S.A.; and Macquarie University, North Ryde, New South Wales, Australia, 1984.

Collected Papers v4.331.

Research Summary 18

The long-term effects of the Maharishi Technology of the Unified Field on the quality of life in the United States (1960 to 1983)

A number of studies had explored the short-term impact of Super Radiance. This time, the researchers wanted to see what happens over the long term. Would the benefits of Super Radiance continue to grow and accumulate or would they drift? This study looked at the combined Super Radiance effect of two main factors:

1. The long-term growth in the numbers of TM meditators in the USA (The 1% effect).
2. The Super Radiance group based at Maharishi International University in Fairfield, Iowa (Now called Maharishi University of Management).

Specifically, The objective of the study was to ascertain whether the rising standard of living in the USA over these years was due to the large increase in the number of people practicing Transcendental Meditation and the existence of the Super Radiance group of TM-Sidhas. To achieve this aim the researchers looked at a range of quality of life (QOL) statistics on an annual basis from 1960 through to 1983. They composed a QOL index covering the following areas of life:

- Crime rate
- Percentage of civil cases reaching trial
- Rate of infectious diseases
- Infant mortality rate
- Suicide rate
- Hospital admission rates
- Cigarette consumption
- Alcohol consumption
- Gross national product
- Patent application rate
- Number of degrees conferred
- Divorce rate
- Traffic fatalities

Surge in TM teaching brings positive shift in QOL trend

Between 1960 and 1975 there had been a nearly continuous negative trend in US quality of life indicators. But in 1975 and 1976 over 350,000 people learned the TM technique bringing the total percentage of meditators to 0.4% of the US population. As predicted by the Hatchard study (Research summary 2) from 1976 onwards, the QOL index started to improve ($t = 2.609$, $p = .009$) albeit rather erratically at first. See charts.

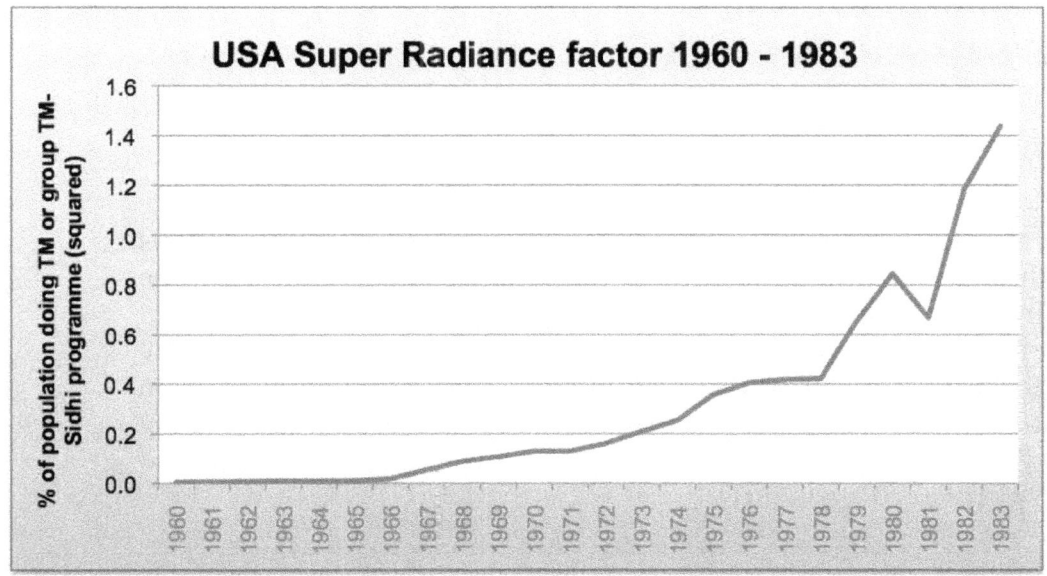

Notes to charts: The two charts illustrate the mirroring of improvements in the USA QOL index in line with increases in the Super Radiance factor. There is however a lag of about one year between the onset of Super Radiance and improvements in the QOL index. The Super Radiance factor is calculated by the aggregate of 1. The percentage of people practising the TM technique individually in their own homes across the country and 2. The square of the number of TM-Sidhas meditating together in groups. Primarily the main US Super Radiance group was in Fairfield Iowa. The improvement in QOL in 1976 was precipitated by a surge of new meditators being taught in 1975. The drop in Super Radiance in 1980 was caused by the temporary departure of a number of TM-Sidhas from the Iowa group.

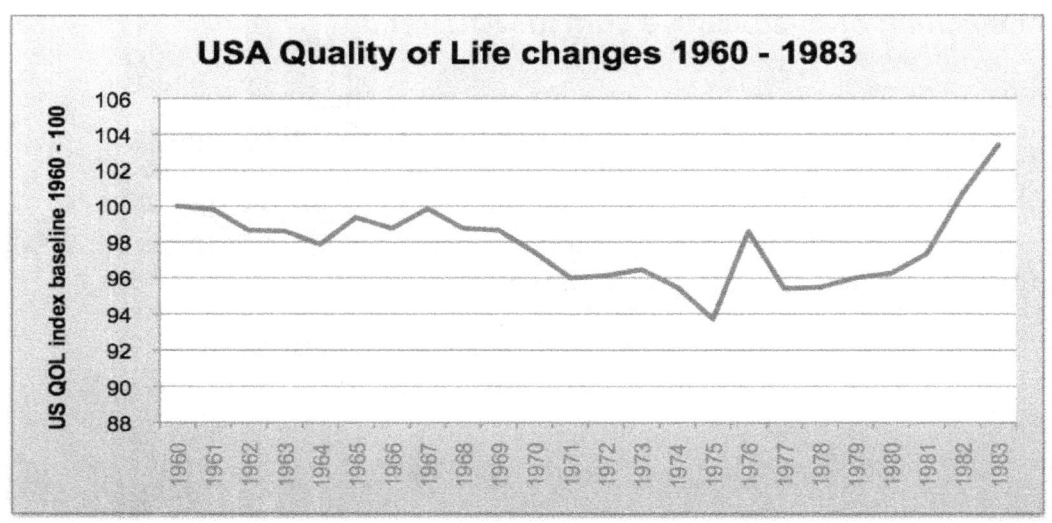

When the growth in the number of meditators stabilized in the late 1970s the growth in the QOL index began to flat line. However, another surge occurred in the QOL index when the TM-Sidhi programme was introduced and a group of TM-Sidhas was formed at Maharishi International University (MIU) in Iowa. As a result of this new input in national coherence, from 1979 onwards improvements in the QOL index began to accelerate showing a 2.443% greater average rate of improvement over the preceding period 1976 to 1981 ($t = 6.704$, $p<.0001$).

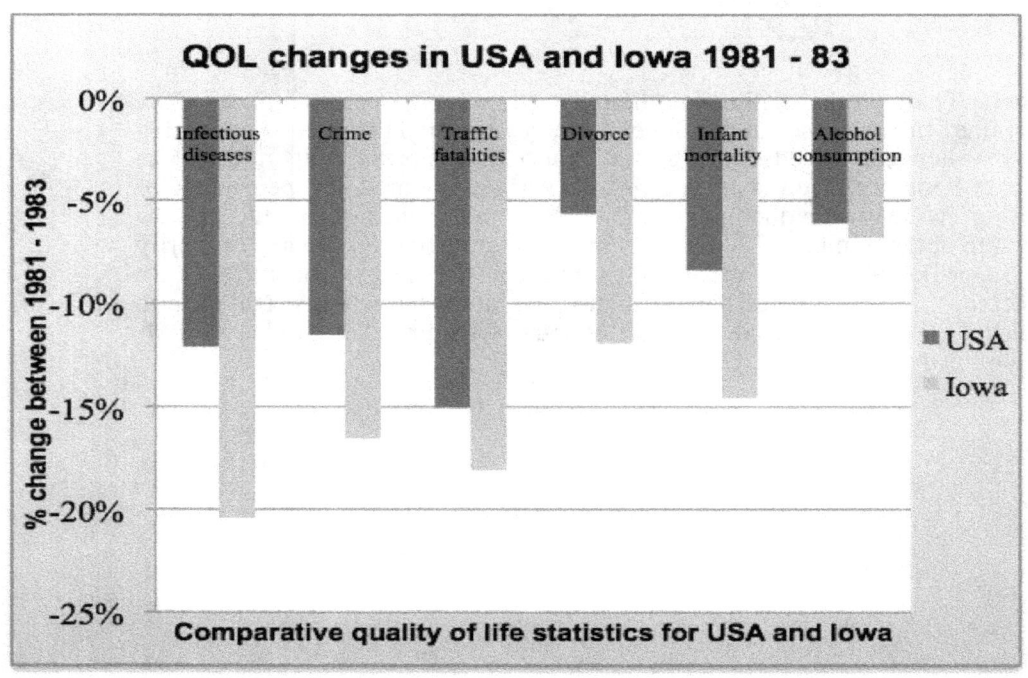

The improvement in the QOL index was further accentuated in 1982 and 1983 when there was a large jump in the numbers of TM-Sidhas meditating at MIU in those years. It is significant that, during this period the combined effect of TM practitioners and the coherence group at MIU achieved the Super Radiance effect for the USA.

An interesting feature of this research study was the comparison made between the US as a whole and Iowa, the state where the TM-Sidhas were grouped. Iowa showed significantly higher improvements to a QOL index during 1982 and 1983 as compared to the rest of the country ($t = 4.476$, $p = .0065$) See chart (QOL changes in USA and Iowa 1981 – 83).

This accentuated rise in Iowa's QOL index in comparison to the national index lends further weight to the argument that the TM-Sidha group in Iowa was the source of the unprecedented surge in national QOL improvement.

Orme-Johnson DW; and Gelderloos P; A version: Orme-Johnson DW; and Gelderloos P; and Dillbeck MC; The Effects of the Maharishi Technology of the Unified Field on the US Quality of Life (1960-1984) was published in *Social Science Perspectives Journal, 2(4), 127-146, 1988.*

Collected Papers v4.332.

Research Summary 19

International peace project in the Middle East: The effect of the Maharishi Technology of the Unified Field

This Middle East study was a prospective one, in that it was set-up in advance of the actual experiment. The study was designed to demonstrate the ability of a Super Radiance group to have a positive impact on a major trouble spot as a direct result of deliberate intervention on the level of the field of consciousness by a group of TM-Sidhas.

At the time of the study, Lebanon was enduring a violent civil war and so the means adopted to intervene was a Super Radiance group based in Jerusalem, the capital of Israel. Thus, during July and August 1983 a group of resident Israeli TM-Sidhas was set-up in Jerusalem to carryout the experiment.

To optimise objectivity the researchers had picked this experimental period arbitrarily to avoid the criticism that they were choosing the timing to coincide with other favourable variable factors. They also presented the proposal, including the criteria for measuring the impact of Super Radiance, to other research scientists in the USA and Israel.

To ensure rigour and objectivity they decided to analyse the effect of the Super Radiance group on independently accessed composite quality of life (QOL) indices for Jerusalem, Israel and Lebanon using Box-Jenkins ARIMA impact assessment analysis. The composite QOL index comprised data on:

- War intensity in Lebanon; (Reduced war deaths of 76% were recorded on days when the group created Super Radiance for Lebanon as well as Israel.)
- Newspaper content providing analysis of Israeli national mood
- The Tel Aviv stock market index
- Automobile accident rate in Jerusalem
- Fire incidences in Jerusalem
- Jerusalem maximum temperature

In their calculation as to the potential impact of the Super Radiance group the researchers took into account the number of TM meditators already meditating around the country in their own homes. They were then able to estimate the number of TM-Sidhas required for each target population.

It was estimated that the requisite numbers for the target populations were:

- 65 TM-Sidhas to impact Jerusalem on its own
- 122 TM-Sidhas to impact the whole of Israel
- 197 TM-Sidhas to impact Israel and Lebanon combined.

In the event, the size of the group fluctuated almost on a day-to-day basis between a minimum of 65 TM-Sidhas and maximum of 241. In general it was observed that as the Super Radiance group grew in size, so there was an increase (improvement) in the composite QOL index.

When the group was at the smaller scale it had a measurable effect on Jerusalem or Israel only. When the group was large enough (over 197) an impact was seen on all composite indices in Lebanon as well; for instance when the group size achieved Super Radiance for Lebanon there were up to 76% fewer casualties and decreased war intensity ($p = .0216$).

Changes tended to happen within a day of the changes in the size of the group.

It was clear from the statistics that the larger the group size in Jerusalem, then the greater the degree of improvement to all the QOL factors. This particular observation reinforced the hypothesis that the Super Radiance group was creating a generalised, underlying coherence effect.

Furthermore, on the days when Super radiance was achieved for the respective localities, significant improvements were seen in <u>each variable</u> in the index. The researchers checked out other possible causes of improvements to QOL such as holidays and temperature but these were found to have no correlation with the improvements in the QOL index.

The chart over shows the strong correspondence between the number of TM-Sidhas in the coherence group in Jerusalem and a composite index of the six variable QOL factors. The volatile fluctuations in group-meditation attendance closely mirror the fluctuations in the QOL index; adding further weight to the argument that the meditators were the causal factor in the QOL improvements.

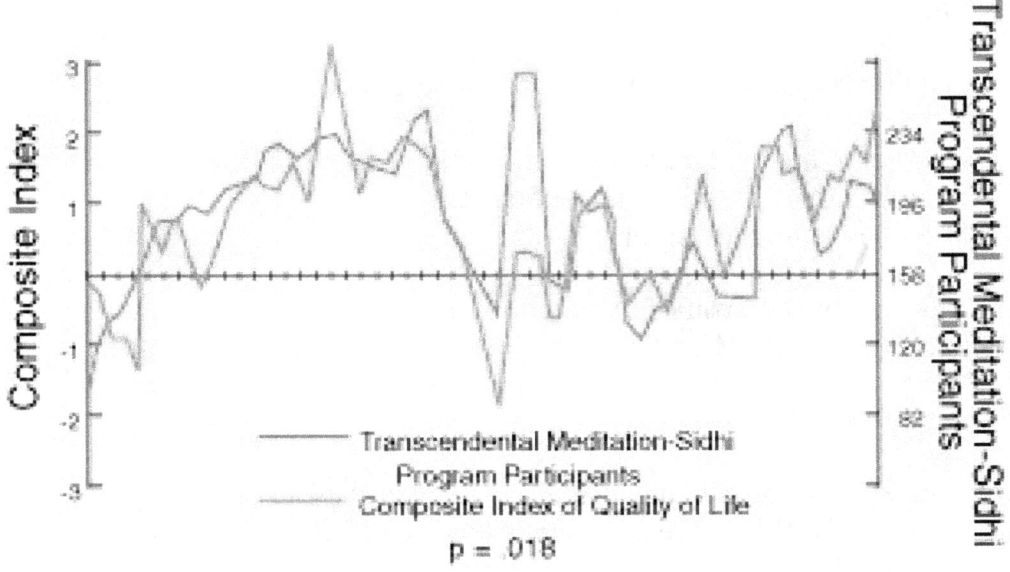

Orme-Johnson DW; Alexander CN; Davies JL; Chandler HM; and Larimore WE; *Journal of Conflict Resolution, 32(4): 776-812, 1988; Journal of Conflict Resolution (34: 756–768, 1990)*

Collected Papers v4.333.

Research Summary 20

A time series analysis of the relationship between the group practice of the Transcendental Meditation and TM-Sidhi Programme and crime rate change in Puerto Rico

The opportunity arose for this study when Maharishi opened an academy in Puerto Rico offering long-term and short-term training courses in Transcendental Meditation and the TM-Sidhi meditation programme. As the academy got underway the number of TM-Sidhas practising together gradually grew until, for two weeks during April 1984, the numbers exceeded the square root of one percent of the island's population.

Time series analysis indicated a significant decrease in crime during this month when the Super Radiance factor had been achieved. In addition, there was an *increase* in crime when the full group of TM-Sidhas finally left the island from July onwards (Joint significance, $p<0.25$). The researchers could find no change in police practices in Puerto Rico to account for the drop in crime during the April experimental period.

Dillbeck MC; Mittlefehldt V; Lukenbach AP; Childress D; Royer A; Westsmith L; and Orme-Johnson DW; Maharishi University of Management, Fairfield, Iowa, USA and Maharishi International Caribbean, Fajardo, Puerto Rico, 1984.

Collected Papers v4.334.

Research Summary 21

The effect of the Maharishi Technology of the Unified Field on the war in Lebanon: A time series analysis of the influence of international and national coherence creating assemblies

This study looked at the impact that three different temporary Super Radiance creating projects had on the Lebanese civil war during a period of about six months in 1983/1984. Each Super Radiance group only met for about two weeks (experimental periods) and comprised:

1. The first ever, global coherence group that met in Iowa in December 1983 – January 1984. This group was large enough to achieve the Super Radiance threshold for the entire world (minimum of 6,900 TM-Sidhas). Hence the researchers predicted, that despite the long distance away it would still have a positive impact on the Lebanese civil war.
2. A local group of 70 TM-Sidhas met during March 1984 in the village of Broumana in Lebanon about 18 km away from the main centre of conflict in Beirut.
3. A regional group of 2,000 TM-Sidhas met in Porec, Yugoslavia during April 1984 located about 1,700 miles from Lebanon.

The researchers measured the impact of the TM-Sidha groups using a Peace/War index to compare the experimental periods with the remaining days of the six-month period that straddled the three different projects. This index involved monitoring daily events reported in major Lebanese newspapers and according these events values on an eight point rating scale from maximum positive conditions + 3 to maximum negative – 4. The researchers also monitored the daily number of war deaths and injuries in the country.

The researchers publicly predicted in advance that the prevailing negative conditions would be reversed and in the event this is exactly what happened.

Average war deaths fell by 55% and war injuries fell by 38% during the three experimental periods as opposed to the control days.

	Peace/war index	P factor	War deaths per day	P factor	War injuries per day
Control period	- 0.83		6.52		20.60
Global	+ 1.41	$p = 0038$	1.67	$p = 00000062$	12.68*
Broumana	+ 2.14	$p = 000036$	3.82	$p = 029$	12.68*
Porec	+ 1.00	$p = 016$	2.50	$p = 007$	12.68*

* This figure is the average for the three groups.

It was also observed that Lebanon experienced an improved foreign currency exchange rate during the local coherence group activity.

The researchers investigated possible alternative explanations to the positive movements during the experimental periods but could not find any that were supported by the data collected.

Alexander CN; Abou Nader TM; Cavanaugh KL; Davies JL; Dillbeck MC; Kfoury RJ; and Orme-Johnson DW; Maharishi University of Management, Fairfield, Iowa, USA, and Massachusetts Institute of Technology, Cambridge, Massachusetts, USA, 1984.

Collected Papers v4.335.

Research Summary 22

The effect of the 'Taste of Utopia' Assembly on the world index of international stock prices

This study focussed on the impact Super Radiance can have on international stock prices. Specifically, the researchers looked at the influence of the global Super Radiance project called the "Taste of Utopia Assembly" reviewed in summary number 23 below (Collected papers 337).

At the height of the Utopia project, 8,000 TM-Sidhas were meditating together in Iowa USA. This figure comfortably created global Super Radiance even though it was only for a brief period of nine days.

The researchers used Box-Jenkins impact assessment methodology for the analysis of time series of daily fluctuations in the world stock index of 20 stock markets worldwide. For comparison purposes, the study covered a period of six and a half months before during and after the experimental period of nine days. They also studied corresponding periods over the previous five-years.

The researchers predicted ahead of the study that global Super Radiance would have a positive impact on the World Stock Index.

In the event, there was a coordinated rise in 19 out of 20 stock markets across the world during the experimental period.

The increase in this World index of stock markets, during the nine-day global Super Radiance period, was 1.58 times greater than the mean change for the previous five years. For the comparable period in the previous five years, the average change in the World index was 2.87% compared to 4.53% during the assembly. The improvements could not be attributed to seasonal patterns common at the time of year or other economic variables ($p = .000033$).

Increase in 19 out of 20 stock markets

During the experimental period the increase of 19 out of 20 stock markets was unprecedented and nearly doubled the mean increase in 9.8 markets seen for the previous five years. The average daily increase was significantly greater than during the period preceding and following the experimental period when on average the World index declined ($p = .0047$)

The researchers held that the study supported the view that:

1. A field of collective consciousness exists that arises from and reciprocally influences the thought and behaviour of the individuals in society
2. Where the group practice of the TM-Sidhi meditation programme achieves the Super Radiance threshold of the square root of 1% of the population, it gives rise to spontaneous improvements in many diverse measures of the quality of life.

Cavanaugh KL; Orme-Johnson DW; and Gelderloos P; Department of Management and Public Affairs and Department of Psychology, Maharishi University of Management, Fairfield, Iowa, USA, 1984.

Collected Papers v4.336.

Research Summary 23

The influence of the Maharishi Technology of the Unified Field on world events and global social indicators: The effects of the 'Taste of Utopia' Assembly

This peace project devised and supervised by Maharishi himself was the culmination of ten years of research on the Super Radiance effect. The stupendous aim of the project was to demonstrate the capacity to create peace across the whole world from one point on earth. As such the sheer scale of the project and its evident success in this objective must rank the study as perhaps the most important scientific social experiment of all time.

At its most intense phase, the project attracted up to 8,000 TM-Sidhas from 50 different countries, who came together to meditate at the Maharishi University of Management (Then called MIU) campus in Iowa, USA in 1984. At the time, 6,900, was the square root of 1% for the then global population of about 5 billion people.

Before the project commenced the researchers predicted that 6,900 TM-Sidhas was the minimum number required to create a significant shift in coherence and consequent shift in positivity in world consciousness.

It is important to note that although the duration of the peace project was three weeks, the number of TM-Sidhas gradually built-up as the project went on. The actual global coherence figure was only reached for a total of nine days during that period.

To monitor the effect of the global Super Radiance group researchers analysed nine 'quality of life' social indicators. These included global statistics, data from international trouble spots including Lebanon and social indicators from several countries including Australia, South Africa, the UK, Pakistan and USA. These countries were selected as they are geographically widely separated from each other and were able to provide comparable statistics at the time.

To allow for seasonal differences the scientists compared all the data for three weeks before, the three weeks during and three weeks after the project period. They also checked similar three-week periods for the five years prior to the project.

The findings are as follows.

Positivity expressed by heads of state

Content analysis of newspaper reports on events relating to heads of state showed a significant shift towards more positive outcomes. Prior to the project period only 35% of statements and actions made by heads of state showed progress towards reversal of prior negative trends. During the project this figure jumped to 71%. After the project, when the number of TM-Sidhas in the group dropped to 2,000 positive statements reverted back to 17% ($p =.02$).

Reduced conflict in Lebanon

As predicted there were impressive improvements recorded in the Lebanese civil war. Total positive events increased from 9.6% prior to the project period to 57.1% during. According to the research authors there was a 'surprisingly rapid evolution of agreement by all parties on a national security plan. After the assembly (peace project) finished, the situation quickly deteriorated.' ($p =.006$).

There was a *"surprisingly rapid evolution of agreement by all parties on a national security plan. After the assembly (peace project) finished the situation quickly deteriorated."* Research authors

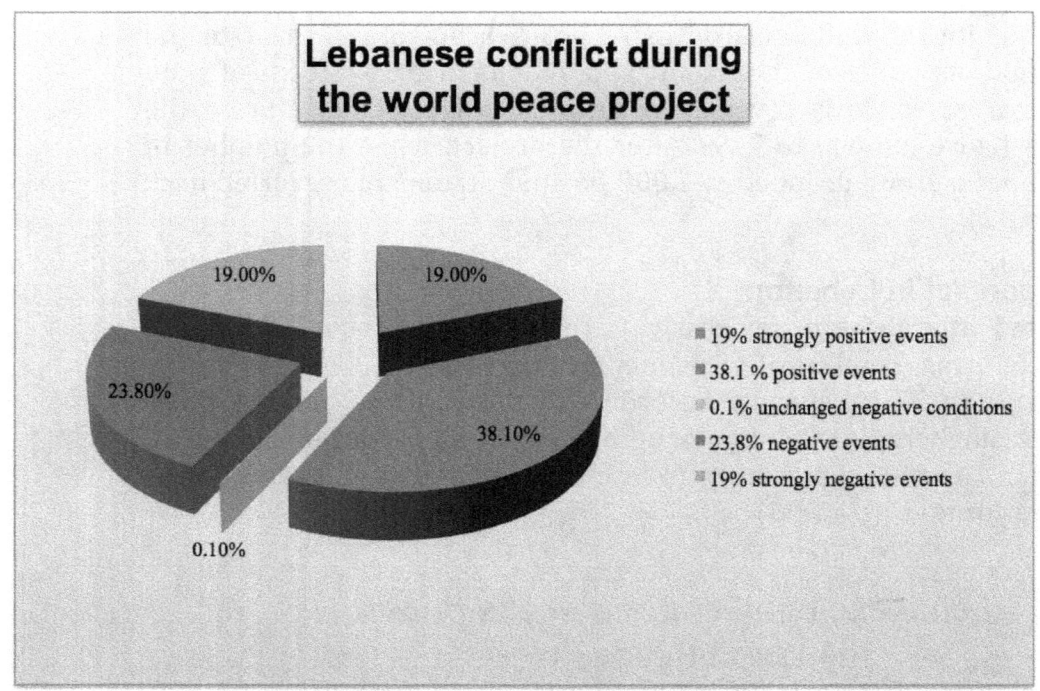

The three tables show the statistics for the periods before, during and after the study period.

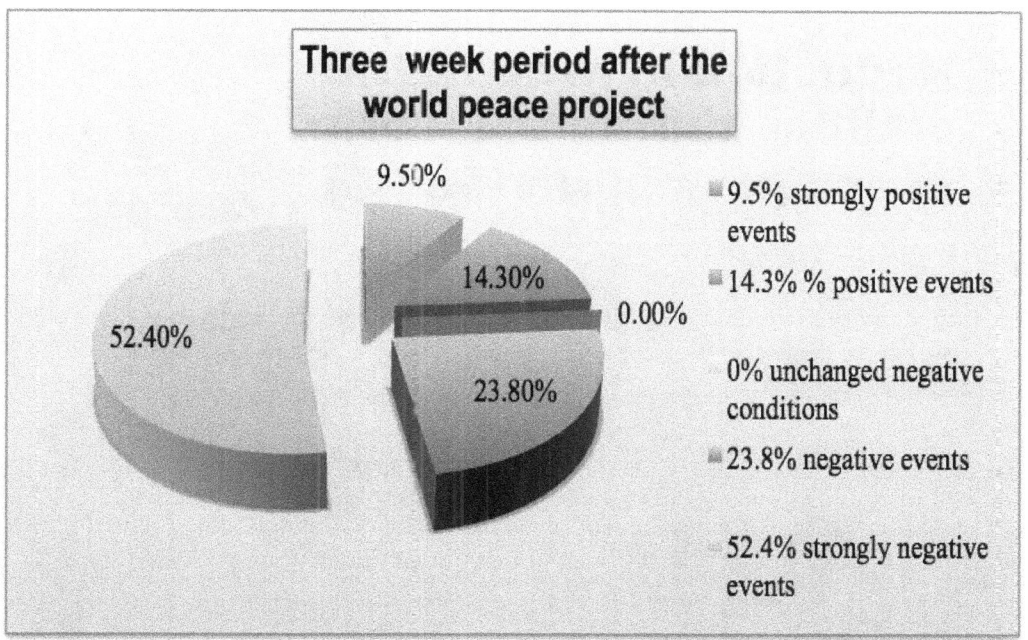

Fewer road traffic fatalities

During the peace project 31.6% fewer road traffic fatalities were seen in the USA than the mean for the prior 16 years. Over the Christmas and New Year holiday periods, road traffic fatalities were at an all time low. This improvement occurred despite an all time high in road mileage travelled.

The researchers also found that fewer than expected traffic fatalities occurred in South Africa (20%) and the Australian states of New South Wales, Victoria, and Western Australia, (11%) compared with the same time of year in previous years ($p = .0001$).

This reduction was all the more remarkable in South Africa as, at the time, the country was otherwise experiencing a significant trend of increases in road traffic fatalities of 7% during this time of year.

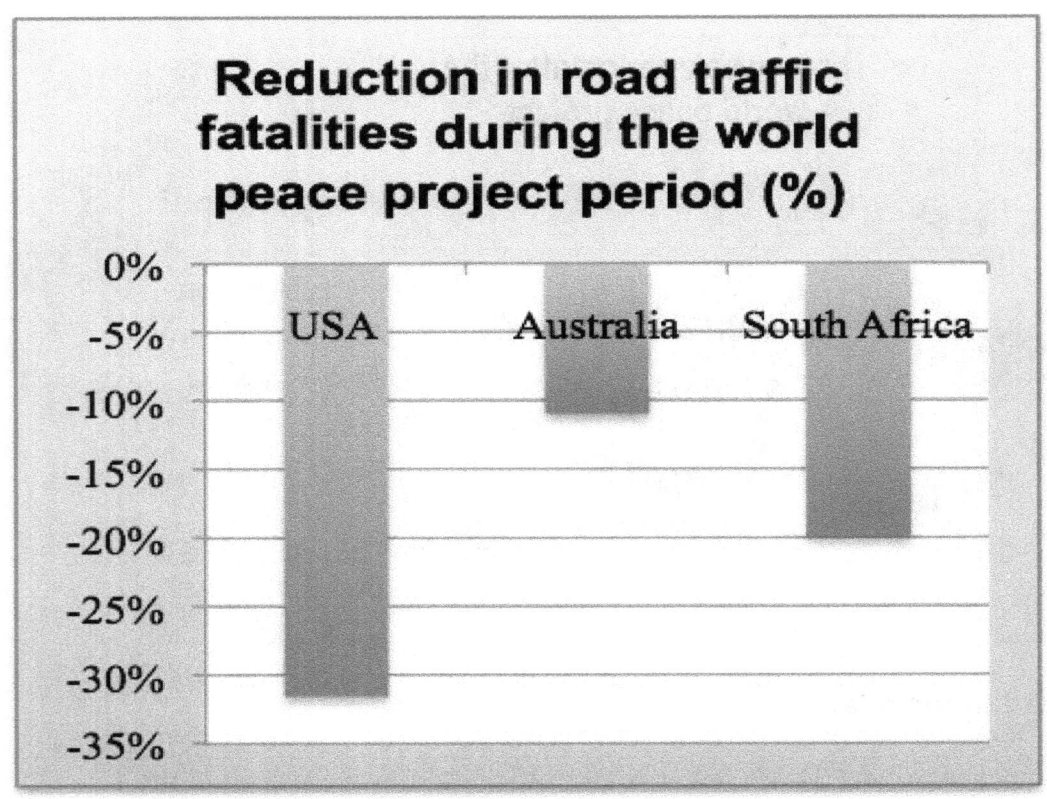

Improvements to economic indicators
Data indicated a significant rise in economic confidence, optimism, and prosperity. The World Stock Index (a measure of the major stocks in 19 countries) reversed a downward trend and instead rose 4.5% ($p = .0001$). 19 out of 20 stock markets in different countries rose by more than 1% during the three-week period; a significantly greater proportion of markets rising than was seen during the previous 5 years ($p = .00004$).

Improvements to the International Conflict scale
There was a significant shift of events in trouble spot countries towards greater positivity as measured by the International Conflict Scale. The percentage of 'Total Positive Events' shifted from 19.8% in the period before to 36% during the project. Total negative events were 80.3% prior to the project period and shrank to 64.10% during the peace project period. Negative events jumped back to 85.4% as soon as the peace project was over ($p = .002$).

Decreased air traffic fatalities
50% decreased air traffic fatalities globally compared with the previous five year period ($p = .0001$).

Fewer notifiable diseases
32% fewer notifiable infectious diseases in the USA and 17.2% fewer in Australia compared to the median of the prior years for the same weeks of the year ($p=.0001$).

Decreased crime

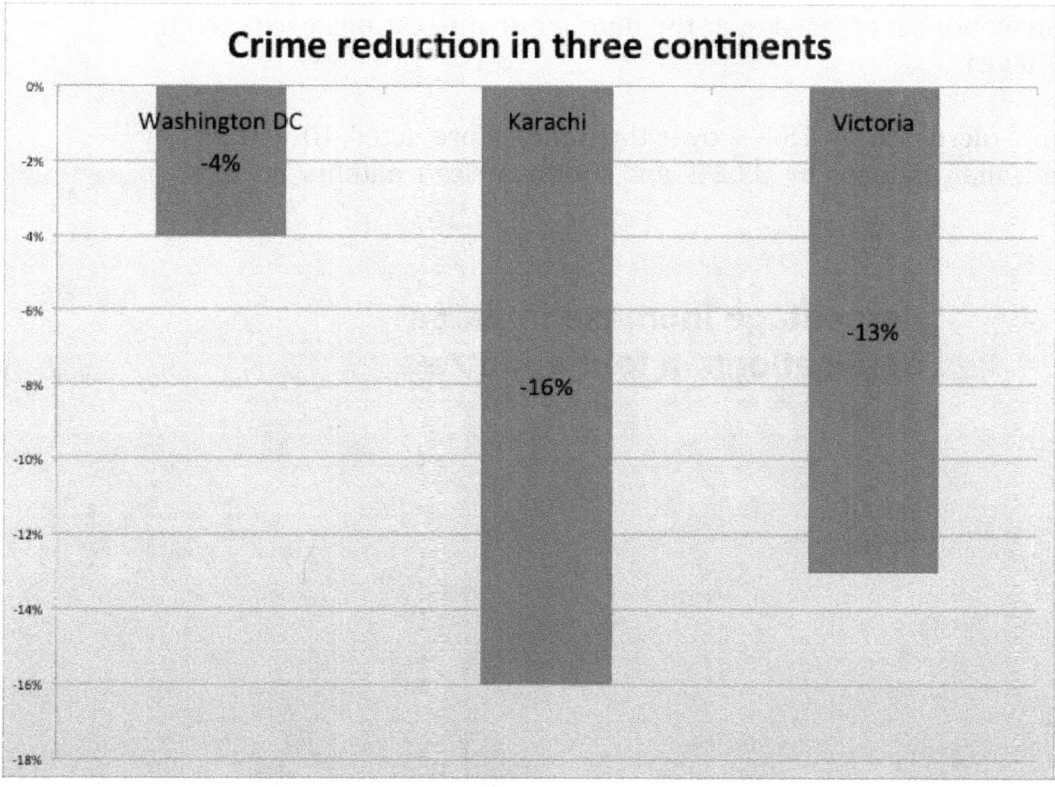

The researchers made enquiries with 165 of the largest metropolitan cities in the world. However few were able to supply the detailed information required for the study in the time available, as the researchers required monthly crime totals back to 1973.

Eventually this depth of crime data became available for three areas. The data was analysed using Box-Jenkins ARIMA time series analysis.

Significantly the results are drawn from three different continents. Even so each study showed decreased crime as follows: Washington DC in the USA (4%), Karachi in Pakistan (16%) and in the State of Victoria, Australia (13%), (p =.000002). The comparison was with crime occurrences for the 24 weeks prior to the three-week project and for 3 weeks afterwards.

The researchers found the reduced crime was not attributable to seasonal variations or prior history of crime trends.

Increased number of patent applications

Patent applications increased over the number of applications predicted for that time of year.

USA patents increased by 15.3% over the number predicted, UK patents by 6.5%, Australian patents by 33.2% and South African patents by 21% (p =.04).

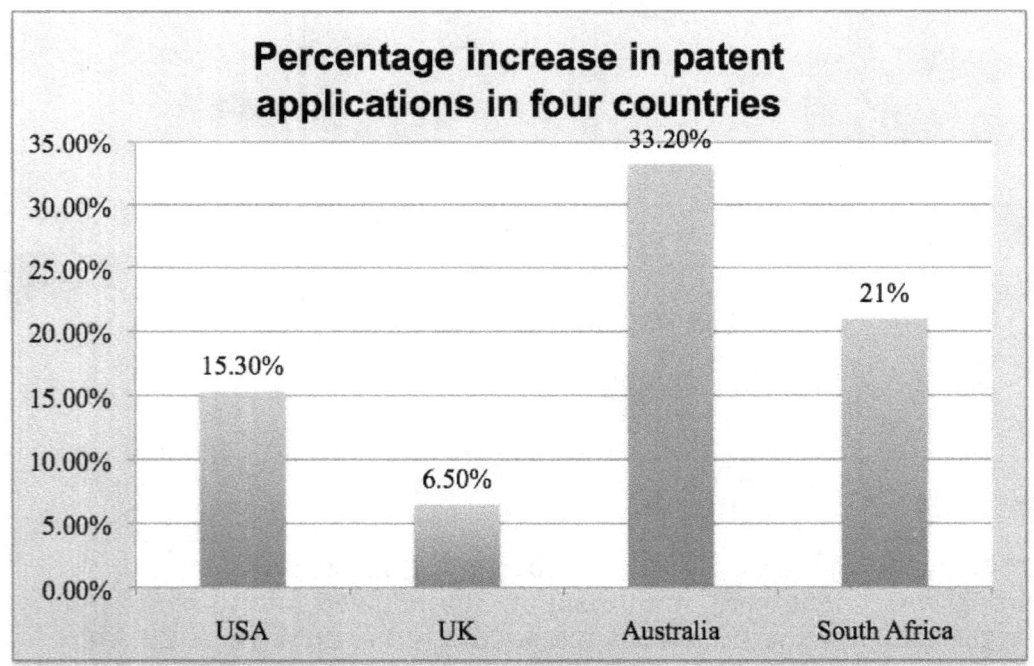

Orme-Johnson DW; Cavanaugh KL; Alexander CN; Gelderloos P; Dillbeck M; Lanford AG; and Abou Nader TM; Department of Psychology and Department of Management and Public Affairs, Maharishi University of Management, Fairfield, Iowa, USA, and Department of Nutrition and Food Science, Massachusetts Institute of Technology, Cambridge, Massachusetts, USA, 1984.

Collected Papers v4.337.

Research Summary 24

A comparative study of dimensions of healthy functioning between families practising the TM programme for five years or for less than a year

Six areas of family functioning were studied to see whether long-term meditating families (over five years of TM practice) were more psychologically healthy than short-term meditating families (less than one-year of TM practice). Comparisons were also made with normal non-meditating families.

The six areas studied comprised:

1. Family structure
2. Mythology
3. Goal directed negotiations
4. Autonomy
5. Family affect
6. Global health pathology scale

The researcher, Martha Chen, studied twenty-three volunteer families from the Washington DC and Pittsburgh areas using an independent interviewer with videotaped recordings. Two psychiatric clinical specialist nurses using the Beavers-Timberlawn Scale then rated interviews with the families independently. Chen then used the Whitney-Mann U Test to verify the statistical hypothesis.

Chen found significant improvements in all six areas ($p = 0.05$) with the five-year plus meditating families scoring consistently better than the one year or less meditating families. The study backed up the hypothesis that long term meditating would improve a family's psychological health and this was reinforced by the fact that the short-term meditating families scores were similar to normal non-meditating family scores.

Chen ME *Dissertation Abstracts International 45(10) 3206B, 1984*

Collected Papers v5.400

Research Summary 25

Consciousness as a field: the Transcendental Meditation and TM-Sidhi Programme and changes in social indicators

This research study comprised five sub-studies, three of which covered projects studied earlier and two covered coherence projects held in the Philippines. With this project the researchers used a direct intervention design with Box-Jenkins time series analysis methodology to assess the effect of coherence creating groups of TM-Sidhas at local level, region, sate and national level.

The five study areas included:

- Union Territory of Delhi, 1980-1981, testing for decreased crime (See summary 12)

- Metro Manila, 1984-1985, testing for decreased crime, as well as a case study on improvement in political stability, (See below)

- Puerto Rico, 1984 testing for decreased crime, (See summary 20)

- Metro Manila Region, 1979-1981, testing for various quality of life (QOL) parameters including decreased crime, foetal deaths, and other deaths,

- State of Rhode Island, US, 1978 testing for QOL including reduced crime rate, motor vehicle fatality rate, mortality rate from other causes, auto accident rate, unemployment rate, pollution, beer consumption rate, and cigarette consumption rate. (See summary number 7)

The research analysis found that the consistent and significant results gained from all five studies confirmed the earlier research and indicated a 'replicable effect of improved quality of life in whole social systems' wherever the square root of 1% of the population are deployed to practice the TM-Sidhi programme together at the same time. The findings were completely in tune with the Maharishi's Vedic theory of the collective consciousness and served to further verify the Super Radiance theory.

The chances of these findings being a coincidence are small. Taking into account the improvements in QOL were achieved over several different time periods with groups spread across the world in different countries with wildly different cultures, the research team estimated that the joint probability of the effects from all five studies being a coincidence was 10^{-9}.

Improvements in political stability

The Metro Manila study of 1984 - 1985 didn't just add to the overwhelming evidence that Super Radiance reduces crime levels. It also provided another useful insight into the positive impact Super Radiance has on political stability. This particular project covered a period during which there was a major, and often violent, political upheaval underway in the Philippines.

In August 1984, 1,500 TM-Sidhas arrived in Manila, capital of the Philippines. Most of these TM-Sidhas were involved in a mass teaching programme focussed around the educational and rehabilitation sectors. As a consequence over the following six months thousands of people learned the TM technique in Metro Manila and the surrounding provinces.

The square root of 1% of the population of the Philippines is 750 and of Metro Manila is 300 people. Unfortunately there was no opportunity for the full contingent of TM-Sidhas to practise together in one group to create a Super Radiance effect for the whole country. Nevertheless, about 250 TM-Sidhas managed to meditate together in a single group in Manila. This group was fifty people short of the magic square root of 1% of Manila's eight million people. However, the gap was more than offset by the thousands of new TM meditators and the numerous small groups of the other 1,250 TM-Sidhas, scattered around the capital.

As outlined briefly above, time series analysis showed a significant drop in crime during the 1984 - 1985 study period, as compared with the baseline period and the post study period. However, perhaps of more interest is the impact that the coherence group had on political events.

Exactly a year before the arrival of the TM-Sidhas, Benigno Aquino, the leader of the main opposition party had been assassinated. The event was widely attributed to government influence. This collective feeling had sparked off a series of mass demonstrations, many of which deteriorated into violent conflicts between the demonstrators and the police. Aquino's assassination had become a focal point of popular opposition to the kleptocratic and authoritarian regime of president Ferdinand Marcos.

A political miracle of sorts

At the time of the TM-Sidhas' arrival, tensions had been mounting with the opposition leaders determined to mark the anniversary of Aquino's death with large-scale demonstrations. From recent past experience it was widely predicted by national and international observers that these demonstrations would degenerate into serious violence.

Instead, as reported by the 'Bulletin Today', "a political miracle of sorts happened ...". A major rally estimated to have half a million participants went ahead without violent incident. Predictions that the huge demonstration would degenerate into rioting were confounded. Instead of fighting, demonstrators were seen to give police officers garlands and flowers. As the Times Journal noted a "festive mood pervaded yesterday's march and rally" (Peaceful, festive 1984).

"Frankly, up to now, we could not believe how a million people who demonstrated to air grievances could have behaved the way they did last Tuesday. Perhaps the law enforcers and organizers of the rally themselves expressed the same disbelief in the peaceful staging of the rally" (What a peaceful rally, 1984) ran the editorial in 'Tempo'

Unfortunately, the researchers were unable to carryout a time series analysis of the political trends, due to lack of appropriate data. However, the relief from tension and violence seen in the days after the arrival of the TM-Sidhas is a predicted trend when there is increased coherence in a society. Just as predictably, the violent eruptions continued once the TM-Sidhas had left the country, as the number of new meditators on their own were insufficient to create the 1% effect.

Dillbeck MC Cavanaugh KL Glenn T Orme-Johnson DW; and Mittlefehldt V; *The Journal of Mind and Behavior 8(1): 67-104, 1987*

Collected Papers v5.401

Research Summary 26

Test of a field model of consciousness and social change: the Transcendental Meditation and TM-Sidhi Programme and decreased urban crime.

In this project, three sub-studies were undertaken to further verify that a small number of people practicing Transcendental Meditation and the TM-Sidhi programme has a causal impact on reduced crime levels. The different studies looked at:

1. A random sample of 160 US cities during the period between 1972 and 1978,
2. A sample of 80 US standard metropolitan areas during the period between 1972 and 1979. These areas included approximately 47% of the total metropolitan population of the USA
3. Washington DC during a two-year period 1981 to 1983 when there were sufficient TM-Sidhas practicing in a group together to achieve the square root of 1% threshold for the area.

In the first two studies, the researchers Dillbeck and co., used cross-lagged panel analysis to correlate the levels of practice of the Transcendental Meditation technique by people in their own homes with levels of violent crime as identified by the FBI Uniform Crime Index. For the Washington study, the researchers adopted time series analysis using the transfer function approach, in order to assess the relationship between weekly variations in the number of TM-Sidhas attending the coherence group and violent crime levels in the area.

Other potentially significant variables were taken into account in the analysis including:

1. Police numbers per population
2. Median years of education
3. Unemployment rate
4. Percentage of population aged over 65 years.

The researchers were able to discount two other alternative hypotheses as to the cause of the reversal in crime trends.

One alternative idea was that the observed crime reduction was due to criminals learning the TM technique and as a consequence changing their behaviour.

The other idea was that there was a significant change in the interaction between meditators and the rest of society that then might have an impact on crime.

In both cases it was considered that the number of people involved in learning Transcendental Meditation was so small as to be insignificant when looked at from the point of view of either direct physical and social interaction or reformed behaviour by criminals.

The inference drawn from the evidence is that the study further supports Maharishi's theory that the wide range of violence and anti-social behaviour seen in a number of western societies today has a common origin – stress in the collective consciousness.

The research confirms that it is relatively easy and highly cost effective to deal with this collective stress without disrupting existing social systems. This can be done by intervening on the level of the collective consciousness by teaching Transcendental Meditation to a relatively small proportion (1%) of the population. Alternatively intervention can be achieved by establishing an even smaller group ($\sqrt{1}$ % of the population) of coherence creating TM-Sidhas.

Dillbeck MC; Banus CB; Polanzi C; and Landrith III GS; *The Journal of Mind and Behavior 9(4): 457-486, 1988*.

Collected Papers v5.402

Research Summary 27

Time series analysis of U.S. and Canadian inflation and unemployment: a test of a field-theoretic hypothesis.

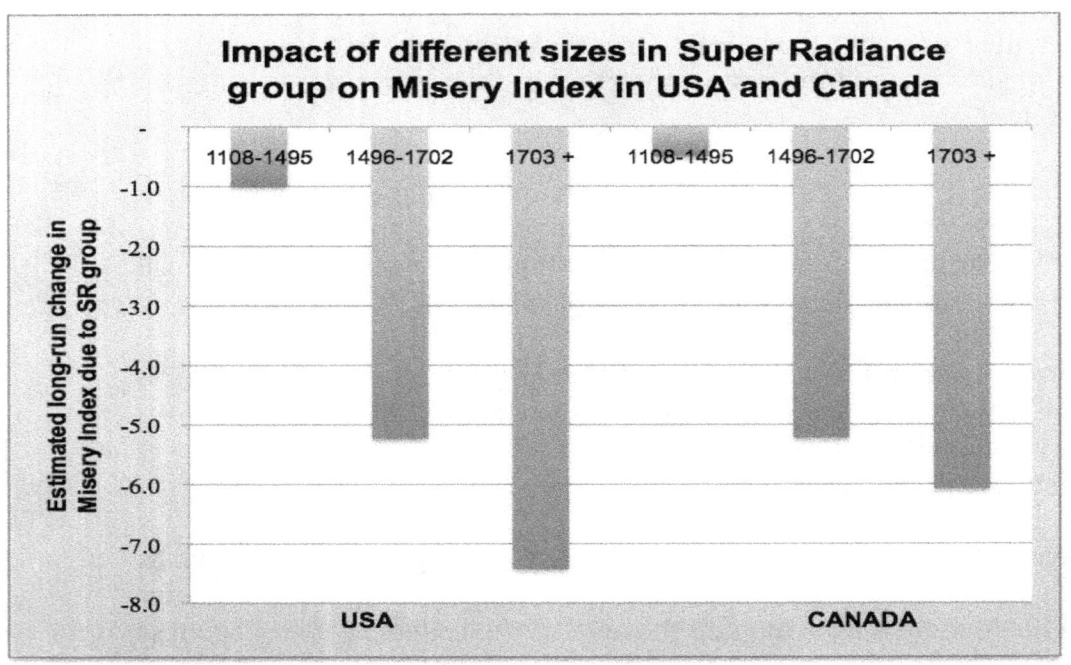

Between April 1979 and January 1987 the researcher, Cavanaugh used Box-Jenkins time series impact assessment analysis on 'Okun's Misery Index' in both the US and Canada.

Okun's Misery Index is a simple composite index that aggregates inflation and unemployment rate. The unemployment rate is used in this instance as it is seen to be a reliable indicator of low economic growth.

Analysis showed that the Misery Index declined (meaning both inflation and unemployment decreased) in both the USA and Canada whenever the group of TM-Sidhas at Maharishi International University (MIU) in Iowa breached the Super Radiance level for the USA. At the time 1,500 TM-Sidhas were enough to achieve Super Radiance, this number being the square root of 1% of the USA population.

Cavanaugh concluded that the TM-Sidha group in Iowa was seen to have a highly significant impact on both the U.S. and Canadian Misery Index. The analysis confirmed the theory that Super Radiance improves the performance of key economic variables, even across national boundaries.

He also found that the analysis confirmed that the effect on the Index was larger when the group grew in size.

When the group size dropped below the Super Radiance level of 1,500 TM-Sidhas but still averaged from 1,100 to 1,500, there were still declines in the Index but these were less pronounced.

Similarly the effect was more extensive in the USA, where the group was located, than across the border in neighbouring Canada. (See chart above)

Cavanaugh KL; This is a revised and updated version of a paper presented at the *Annual Meeting of the American Statistical Association, San Francisco, California, August 17-20, 1987*, and published in *Proceedings of the American Statistical Association, Business and Economics Statistics Section (Alexandria, Virginia: American Statistical Association): 799-804, 1987.*

Collected Papers v5.403.

Research Summary 28

Simultaneous transfer function analysis of Okun's Misery Index: improvements in the economic quality of life through Maharishi's Vedic Science and technology of consciousness.

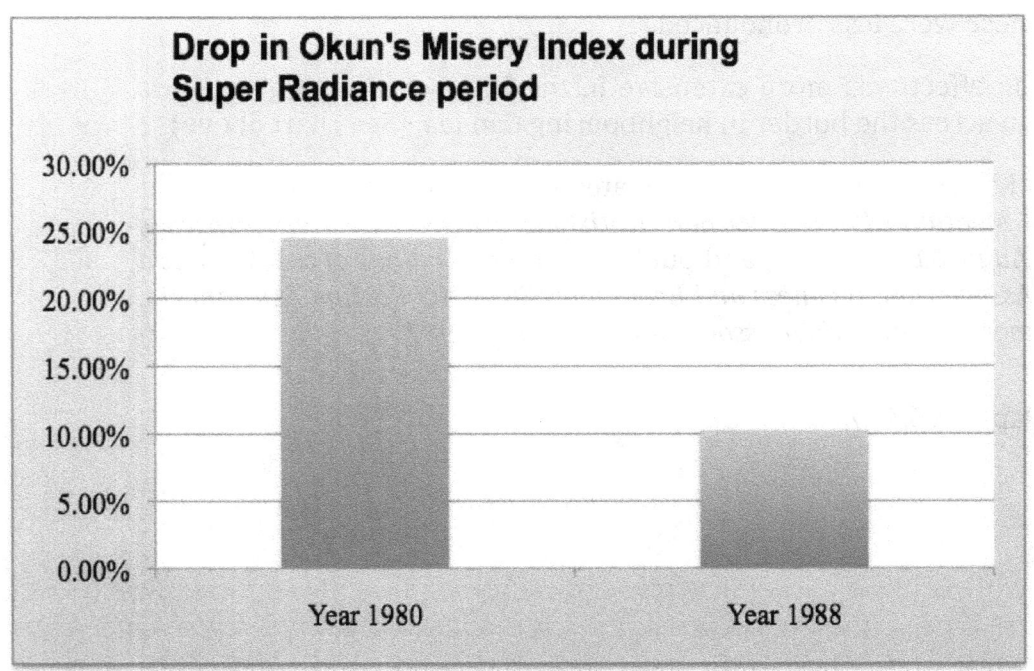

From the 1960s through to 1980 the United States of America experienced the relatively new economic phenomenon known as 'stagflation'.

The term stagflation is used to describe the phenomenon of an economy suffering from the twin evils of stagnation and inflation both at the same time. The USA's problem all changed however in early 1980 when there was a surprise, sudden and sustained reversal of the stagflation trend.

Stagflation as measured by Okun's Misery Index peaked at 24.5% in early 1980. By August 1988 the index had fallen to only 10.3% (As mentioned in summary 27, Okun's Misery Index is an aggregate of both inflation and unemployment rates and provides a helpful indicator of the prevalence of these two problems for a society).

It was the researchers assertion that this sudden and happy reversal was caused by the advent of Super Radiance in the USA. By 1980 there was a sizeable coherence group of TM-Sidhas meditating at MIU in Iowa.

Incidentally, by that time there was also a significant fraction of the general population practising Transcendental Meditation in US society at large reinforcing the coherence effect.

Super Radiance neutralises stress in the collective consciousness

It was thought the two coherence factors combined were enough to simultaneously enliven the collective consciousness and purify it from accumulated stress.

According to Maharishi's Vedic Science theory, consciousness is an underlying field of non-localised intelligence that is the source and sustenance of the whole material universe including the human physiology, human thoughts and behaviour. The collective experience of pure consciousness during Transcendental Meditation and the TM-Sidhi programme neutralises stress in the collective consciousness.

As the collective consciousness becomes both purified of stress and enlivened, so the thoughts and behaviour of every individual in society become more attuned with fundamental laws of nature.

In turn this results in a holistic improvement in the quality of life for the whole society. Just as an individual when he is less stressed starts to take more rational decisions, expresses better moral judgement, has better access to his creative imagination, empathises better with those around him and so on, so society collectively benefits in the same way from everyone experiencing the same transformation in their thinking patterns, emotional wellbeing and daily activity.

Many studies, as we have seen in the summaries above, already testified to the impact Super Radiance has on social problems such as crime, violent or accidental fatalities and other indicators of social disorder. In this study the researchers set out to validate the idea that the Super Radiance effect was also responsible for the reversal of the stagflation trend from 1980 onwards.

After detailed analysis of economic statistics and correlating these to the fluctuating numbers in the coherence group in Iowa, the study concluded that the impact of Super Radiance on economic variables is large and highly significant. Part of the analysis involved controlling for other key variable economic factors.

For instance, the researchers found that increases in the size of the coherence group had significant beneficial effects on the growth of crude materials prices. They reckoned that this impact suggested that increased coherence in collective consciousness might help to ease supply side shocks and so in turn contribute to lower inflation and unemployment

Cavanaugh KL; and King KD; Paper presented at the *Annual Meeting of the American Statistical Association, New Orleans, Louisiana, August 22-25, 1988.* An abridged version of this paper appeared in *Proceedings of the American Statistical Association, Business and Economics Statistics Section: 491-496, 1988.*

Collected Papers v5.404.

Research Summary 29

A multiple-input transfer function model of Okun's Misery Index: an empirical test of the Maharishi Effect.

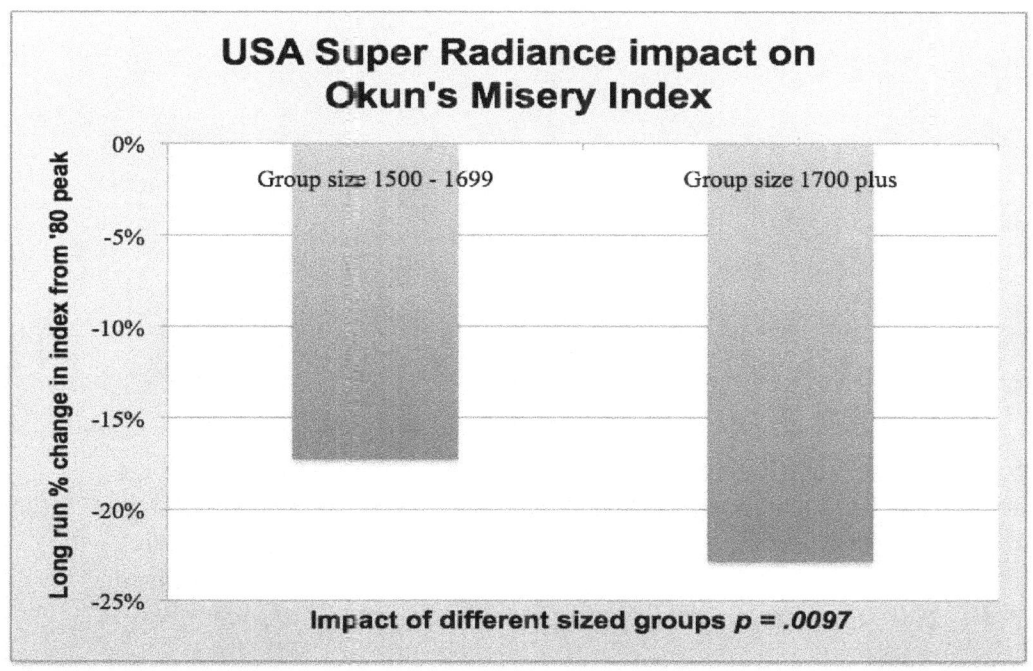

In this study, the researchers found that during the periods between 1979 and 1988 when large numbers of TM-Sidhas were at Maharishi International University in Iowa there was a marked reduction in 'Okun's Misery Index' in the USA and Canada.

As mentioned above, Okun's Misery Index is a composite index aggregating inflation and unemployment.

The study was controlled for the rate of change of industrial production, crude materials prices, and a measure of the money supply. By 1988 the Misery Index had fallen to 40% of the 1980 peak value. The researchers attributed 31.1% of the decline to the Super Radiance group at MIU group ($p < 3.2 \times 10^{-9}$).

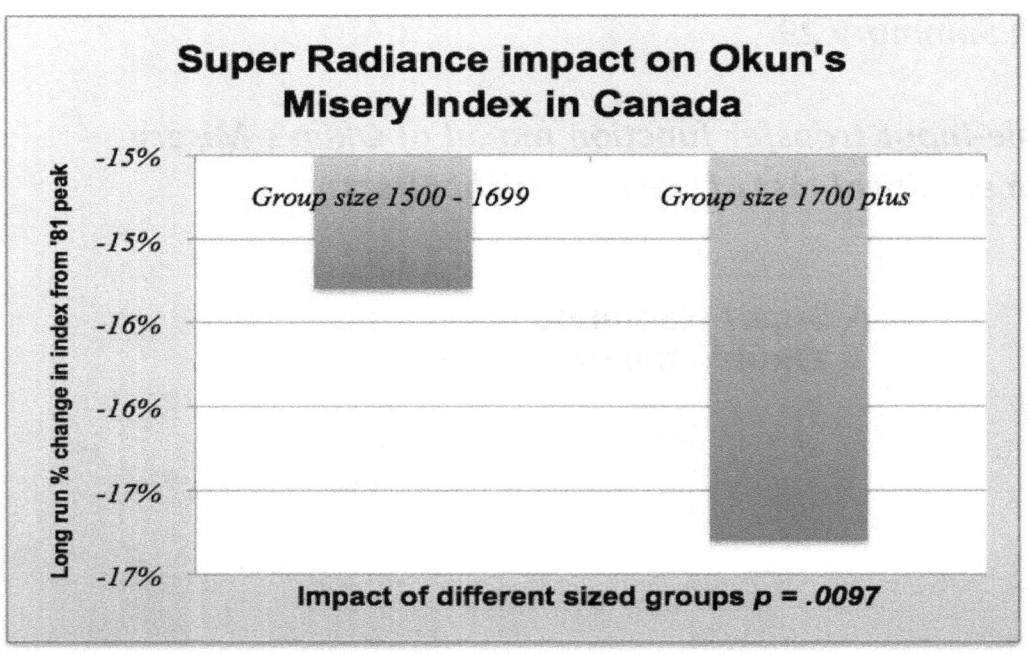

The charts show the relative impact that different sized Super Radiance groups had on the Index in both USA and Canada. Basically the scientists found that the bigger the Super Radiance group the larger the negative impact on the Index in both countries. In this model the scientists estimated that for each 100 additional participants in the Super Radiance group produced there was a further decrease in the Misery Index of .31% in US.

Cavanaugh KL; King KD; and Ertuna C, Paper presented at the *Annual Meeting of the American Statistical Association, Washington, D.C., August 6-10, 1989.* An abridged version of this paper appears in *Proceedings of the American Statistical Association, Business and Economics Statistics Section (Alexandria, Virginia: American Statistical Association): 565-570, 1989.*

Collected Papers v5.405.

Research Summary 30

Consciousness and the quality of economic life: Empirical research on the macroeconomic effects of the collective practice of Maharishi's Transcendental Meditation and TM-Sidhi program.

This study replicates and gives further support to earlier macroeconomic research carried out by Cavanaugh and King. This time, the idea was to further explore the dynamic relationship between the size of a TM-Sidhi group in any given population and Okun's misery index which measures the degree to which western society is afflicted by the perennial problems of inflation and unemployment.

From the late 1960's onwards the USA had experienced an upward trend in the Misery Index and this was reflected in a growing dissatisfaction with the country's economic performance and a gradual deterioration in the sense of general wellbeing. The researchers found that during the period 1979 – 1988 there was a statistically significant reduction in the US Misery Index made by an appropriately large TM-Sidhi group with a lag of about 4 – 5 months. It was evident from the figures that the size of the TM-Sidhi group leads the misery index rather than the other way around. Controls were introduced for both the effect of monetary growth and the rate of change of crude materials prices.

The overall findings concluded that the collective practice of the TM-Sidhi programme had been contributing to a significant improvement in the economic quality of life in the USA during the research period.

Cavanaugh KL; King KD; and Titus BD This is a revised version of a paper presented at the *Annual Meeting of the Midwest Management Society, Chicago, Illinois, March 1989, and published in R.G. Greenwood (ed.), Proceedings of the Midwest Management Society (Chicago, Illinois: Midwest Management Society): 183-190, 1989.*

Collected Papers v5.406.

Research Summary 31

Test of a field theory of consciousness and social change: time series analysis of participation in the TM-Sidhi Programme and reduction of violent deaths in the USA.

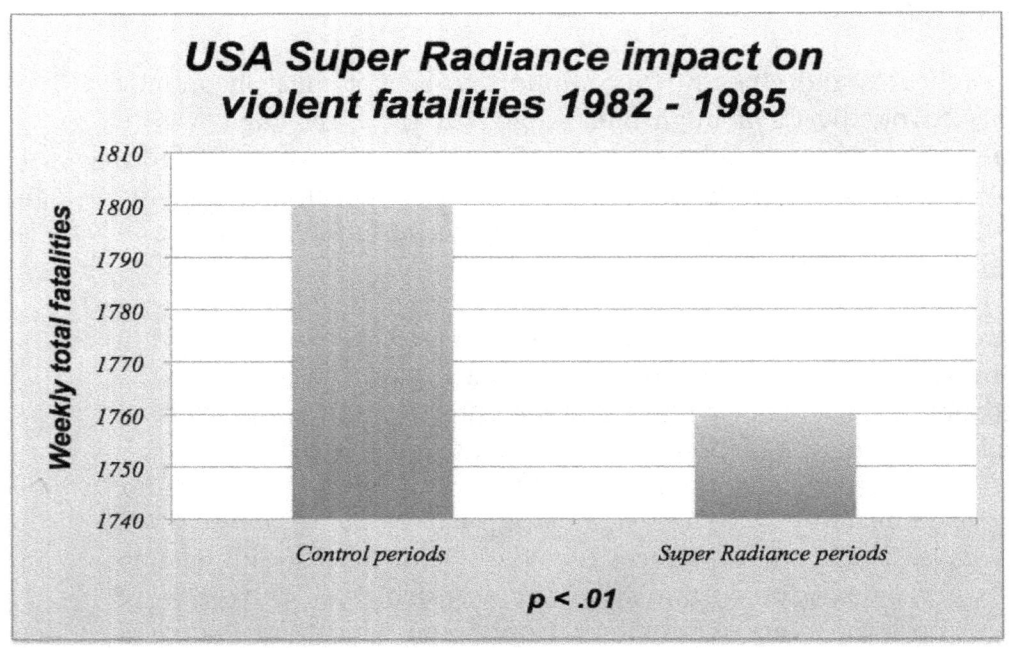

This study looked specifically at the impact of the largest Super Radiance group in the USA based at Maharishi International University (now called MUM) in Iowa.

The research period for the major part of the study is from 1982 to 1985. During this time the MIU group often breached the square root of 1% threshold needed for a positive impact across the whole of North America including the USA and Canada.

At that time the number of TM-Sidhas required for Super Radiance for the USA was about 1,550.

A secondary analysis was also carried out for the years 1979 – 1985 coinciding with the inception and growth of the MIU group. The study focussed on an index of violence in the USA comprised of statistics for fatalities arising from motor vehicle accidents, homicides and suicides. Box Jenkins time series analysis using the impact assessment approach showed a statistically significant decline in violent deaths in the weeks immediately after the group of TM-Sidhas achieved the square root of 1% threshold.

During periods when the size of the groups was smaller than the square root of one percent of the U.S. and Canadian populations, fatality rates were higher.

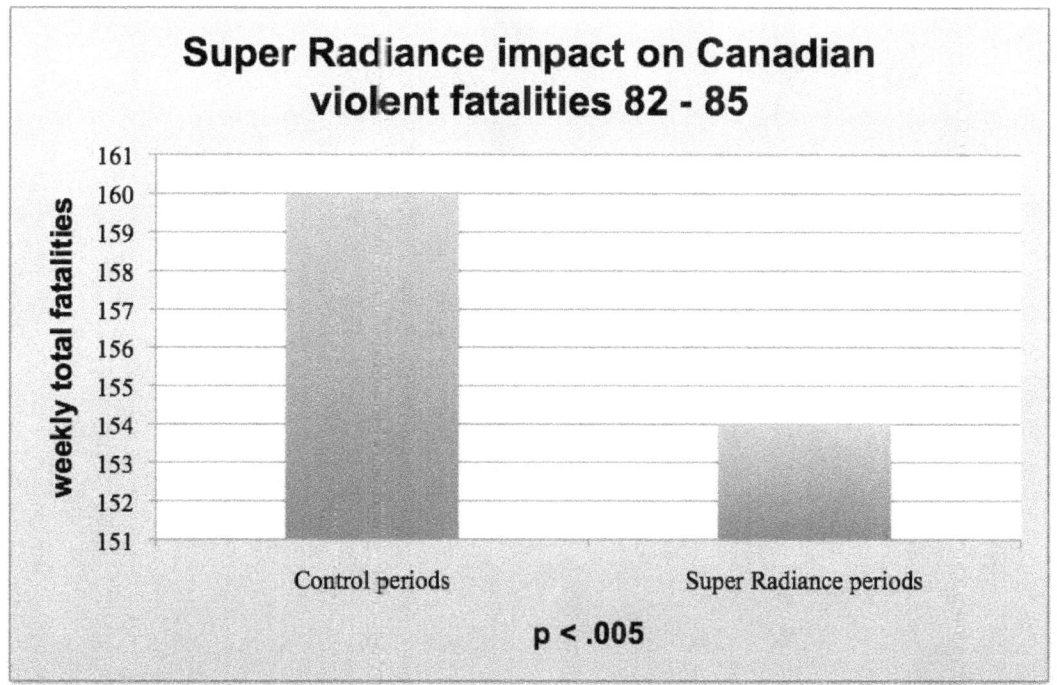

The use of time series methodology ensures that these effects could not be due to random variation, seasonal cycles, or long-term trends in the two countries.

Identifying cause and effect

The researchers carried out a separate transfer function analysis (STF). This indicated that it was not a question of changes in the violence index leading to reciprocal changes in the number of TM-Sidhas in the MIU group, but the other wary around. In other words, this STF analysis reinforced the understanding that the Super Radiance effect is the causal factor behind the drop in violent fatalities.

Dillbeck MC Summary of a paper in *Social Indicators Research 22: 399-418, 1990*

Collected Papers v5.407.

Research Summary 32

Change in the quality of life in Canada: intervention studies of the effect of the Transcendental Meditation and TM-Sidhi program.

This study is a useful demonstration of how, once the Super Radiance effect has been achieved for one country, that country can improve not only their own wellbeing but also that of a neighbouring country relatively easily. In this way Super Radiance provides a highly cost effective method to underpin a nation's own security without in any way intruding or interfering in political, social or economic activities across national borders.

The idea behind the study was to study those weeks and months (the experimental periods) when the US TM-Sidha group in Iowa was large enough to reach the Super Radiance threshold for both the USA *and* Canada. The researchers then compared these periods with those periods when the US group was insufficiently large to achieve Super Radiance for the Canadian population.

The researchers used Box Jenkins time series impact assessment analysis to study improvements to the quality of life (QOL) in Canada. They measure QOL by a range of social indicators including traffic fatalities, homicides, suicides, other accidental deaths, cigarette consumption and days lost due to industrial strikes.

Essentially there were two sub-studies that compared the irregularly spaced and varied time periods when Super Radiance was in place:

Sub-study 1 – *Weekly* data from Canada between the years 1982 and 1985
Sub-study 2 – *Monthly* data from Canada between the years 1972 and 1986

As anticipated, when they looked at the data, the researchers found that violent events of one sort or another in Canada dropped significantly every time the coherence group in Iowa achieved Super Radiance for the combined USA and Canadian populations.

Weekly data

The violence index for the weekly data in Sub-study 1 showed a 4.1% drop during the experimental periods ($p < .01$). Similarly there was a 5.1% drop in other accidental deaths $p = < 0.005$.

Monthly data

The monthly data collecting study also showed similar improvements

- 4.1% drop in violent fatalities ($p < 0.025$)
- 10.1% drop in cigarette consumption ($p < 0.001$)
- 18.8% less days lost in strikes ($p < 0.05$)

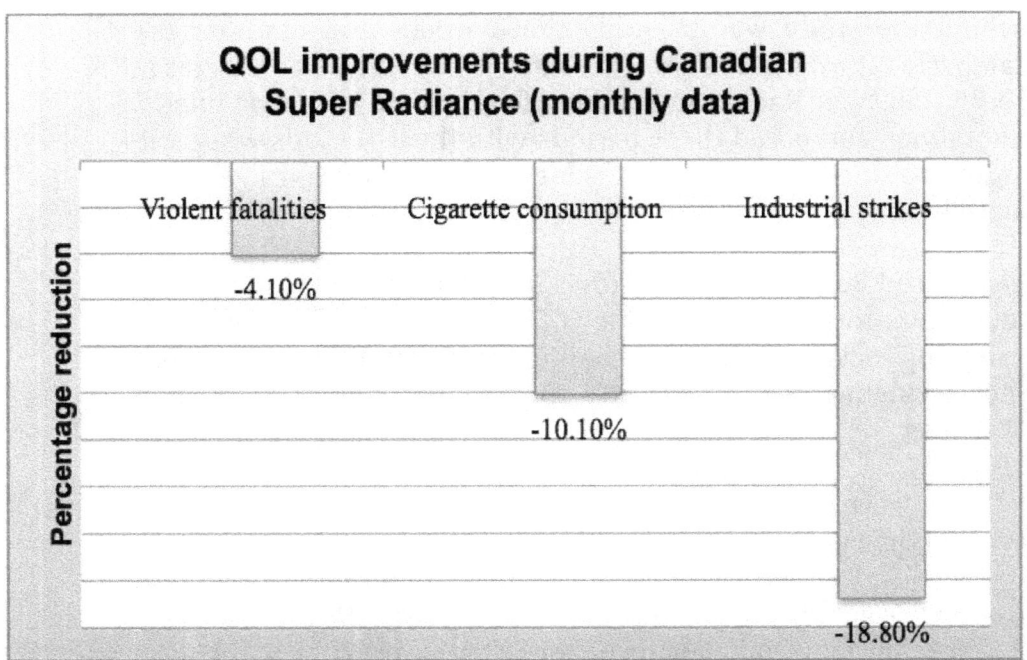

The researchers checked for other possible causes such as population changes and seasonal changes. None of these other variable factors correlated with improvements seen to the QOL statistics.

Policy implications

There is an interesting policy implication here.

The difference in numbers required for USA Super Radiance and the combined Super Radiance of both USA and Canada are very small.

Today, the USA Super Radiance factor is 1,767 TM-Sidhas. The Canadian Super Radiance factor on its own is 588 TM-Sidhas. However the Super Radiance factor required for both countries is only 1,862 TM-Sidhas. In other words, once the USA achieves Super Radiance it only needs to attract an extra 95 TM-Sidhas to the coherence group to impact the whole neighbouring Canadian population.

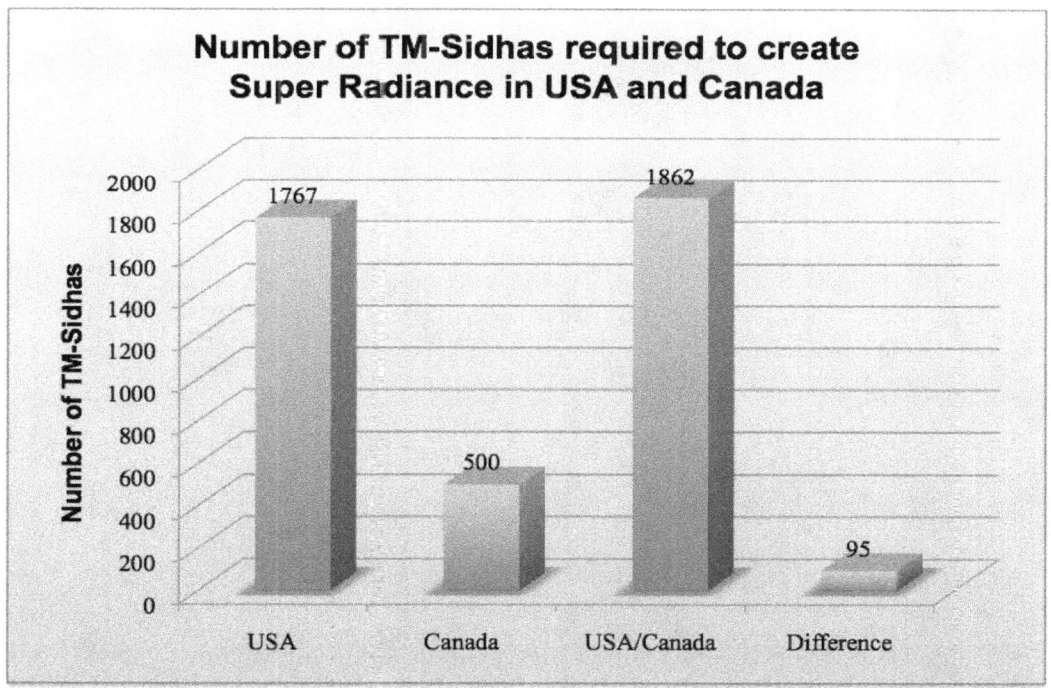

Add in another 281 TM-Sidhas and the USA will provide coherence for Mexico as well, whereas on its own Mexico would require over a 1,000 TM-Sidhas to pull off the same effect.

The implications for the US's ongoing struggle against the illegal drug trade channelled through Mexico, illegal immigration and other related law and order issues are obviously massive.

Assimakis PD; Abstract published in *Dissertation Abstracts International 50(5) Sec. B, p. 2203, November 1989.*

Collected Papers v5.408.

Research Summary 33

Creating world peace through the collective practice of the Maharishi Technology of the Unified Field: improved US-Soviet relations.

In this study, the researchers used time series analysis to study the implications of public statements made by President Reagan about the Soviet Union. The study period ran from 4th April 1985 to 23rd September 1987.

Since the Second World War the two superpowers had lived in a poisonous atmosphere of suppressed hostility underpinned by a mutual race for supremacy in military capability. The resultant 'Cold War' involved almost continual surrogate violent conflicts across the globe and the ever-present threat of nuclear annihilation and had continued unabated for thirty-five years. With the advent of coherence creating groups of TM-Sidhas in the USA it was predicted that relations might ease, as reflected by a more conciliatory attitude being taken by the US towards the Soviet empire.

Government leaders are perceived as instruments of the collective consciousness rather than initiators of new developments, so the researchers matched fluctuations in the size of the coherence groups with changes in attitude expressed by the US president. The results showed that when the groups exceeded their average size there was a substantial positive effect on presidential statements towards the Soviet Union as compared to the times when the groups were below their average size.

The biggest differentials occurred however when the US coherence group in Iowa achieved the square root of 1% Super Radiance threshold of 1,560 TM-Sidhas.

Gelderloos P; Frid MJ; Goddard PH; Xue X; and Löliger SA *Social Science Perspectives Journal 2(4): 80-94, 1988.*

Collected Papers v5.409.

Research Summary 34

Alleviating political violence through enhancing coherence in collective consciousness: impact assessment analysis of the Lebanon war.

This study looked at the impact that seven temporary Super Radiance groups had on the civil war in Lebanon between June 1983 and August 1985.

Although the groups had not been set up to deal specifically with the Lebanon conflict, the researchers predicted that each were of a size and proximity that, according to the Super Radiance theory, would enable them to have a significant and tangible impact.

The seven different Super Radiance groups were spread out across five different locations and were in place at different periods and for different durations of time. (See table below)

	Seven Super Radiance groups for Lebanon		
	Location	TM-Sidha group	Date
1	Israel	425	Summer 1983
2	Iowa USA	8,000	Winter 1983/84
3	Iowa USA	7,000	Summer 1984
4	Washington	7,000	Autumn 1984
5	The Hague	7,000	Winter 1984/85
6	Broumana Lebanon	150	March 1984
7	Porec Yugoslavia	2,500	July 1984

In aggregate at different times, the total duration of the Super Radiance effect for Lebanon was 93 days (11.3%) during the 821-day study period.

The study method was a Box-Jenkins impact assessment analysis to compare events during and outside the various Super Radiance periods.

The specific events monitored were from daily records of:

- Cooperation and conflict between the antagonists
- War fatalities
- War injuries

These events were rated on a 16-point composite scale. To validate the findings further these recordings were made by an independent Lebanese statistician who was 'blind' to the purpose of the study or the existence of the Super Radiance groups and their timings. Data was drawn from eight different international sources including local broadcasts from different sides to the conflict.

Significantly, each project had a positive impact on the war in Lebanon on its own.

However, the findings for the combined study of all seven projects show a remarkable consistency with an almost impossible probability of coincidence. During those 93 days when there was a Super Radiance effect for Lebanon, the analysis showed:

1. A 66% mean increase in levels of cooperation among antagonists ($t = 4.96, p = 4 \times 10^{-7}$);
2. 47% reduction in the level of conflict ($t = -5.81, p = 3 \times 10^{-9}$);
3. 71% reduction in war fatalities ($t = -6.45, p = 1 \times 10^{-10}$);
4. 68% reduction in war injuries ($t = -4.91, p = 5 \times 10^{-7}$);

As usual, the researchers tested for other variable factors that might have had an impact on the conflict. These variables included the weather, holiday periods, seasonal cycles and pre-existing trends. They could find none that correlated in any way with the results. The probability of a coincidence arising from all the seven Super Radiance periods combined is $p = 9 \times 10^{-20}$. In English this means that the probability of the consistent effect being a coincidence is one in billions.

It should be pointed out that there was no media announcements or other publicity about the Super Radiance activity prior to or during the study periods. Similarly, there were no social, diplomatic or political interactions between the project participants and the population of Lebanon.

It should also be noted that six out of the seven projects were carried out in other countries and even on different continents. Only the local group would have had any possibility of physical interaction.

In actuality the group in Broumana confined their activities and interaction with non-participants to a small village community near the centre of conflict. During these peace projects the participants are anyway spending most of their waking hours in deep meditation and have little or no contact with people outside the meditating facility.

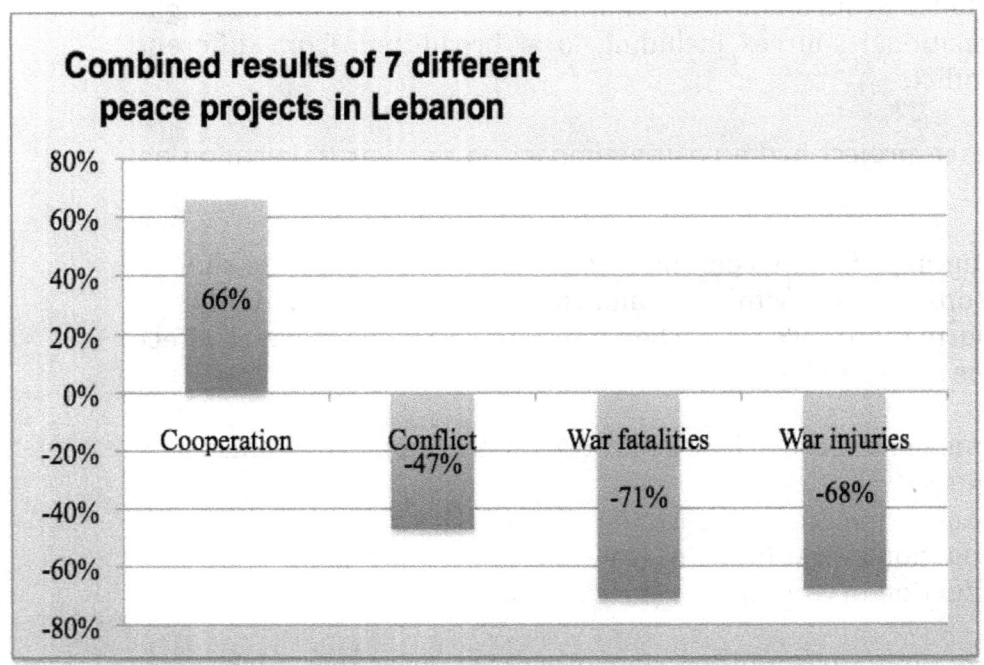

Davies JL, and Alexander CN Summary of a paper presented at the *85th Annual Meeting of the American Political Science Association, September 1989.* (Refer also to *Dissertation Abstracts International 49(8): 2381A, 1988.*)

Collected Papers v5.410.

Research Summary 35

Time series impact assessment analysis of reduced international conflict and terrorism: Effects of large assemblies of participants in the Transcendental Meditation and TM-Sidhi program.

This study used time series analysis to verify the impact that three global Super Radiance groups had on world events.

Three large groups of TM-Sidhas met between 1983 and 1985 at three different locations; the first in Fairfield, Iowa USA, another in The Hague in the Netherlands and the third in Washington DC. Each project period lasted from between eight to eleven days only.

Despite the short duration of the projects, each group attracted over 7,000 participants. Therefore each group achieved the Super Radiance effect (square root of 1%) for the whole world population, which was at that time about 5 billion people.

The researchers adopted three sources of data to monitor changes occurring before, during and after the duration of the 3 different projects. These sources were:

1. Blind ratings of news events, which were drawn from two major international newspapers (New York Times for the two US projects and the London Times for the Netherlands project). The data was then treated by standard methodology for scoring international conflict events.
2. Casualties and injuries caused by international terrorist acts recorded by the Rand Corporation.
3. Capital International's World Index of stock prices to measure global short-term economic confidence.

The results when they occurred were immediate, impressive and lasted only for the few days that the groups were in place.

Decline in terrorist activity:

The data collected from the Rand Corporation showed a 72% reduction in terrorism across all three projects $p < 0.025$

Rise in stock prices:

A small but statistically significant increase occurred in international stock prices $p < 0.023$

International conflict scale recorded:

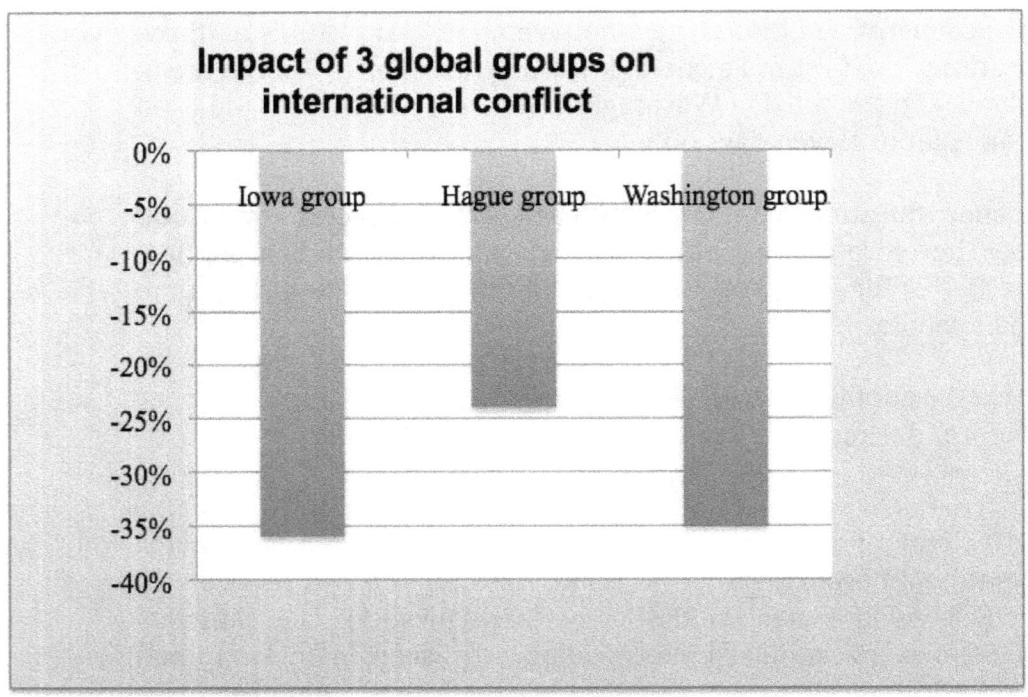

36% reduction during the Iowa project $p < 0.25$

24% reduction during the Hague project $p < 0.005$

35% reduction during the Washington project $p < 0.01$

Comparisons with five other years indicated that the times of year that the projects were carried out were irrelevant in terms of causality of the improvements.

The researchers concluded that these projects showed yet again that any country could instigate significant improvements in the international diplomatic and political situation without intruding in the life of other countries and at a cost that would be an insignificant fraction of the usual defence costs of the major powers.

Orme-Johnson DW; Dillbeck MC; Alexander CN; Chandler HM; and Cranson RW; A summary of a paper presented at the *Annual Conference of the American Political Science Association, Atlanta, Georgia, USA, August 1989. Journal of Offender Rehabilitation 36 (1-4): 283-302, 2003.*

Collected Papers v5.411.

Research Summary 36

Time series analysis of improved quality of life in Canada: Social change, collective consciousness, and the TM-Sidhi program – Research abstract.

Two replication studies in Canada tested a field theory of the effect of consciousness on social change. The hypothesis proposed that the one extraneous variable driving social change in US society is the number of TM-Sidhas in the US Super Radiance group at Fairfield in Iowa.

The first study, using both time series intervention analysis and transfer function analysis methods, indicated a significant reduction in violent deaths (homicide, suicide, and motor vehicle fatalities), in weeks following change in the extraneous variable during the period between 1983 and 1985.

The second study, using time series intervention analysis, during and after intervention periods showed a significant improvement in quality of life on an index composed of the behavioural variables available on a monthly basis for Canada from 1972 to 1986. In this instance the variables were: homicide, suicide, motor vehicle fatalities, cigarette consumption, and workers' days lost due to strikes.

Assimakis PD, and Dillbeck MC *Psychological Reports 1995*

Collected papers v6.493

Research Summary 37

The dynamics of US-Soviet relations, 1979-1986: Effects of reducing social stress through the Transcendental Meditation and TM-Sidhi program.

Using a monthly index of events provided by the Zurich Project on East-West Relations, researchers observed significant increases in the positivity of statements and actions made by United States politicians and senior officials toward the Soviet Union during the periods from 1979 to 1986.

This enhanced positivity occurred during the times when the size of a group of TM-Sidhas in the United States at Maharishi International University in Fairfield, Iowa, had achieved the Super Radiance figure of the square root of one per cent of the US population. (See chart below)

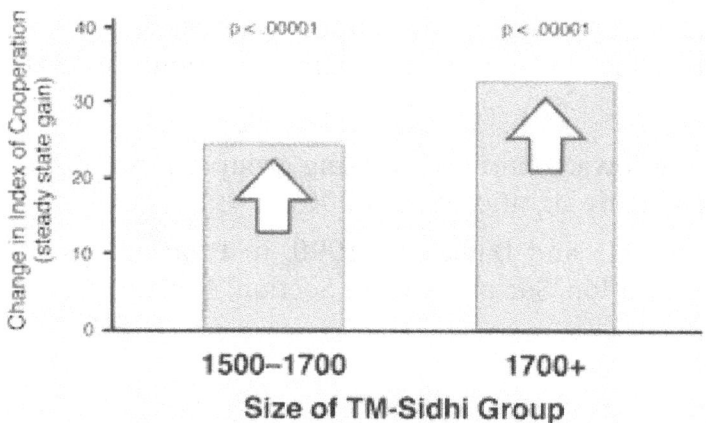

Similarly, during those times between 1979 and 1986 when the MIU group at Iowa increased further in size, researchers noticed significantly improved statements and actions by the government of the Soviet Union towards the USA. The second chart compares levels of cooperation during periods of

Super Radiance and periods where the TM-Sidhi groups were not large enough to achieve the Super Radiance effect.

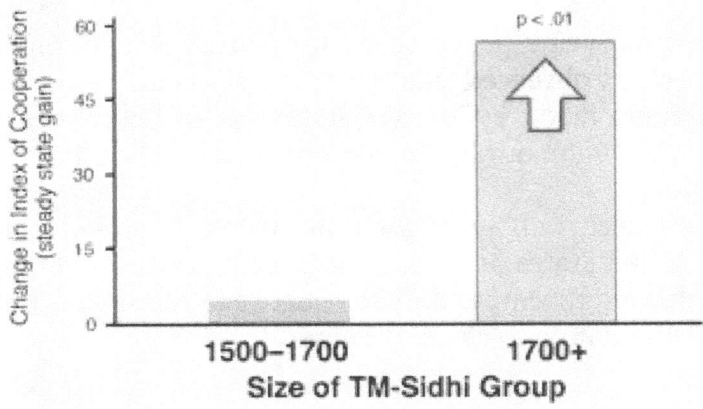

USSR shift independent of US government action

This positivity, identified by Box-Jenkins time series impact assessment analysis of an independent data bank of international statistics, was seen to be independent of the effect of any US government actions toward the Soviet Union.

The overall impact of the Iowa coherence-creating group on the USA-USSR interaction was rated as highly significant (p<.00001).

Gelderloos P; Cavanaugh KL; and Davies JL, 1990. In Proceedings of the American Statistical Association, Social Statistics Section, Alexandria, VA

Collected papers v6.497

Research Summary 38

The effects of the Maharishi Technology of the Unified Field: Reply to a methodological critique – Research abstract.

This study was a reanalysis, using alternative statistical methods, of the data published in 1988 on an index of war intensity and war deaths in neighbouring Lebanon during the period in which an Israel Maharishi effect (Super Radiance) group was created in the summer of 1983 (see summary 19). The Akaike Information Criterion was used to choose objectively among 14 alternative time series transfer function models, including the one used in the original study.

Original study reworked 14 different ways to check for consistency

The findings of the original study of reduction of the war index were replicated in all 14 alternative statistical models. Interestingly, the models that were more suitable according to the Akaike Information Criterion also yielded more significant effects of the TM-Sidhi program group ($p < .0001$).

Also, use of random sequences as alternative or control variables did not have any significant relationship to the war index. This result is another indication that the results from the original 1988 study were not due to chance.

Orme-Johnson DW; Alexander CN; and Davies JL *Journal of Conflict Resolution 34(2): 756-768, 1990.*

Collected papers v6.496

Research Summary 39

Improved quality of life in Iowa through the Maharishi Effect.

The researcher used time series transfer function analysis to relate the size of the MIU Super Radiance group in Iowa USA to an index of monthly rates of unemployment, traffic accidents, crime and a quality of life between the years 1979 - 1986.

The findings showed that as the group increased so:-

- Unemployment fell ($p < .004$).
- Crime fell ($p < .0001$).
- Traffic fatalities fell ($p < .0001$).
- Quality of life improved ($p < .006$).

Reeks DL Abstract of Doctoral Dissertation, Maharishi University of Management, U.S.A. *Dissertation Abstracts International 51(12), 1991.*

Collected papers v6.490

Research Summary 40

The Maharishi Effect (Super Radiance effect): A model for social improvement: Time series analysis of a phase transition to reduce crime in Merseyside metropolitan area.

In the late 1980s and early 1990s there arose an opportunity to carryout a long-term study on crime prevention, in metropolitan Merseyside in the UK. This opportunity arose due to the establishment of a community of TM-Sidhas in nearby Skelmersdale.

For about five years the whole of this metropolitan area benefited from the Super Radiance effect due to the combined effect of the 140 or so TM-Sidhas meditating together in their community meditation facility and the large numbers of people locally being taught the Transcendental Meditation technique. At the time there was a very active TM teacher working in Liverpool.

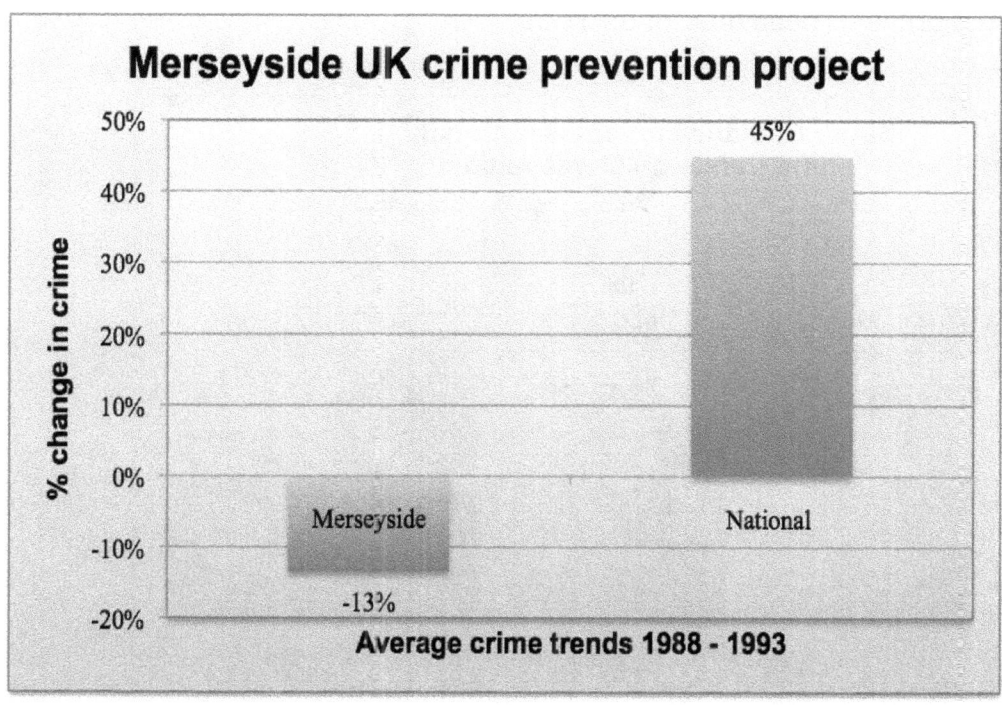

The study is particularly interesting as it shows the accumulative impact on crime over a long period of time (five-years).

Analysis of Merseyside monthly crime data and the number of TM-Sidhas meditating together in Skelmersdale from 1978 to 1991 shows that 'a phase transition to increased orderliness' occurred during March 1988.

At this point the combination of the local meditators and the TM-Sidhi group size first exceeded Merseyside's Super Radiance threshold. During the next five years the Super Radiance threshold was maintained for the area and crime dropped by a figure of 13.4% ($p < 0.00006$).

Although this reduction may seem small, the drop must also be viewed in the context of crime rising generally everywhere else in the UK over the same period. During the study period, crime in the UK as a whole experienced a 45% rise.

In 1987 and before the Super Radiance threshold had been reached, Merseyside had the third highest crime rate of the eleven largest Metropolitan areas in England and Wales; by 1992 it had the lowest crime rate of this group of cities. The new crime level was 40% below levels predicted by the previous behaviour of the series.

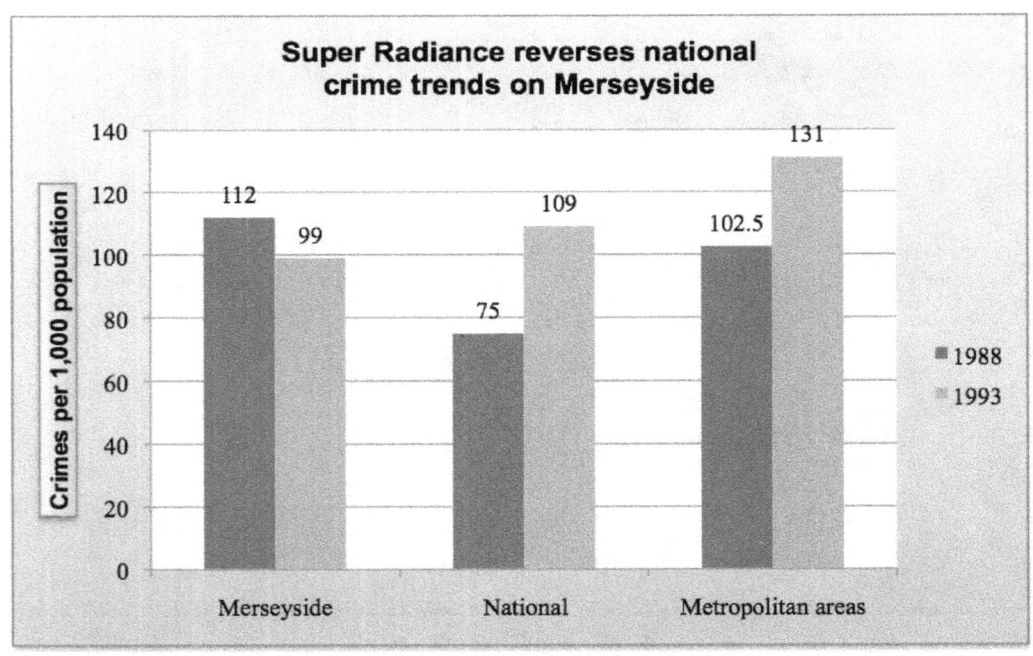

As a result of the Super Radiance effect, researchers estimated that there were 255,000 less crimes in Merseyside from 1988 to 1992 than would have been expected had Merseyside continued to follow the national crime trend.

Based on Home Office figures on the costs of crime this reversal of the crime trend probably saved Merseyside in excess of £1,250 million for the five-year period.

Lead lag analysis showed that demographic changes, economic variables, police practice, and other factors could not account for the changes.

One obvious objection to the Super Radiance theory, that the TM-Sidha group was impacting crime trends is that over this time police practice and in particular methods to rehabilitate drug addicts, improved.

This objection can be overruled, as it is clear from the evidence that such improvements in policy-making and organisational processes that occurred in the area actually *followed* the establishment of Super Radiance in the area. These technical improvements did not lead or precede the Super Radiance effect created by the TM-Sidha community in Skelmersdale.

In point of fact, Super Radiance theory predicts that successful interventions in prevention and rehabilitation by police, probation services and other agencies are to be expected in the more coherent atmosphere created by the Super Radiance effect.

The enhanced brainwave coherence radiated by TM-Sidhas in a Super Radiance group does not just influence criminals but of course all elements of society. The reduced stress in the collective consciousness is always going to lead to enhanced creativity and more harmonious relationships within the community. This improvement in emotional and intellectual functioning by community members will naturally translate into more productive cooperation between government agencies and other crime prevention experts.

In essence, the Super Radiance effect does not act independently of, or separately to other initiatives to improve quality of life in a society but instead provides the ground state that best supports success for those activities.

Hatchard GD; Deans AJ; Cavanaugh KL; and Orme-Johnson DW Psychology, *Crime, and Law (1995, in press)*. Also presented by invitation to the *Annual Conference of the British Psychological Society on Criminal and Legal Psychology*, 1-3 March, 1993,

Harrogate, England.

Collected papers v6.488

Research summary 41

Results of the national demonstration project to reduce violent crime and improve governmental effectiveness in Washington, D.C.

An experiment in Washington DC to study the effect of a large group of meditators on social trends, saw a rapid reduction in violent crime during the project period.

The researchers, led by John Hagelin a renowned quantum physicist, set up this major prospective social study in Washington DC. The objective was to show how easy and simple it is to reduce crime and social stress and improve the effectiveness of government if you can intervene from the field of consciousness.

In essence the idea was to instigate a high profile demonstration of the effectiveness of reducing stress in the collective consciousness of a population. As with earlier studies, the method for achieving this effect was the deployment of a coherence-creating or Super Radiance group of TM-Sidhas.

As we have seen, about forty earlier field studies had already demonstrated the power of the Super Radiance effect and so the understanding of the mechanics of coherence creation was already well established. What the researchers wanted to do was try and make a big impression in the most important capital city of the world. The idea was to attract attention from the relevant authorities as to the immense possibilities for crime fighting and war prevention.

Police ridicule prediction

The project took place between June 7th and July 30th 1993. Based on previous experience, the researchers predicted in advance that the TM-Sidha group would reduce crime by over 20% in the city during the study period. At the time the local police authority ridiculed this prediction. The police chief actually went on record to assert that the only event that would reduce crime that much in Washington during the summer months would be 20 inches of snow.

Undeterred by this professional cynicism, 800 TM-Sidhas arrived in the first week of the trial period. This influx gave the group a comfortable Super Radiance level straight away for the conurbation around Washington. By the last two weeks of the two-month trial period the group had grown to 4,000 in number.

Although the Super Radiance threshold for an area is normally the number of TM-Sidhas it takes to equal or exceed the square root of 1% ($\sqrt{1}$ %) of the local population, (About 173 TM-Sidhas for Washington DC), in this instance it was felt safer to create or exceed the Super Radiance effect for the whole country (About 1,750 TM-Sidhas). So instead of aiming to attract 173 TM-Sidhas, the $\sqrt{1}$ % of the Washington area population, the study team set out to attract in excess of 1,750 TM-Sidhas, the $\sqrt{1}$ % of the entire US population. There were important reasons for this change in the Super Radiance strategy.

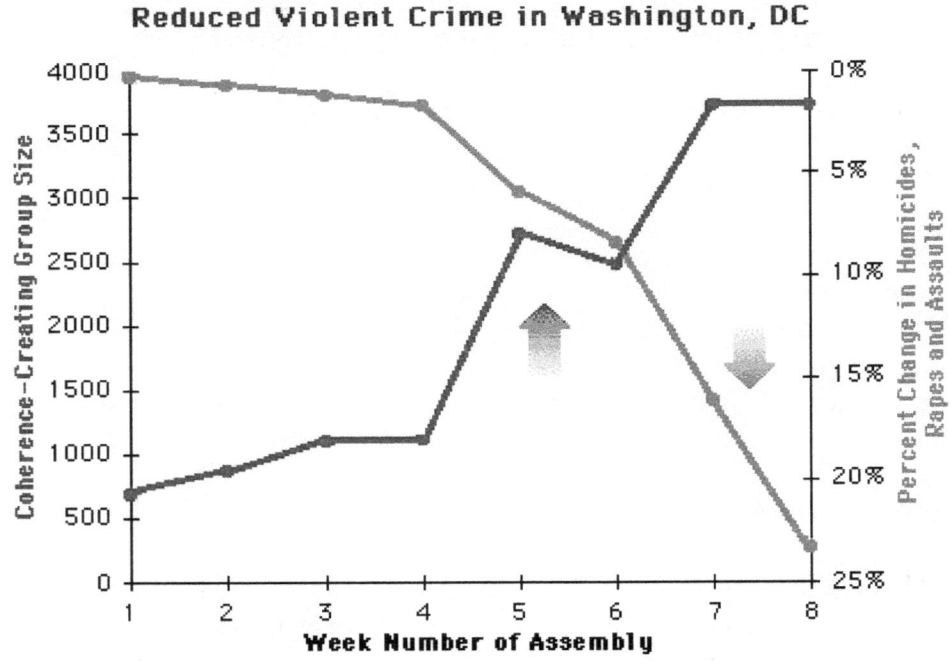

As with the earlier Washington crime prevention project, (See summary 14) the reasoning the researchers departed from the normal formula was based on Washington DC's prominence as the national capital of the world's major super power.

The city not only includes national institutions such as the Presidency, the Supreme Court of Justice, Congress and many other government organisations, but nearby are also the Pentagon, The State Department and the CIA headquarters.

These latter institutions spread their influence across the world. And on the level of consciousness this influence is entirely reciprocal. Unfortunately for the US it is a case of "As you sow, so shall you reap."

Washington's crime rate is three times the national average

As such, the researchers saw the city, as a focal point of collective stress both from the nation and the international community. They surmised that it was this exposure to global collective stress that provoked such a high level of crime within the area - over three times the national average crime level.

In other words, the researchers reckoned that to instigate a rapid decline in local crime, the TM-Sidha group would have to be able to handle a lot more than just the locally generated level of collective stress.

Recent history of climbing crime rates

Washington's immediate history showed that during the first five months of the year prior to the research project, violent crime had been steadily increasing. This increase continued on into the first week of the project. But after the first week or so and as the numbers of the meditating group grew, violent crime began a steep decline (violent crime is defined here as HRA crime: homicides, rapes and aggravated assaults, measured by FBI Uniform Crime Statistics).

From that time on until the end of the two-month experiment, HRA crime stayed well below the time series prediction.

23.6% drop in crime during the demonstration

The maximum impact was an unprecedented drop in crime of 23.6%, occurring when the size of the group was at its largest in the final phase of the project.

The statistical probability that this result could reflect chance variation in crime levels was less than 2 in 1 billion (p < .000000002). After the project and as predicted by the researchers, HRA crime began to rise again. The researchers were unable to attribute the effects to other possible causes, such as temperature, precipitation, weekends, and police and community anticrime activities.

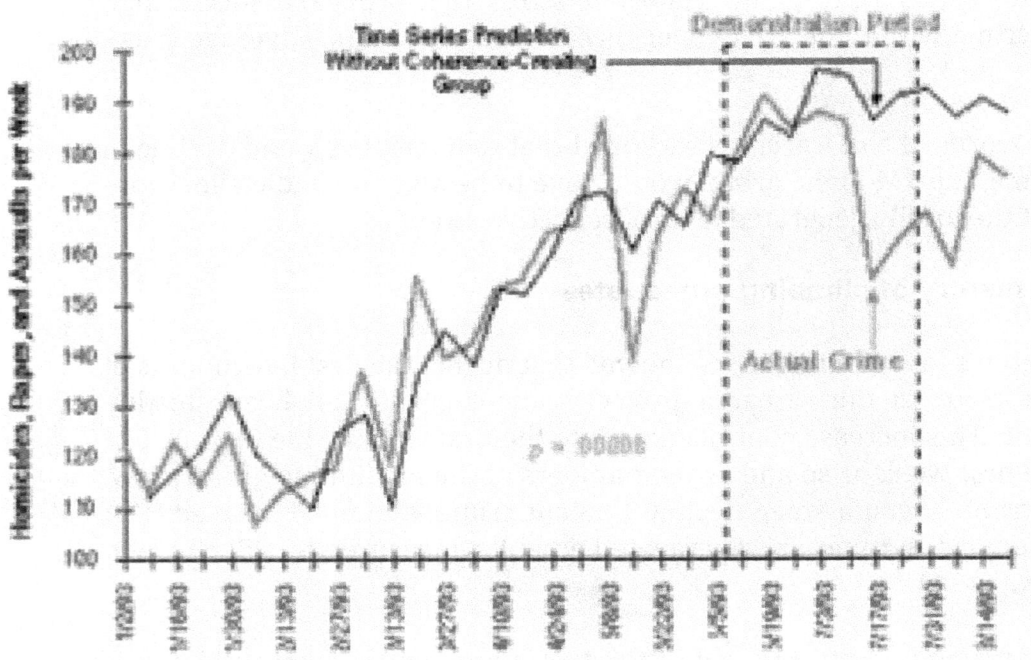

Contrary to the Police chief's predictions, Washington did not benefit from 20 inches of snow. In fact throughout the project the city experienced extremely hot weather conditions.

A range of other improvements

Also, as predicted by the researchers before the project, there was a range of other improvements during the study period.

- President Clinton experienced improved approval ratings ($p = 5.29 \times 10^{-8}$).
- Media positivity toward President Clinton showed a net change increase ($p = .01$).
- Emergency psychiatric calls decreased ($p = .009$).
- Hospital trauma cases decreased ($p = .02$).
- Complaints against the police decreased ($p = .01$).
- Accidental deaths decreased ($p = .05$).
- Quality of life index improved ($p = 3.22 \times 10^{-5}$).

Hagelin JS; Orme-Johnson DW; Rainforth M; Cavanaugh K; Alexander CN; Shatkin SF; Davies JL; Hughs AO; Ross E; Institute of Science, Technology and Public Policy Technical Report 94:1, 1994. *Social Indicators Research (47: 153–201, 1999)*

Collected Papers v 6.489

Research summary 42

The Peace and Well Being of Nations: An Analysis of Improved Quality of Life and Enhanced Economic Performance Through the Maharishi Effect in New Zealand and Norway. A Longitudinal, Cross-Country, Panel-Regression Analysis of the IMD Index of National Competitive Advantage

The two researchers, Guy Hatchard and Ken Cavanaugh used the IMD (International Institute for Management Development based in Switzerland) index of National Competitive Advantage to track economic improvements in Norway and New Zealand. By 1993 these two countries had achieved the Super Radiance threshold of 1% of the population learning Transcendental Meditation. The researchers used the IMD scores to monitor each country's progress over the next five years. Findings were crosschecked with OECD reports.

The background to the IMD index is that it analyses 46 countries across 224 social and economic factors in eight categories and 41 sub-scales. The objective of the index is "to capture in a single index the capacity of a country's economic structure to promote growth".

Dramatic improvements to economic competitiveness

The IMD index shows that when New Zealand and Norway achieved the Super Radiance effect, by means of a surge in TM teaching and TM-Sidhi training, there followed dramatic improvements in the economic competitiveness of both countries.

The statistics show that from 1993 through to 1995, out of a league of 46 countries Norway came second and New Zealand third in terms of the percentage improvement in their IMD scores.

The average annual improvement for Norway was 54.16% pa and for New Zealand was 40.93% pa for the three subject years immediately after achieving the Super Radiance threshold.

These improvements compared with an improvement of 11.61% pa for the UK and 4.29% pa for the USA.

During the study period, 20 of the 46 countries on the index rated negative percentage scores. Interestingly one of these countries experiencing a negative IMD score was India with minus 6.73% pa where a Super Radiance group had just recently disbanded.

The only country that achieved a higher score was Finland. However the team found this was as a result of special circumstances. Finland had fallen on hard times since the collapse of its major trading partner the Soviet Union in 1990. With the revival of the newly established Russian free economy Finland started catching up fast with a surge in economic activity.

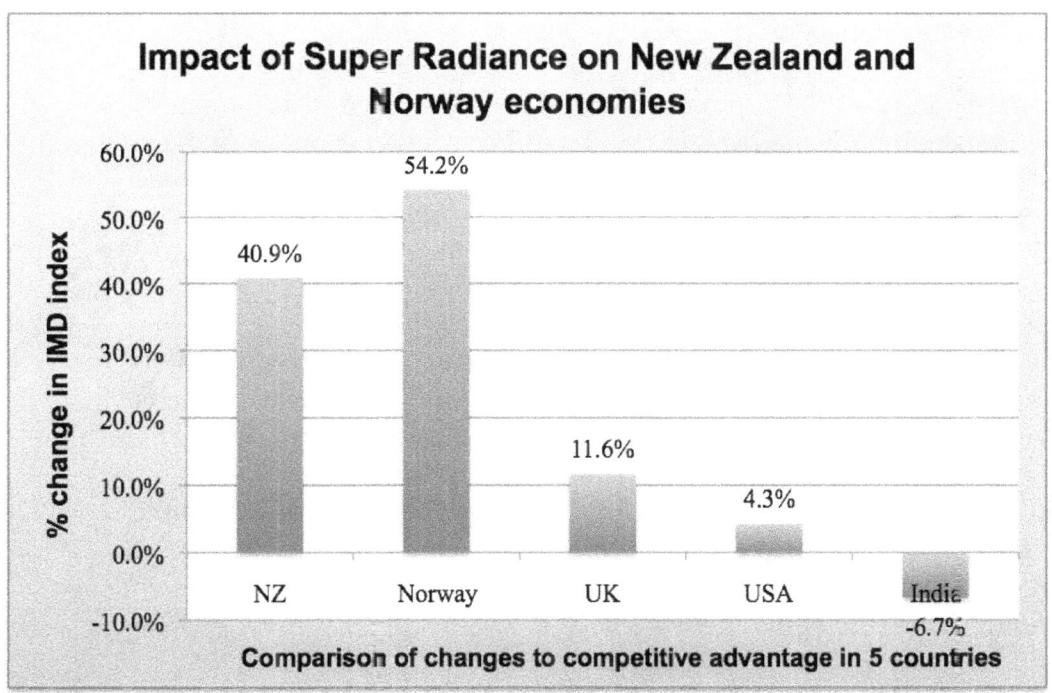

Highlights of economic recovery

- OECD forecasts failed to predict the speed, timing and depth of the Norwegian and New Zealand improvements. Specifically even as late as 1992 the OECD did not believe that the radical economic liberalization undertaken in New Zealand in the mid 1980s would correct what it saw as fundamental imbalances in the economy.

- Subsequent OECD biannual country surveys commented on the 'unusual, far reaching, unexpected, and sustained nature of the economic resurgence in both countries', reporting that both New Zealand and Norway experienced sustained periods of low inflation, high economic growth, and low unemployment after 1993.

- Norway and New Zealand had similar improvements in GDP, inflation and unemployment. In five years the Norwegian GDP lifted 20% (OECD economic survey 1999).

- The increase in the New Zealand GDP growth rate was an average of 3.28% for the period 1993 – 97.

- From the end of 1994 there was a rapid growth in overseas investors confidence in both the New Zealand and Norwegian economies. New Zealand experienced the second largest per capita overseas investment in the world (behind Singapore) in company stocks. The net overseas investment was equivalent to US$3,500 for every person in country.

- The net inflow of overseas investment in Norway rose from US$3.16 billion in 1992 to US$14.33 billion in 1994. The net overseas investment was equivalent to US$2,249 for every person in Norway.

- OECD identified a sharp widening of Norway's current account surplus.

- Unemployment dropped below 3%.

- The New Zealand government reduced its debt by 41%, in the period 1993 – 97, a reduction of US$8.7 billion. Previous to 1993, the government had been facing a persistently high debt to GDP ratio that had failed to respond to fiscally conservative reforms.

- New Zealand government treasury and OECD sources show that after the Maharishi Effect (1%) threshold was passed in 1993, the government retired 23.5% of GDP in net total debt over a four-year period. During this time real GDP increased from US$42.6 billion to US$47.5 billion.

Hatchard GD, Cavanaugh KC.

Research summary 43

Case study on the impact on the quality of life in Cambodia due to the Maharishi effect

The opportunity to carryout this study arose from a joint venture between three very different institutions:

1. The Royal Cambodian Government,
2. The Australian Aid to Cambodia Fund (AACF),
3. Maharishi Vedic University (MVU) Holland.

The joint venture set-up a new Maharishi Vedic University (MVU) in Cambodia (formerly Kampuchea), and this was established in 1992. The objective was to provide a Consciousness-Based Education to rural youth who would not otherwise have access to higher education.

By 2004, MVU Cambodia had grown to occupy four campuses with a total of over 1,000 students. The unique feature of the education system at the university is the daily group practice of the Transcendental Meditation technique and TM Sidhi programme.

As Cambodia has a population of 10 million, the 1,000 group at MVU was therefore sufficiently large enough to pass the $\sqrt{1\%}$ Super Radiance effect threshold.

Prior to 1993, there were few reliable measures of social and economic factors available. However one economic statistic that was available was for inflation rates. Recorded trends show a dramatic drop in inflation at the point the Super Radiance effect commenced. (See table over).

In addition Cambodia has emerged from being one of the poorest countries in the world. The country experienced a dynamic average real GDP growth between 1994 and 2001 in excess of 5.5% p.a.

See table over:

Cambodian transformation since 1993 Super Radiance

Before 1993	After 1993
• Civil war	• Democratic government with a restored monarchy
• Martial law	• Freedom of expression and civil rights
• Rule by military dictatorship,	• Substantial foreign investment
• Censorship and repression of civil rights	• Greater economic self-sufficiency
• Weak economy reliant on external assistance	• Much improved relations with neighbours
• Poor relations with neighbours	• Member of the ASEAN group of nations
• Prevailing sense of fear, intimidation and helplessness. The country was still recovering from the previous Khmer Rouge communist regime (1975 – 79) whose social engineering and genocide had wiped out over 20% of the population	• Much greater sense of confidence, security and optimism. Thousands of Khmer Rouge guerrillas surrender in a government amnesty.

To summarize, since 1993 since the onset of Super Radiance, Cambodia has realized a genuine base for:

- The harmonization of conflicting groups
- Social cooperative behaviour,
- Strong economic growth
- Relatively stable political institutions.

Many MVU graduates now occupy leading roles in Cambodian society.

"MVU is playing an important role in human resource development and in restoration of peace and expansion of prosperity throughout the country." His Majesty King Norodom Sihanouk

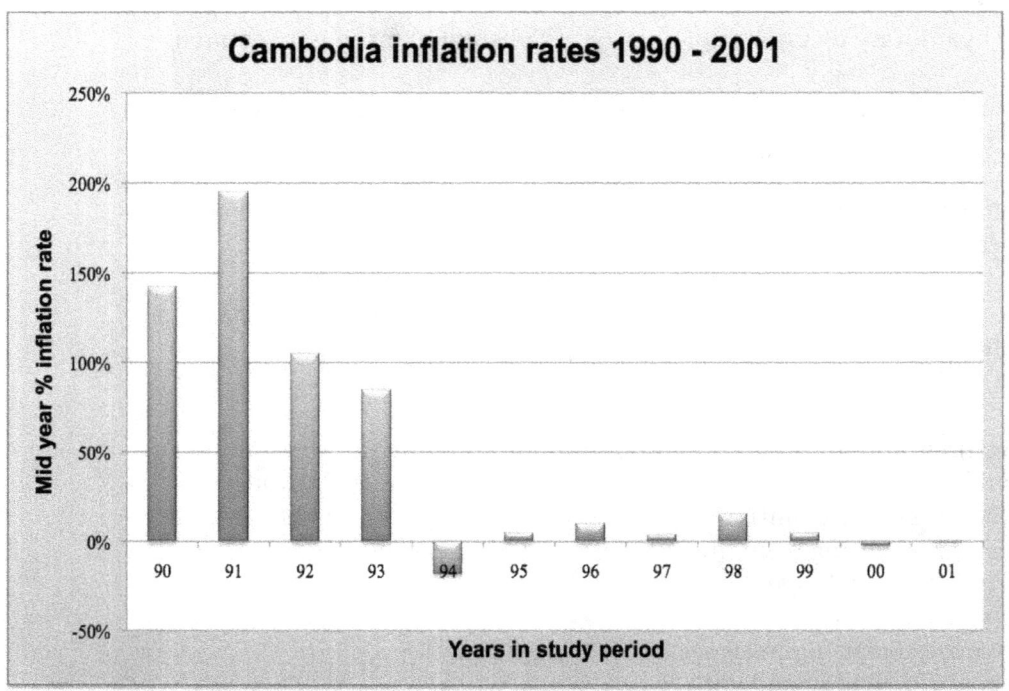

As we have seen from previous studies in other countries, the resolution of conflict, the emergence of cooperative behaviour and the resurgence of economic activity is typically the hallmark of the Super Radiance or Maharishi Effect.

Case study from Hatchard GD, KC Cavanaugh, The Peace and Well Being of Nations: An Analysis of Improved Quality of Life and Enhanced Economic Performance Through the Maharishi Effect in New Zealand, Norway. A Longitudinal, Cross-Country, Panel-Regression Analysis of the IMD Index of National Competitive Advantage. See research summary 42.

Research Summary 44

Mozambique transformation study

The Mozambique transformation from devastating civil war and aid dependency is a remarkable story of our times.

Mozambique illustrates that, however hopeless the situation appears, however intractable the problems are, a government, national leader or NGO now has the capability to quietly instigate a shift in the collective consciousness of the population and so initiate a powerful, positive and permanent impact on the destiny of their country.

Summary

In the early 1990s, Mozambique benefited from the global coherence groups that had been set-up briefly in India that greatly reduced the fighting across the world. Shortly after this easing of the situation, President Chissano created a number of TM based super radiance groups in the country itself. The immediate effect of these groups was to further reduce the fighting so that it ended altogether and precipitate an economic revival.

Essentially, the more peaceful atmosphere created by the coherence groups paved the way for the two main rival factions to negotiate permanent settlements. With peace breaking out, the government could then develop mutually acceptable economic and constitutional reforms that took hold and prospered. The results, among other factors were a 12.4% economic growth rate, inflation reducing from 70% to 2% and a liquidation of the national debt.

Starting point - Mozambique's desperate plight

By 1992, the Mozambique people had endured twenty-seven years of almost continuous warfare. First came the fight against Portuguese colonial rule. This culminated in the withdrawal of the Portuguese in 1975.

Unfortunately independence was largely nominal as powerful external forces constrained Mozambique's true 'independence'. The country became a pawn in ruthless Cold War rivalry and like many other former colonies, became a surrogate battleground for the Super Powers.

A terrible civil war then raged between the Marxist leaning government, backed by the Soviet Union, and the rebel organisation Renamo, sponsored by the West-supporting South African apartheid regime. At the time, South Africa was not only fearful of having a Marxist controlled neighbour but was also determined to destabilise any possible supporters of the African National Congress Party at home.

The ongoing war devastated Mozambique.

Out of a population of 19 million, at least one million are reckoned to have lost their lives and five million people became displaced as a consequence of the war. The Mozambique economy went to rack and ruin, the basic infrastructure was wrecked and the countryside became carpeted with land mines that debilitated both agriculture and village life.

Here in Mozambique we also saw the arrival of a sinister new military weapon, the child soldier. Renamo indoctrinated thousands of teenage children into becoming robotic, fearless, heartless butchers rampaging the countryside, pillaging and murdering. Child soldiers had dragged Africa another step down the road of brutality and dehumanisation.

By 1987 the disintegration had levelled Mozambique to being the world's poorest country. The combination of war, ideological zealotry and drought meant this otherwise fertile country had become dependent on international relief and emergency food aid simply to feed itself.

Inflation was rampant at 70%, there was zero economic growth and the threat of starvation had become an oppressive reality haunting most of the inhabitants. To compound the misery, by the early 90s, the Whole of South East Africa was suffering the worst drought for over a century.

Breakthrough

Mozambique finally got a break for two reasons.

Firstly in 1989 there was an upsurge in world coherence. This was caused by the first group of 7,000 TM-Sidhas to achieve a degree of sustained world

Super Radiance. This Indian based group precipitated a chain of seismic events globally. One major result was the unprecedented and rapid cessation of the Cold War and the subsequent collapse in 1990 of the Mozambique government's external sponsor, the Soviet Union.

This seminal event in world history had an immediate knock-on effect for Mozambique. The reduced pressure from external forces that had previously fuelled local hostilities combined with the calamitous economic situation enabled the government to negotiate a fragile peace with the rebels.

> *"First I started the practice of Transcendental Meditation myself, then introduced the practice to my close family, then to my cabinet of ministers, then to my government officers, and then to the military. The result has been political peace and balance in Nature in my country ... "* Former President Joaquim Alberto Chissano of Mozambique

Secondly, during 1992 Mozambique's then President, Joaquim Alberto Chissano, learned the Transcendental Meditation (TM) technique. This proved to be a formative event in his life, as the experience led him to persuade, first his immediate family, and after that, his cabinet to take up the daily practice as well.

Chissano soon began to integrate the practice of TM in the administration of his country.

"I had a group of coherence creating individuals next to my office. When representatives from other organizations came to me for a meeting, they were all expecting strong disagreements.

However, the atmosphere was so relaxed, we were like old friends meeting after a long time."

(Read research summaries 46 and 49, showing the impact of TM on the cortisol and serotonin levels of people nearby to a group of meditators and the phenomenon of inter-subject EEG coherence)

It was during this period that Chissano managed to secure the General Peace Agreement in 1992 that finally ended the war and began the process of demobilisation.

Introduction of TM to the armed forces

Building on this initial success, Chissano and his government decided to introduce Transcendental Meditation to the armed forces and the civilian population. During 1992 and 1993, all military and police recruits were ordered to meditate for 20 minutes, twice a day.

Within a short space of time more than 16,000 soldiers and 30,000 civilians were taught TM. 3,000 of these meditators were trained in the TM-Sidhi programme. This figure of 3,000 is highly significant as the Super Radiance factor Mozambique is actually only 435 TM-Sidhas grouped in one place.

Initially many of these people meditated in large groups. However, when the military demobilisation got underway from about 1994 onwards, as stipulated in the General Peace Agreement, the larger groups started disbanding. As the military demobilized, Lt. General Tobias Dai, then Commander of the Armed Forces, and more recently the General Secretary of the Ministry of Defence, noticed a negative trend emerging.

"What is very clear is that once the positive effect is created, if group practice (of TM) is stopped, the previous tendencies of higher collective stress, as determined from the crime indexes and the tense situations in the country, began to rise again. In 1994, there was a remarkable decrease in coherence in the country as a result of decreased participation in the group practice of the Transcendental Meditation and TM-Sidhi Programme..."

Even so the initial uplift in coherence created by the larger groups of TM-Sidhas and the surge in teaching TM and the TM-Sidhi programme across the country had a lasting impact. From 1992 onwards there started a rapid process of economic renewal.

Economic renewal

By 1993 the effects were being observed from outside the country. For instance on 22nd February 1993 The New York Times reported: "Mozambique has unexpectedly emerged as a candidate for an African

Success story. We have a combination of peace and rain which has not been seen in Mozambique for a quarter of a century."

> *"Mozambique has unexpectedly emerged as a candidate for an African Success story. We have a combination of peace and rain which has not been seen in Mozambique for a quarter of a century".* New York Times

President Chissano certainly attributes the cessation of civil conflict in Mozambique and the ensuing development of his country to the effect of Transcendental Meditation.

Here are some of the highlights from the transition.

Situation prior to achieving global and then national Super Radiance

- Prolonged civil war and violent political rivalry
- One million people killed and 5 million displaced as refugees
- Radical Marxist policies inhibiting economic activity
- Zero growth rate
- Inflation at 70%
- Massive overseas debt
- Unrelenting drought
- Chronic dependence on overseas food aid to stave off starvation

Benefits achieved once Super Radiance for Mozambique had been reached

- Conversion to stable democratic government and free market reforms
- The only successful UNO mission in the world at the time
- Annual growth rate of 12.4%, the highest in Africa
- Inflation dropped to 2% by 1999
- Reduction of national debt to zero
- Drought ending in November 1992
- Overall drop in crime level
- Drop in car accidents despite a tripling of road traffic mileage
- Resurgent agriculture with foreign food aid no longer needed
- The most stable currency in Africa

Chissano, a committed Roman Catholic says, "People ask me if this (TM) is a religion. I have explained to them that I may keep my religion but I should take advantage of this science and make maximum use of it. We will not stop praying in our churches, we will not stop praying in our mosques, we will not stop praying in our synagogues, but we will make an appeal to the support of Nature through the application of this technology (of consciousness)."

It could have been a lot worse – A comparison with Angola ...

We must remember that the unfolding of events in Mozambique could have been a lot worse. Mozambique's experience is in stark contrast to the hapless Angolans who had also suffered a civil war following independence from Portugal. Exacerbated by international rivalry and entanglements, and lacking in the key Super Radiance factor, the civil war dragged on for a further ten years after Mozambique's had subsided.

Angola's ongoing conflict spawned a disastrous humanitarian crisis with a harrowing 4.28 million people or one-third of the total population displaced. According to United Nations' estimates in 2003, 80% of Angolans still lacked access to basic medical care, 60% lacked access to water, and 30% of Angolan children would die before the age of 5, with an overall national life expectancy of less than 40 years of age.

And also Somalia ...

Another sorry example of the best international intentions being dashed by the lack of coherence in national consciousness is in Somalia.

Peace negotiations in Somalia began in January 1993 under the auspices of the UN and these were aimed at a transition to democracy. The UN involvement meant the agreement was backed by the presence of 28,000 UN peacekeeping troops. But the presence of this many troops still failed to lead to progress. The UN contingents were forced to withdraw and the country suffered civil conflict and fragmentation throughout the 1990s.

All the Somalians needed to create peace, harmony and prosperity was not 28,000 UN peacekeepers, but a permanent group of just 310 TM-Sidhas.

Case study sources

Much of the material in this section is derived from a case study by Hatchard GD, KC Cavanaugh, "The Peace and Well Being of Nations: An

Analysis of Improved Quality of Life and Enhanced Economic Performance through the Maharishi Effect in New Zealand, Norway, USA, Cambodia, and Mozambique. A Longitudinal, Cross-Country, Panel-Regression Analysis of the IMD Index of National Competitive Advantage. See research summary 42.

See also Case study - Maharishi's formula for a prevention wing in the military— applied and found successful in Mozambique: case study, 1993–1994. Lt. Gen. Tobias Dai

Collected papers v6.495

Research Summary 45

Preventing terrorism and international conflict: Effects of large assemblies of participants in the Transcendental Meditation and TM-Sidhi programs.

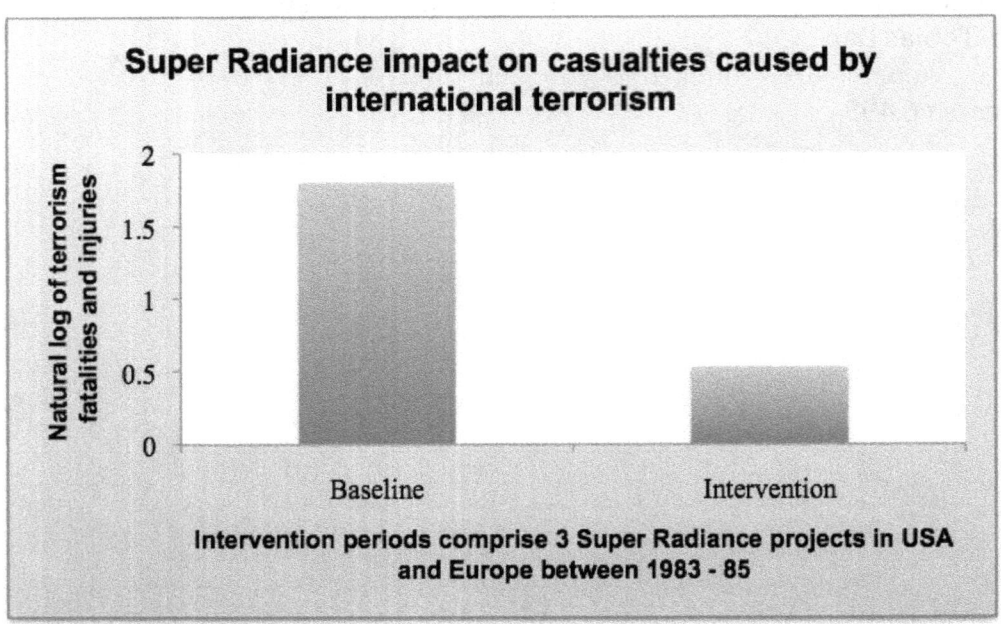

A study in how to defeat terrorism quickly and quietly

Since Al Qaeda attacked the Twin Towers in New York, the global war against terrorism has consumed more and more resources and has curtailed more and more freedoms for the average peaceful citizen. All this heavy-handed security appears somewhat unnecessary when viewed in the context of research into the impact of Super Radiance on terrorist outbreaks.

What is terrorism?

But first it might help to clarify what terrorism is.

Terrorism is a particularly virulent form of antisocial behaviour. As the name implies it is designed to terrorise the subject population, to an extent where they will induce their legitimate government to take counter-measures that are of necessity oppressive. (In this sense terrorists are distinct from freedom fighters, who strive to free the population from a tyrannical regime or foreign invader). The idea is that the government's counter measures become so unpopular that the populace grow sick and tired of the oppression and paranoia and revolt against the legitimate government.

What is supposed to happen next is that in the ensuing chaos and power vacuum the terrorist organisation slips into power on the back of quasi-legitimate political supporters or in the guise of freedom fighters.

As a political theory for creating a transition to a better society, terrorism is spectacularly useless.

Unfortunately terrorism's poor track record of success in achieving its goals has not prevented deranged and criminalised political ideologues from indulging in fruitless but violent attempts to undermine the rest of society. Unfortunately, all too often governments take the bait and wherever there is a threat of terrorism they understandably rush in and introduce oppressive measures to try and protect society from harm.

Many anti-terrorist measures are costly, repressive and counter productive

The present global war against terrorism is a good case in point.

Ever since 9/11, Western governments and the USA in particular have imposed measures that increasingly restrict what are supposed to be inviolable rights and freedoms in an attempt to protect the general population. Unhappily this attempt to protect civilisation has degenerated to such a level where we now have routine counter measures that include covert ops in other countries' sovereign territory, highly intrusive surveillance, extreme interrogation measures, imprisonment without trial and remote execution of suspects by predator drones. The added problem is that such measures are invariably counterproductive as they incite further hatred and hostility between the antagonists.

Society seems stuck in a conundrum.

Do we opt for counter measures that are in many ways a travesty of civilised values and ultimately lead to oppression and tyranny?

Or do we just have to put up with the interminable random outbreaks of violence, chaos and anarchy unleashed by the terrorist?

Happily the Super Radiance effect provides a third alternative.

Defeating terrorism at the level of consciousness

In this study, a meta-analysis of three earlier global peace projects specifically tested the hypothesis that the Super Radiance effect also impacted terrorism. The result shows that, as predicted, Super Radiance, acting on the level of the collective consciousness, quickly and quietly reduces the level of terrorist activity. Importantly, success is achieved at minimal cost to society and without violating any freedoms, rights or civilised values.

The reason behind this seemingly effortless success is that Super Radiance diffuses stress levels in the collective consciousness. The simple mechanics are that, stress in the individual consciousness creates stress in the collective consciousness. Just as happiness infects other members of society and just as individual stress influences every part of the individual physiology, so the stress of an individual also permeates society and influences everyone else's behaviour. When stress in the collective consciousness accrues beyond a certain level it manifests in the form of outbreaks of anti-social behaviour, social disorder, disease and crime. In the more extreme cases of stress, we see eruptions of violent conflict, terrorism and ultimately open warfare.

The relationship between the individual consciousness and the collective consciousness is reciprocal. This means that the collective consciousness also has an influence on each individual member. So, where we are able to create Super Radiance with a large group of TM-Sidhas their collective meditation enlivens the collective consciousness and serves to lessen the individual stress of everyone in society. When this happens the incidents of conflict, violence, criminal activity and so on goes down.

This particular study focussed on the impact of three Super Radiance groups comprising 6,000 to 8,000 TM-Sidhas. The groups were separate both in time and in place and, at the time, either achieved or approached the Super Radiance figure required for an impact on global consciousness. (See table)

Location	No of TM-Sidhas	Start date	Finish date
Fairfield Iowa USA	8,000	27th December 1983	6th January 1984
The Hague Holland	6,000 +	28th December 1984	6th January 1985
Washington DC	5,500	9th July 1985	17th July 1985

The research methodology comprised a meta-analysis of data acquired from the Chronology of International Terrorism (Extract) complied by the Rand Corporation. This data was derived from public domain sources including about 100 newspapers, journals and periodicals using independent assessors who were blind to the dates of the projects.

To provide a control for the experiment, records of fatalities and injuries caused by international terrorism were monitored over a two-year period (2nd January 1983 – 31st December 1985). This was undertaken in a series of five-day periods to match the 'intervention' periods when one of the three Super Radiance groups was in operation. The data was then subjected to time-series analysis.

Super Radiance creates a 72% drop in international terrorism

The results showed a dramatic decrease in international terrorism of a mean 72% compared with terrorist activity during the non-intervention periods. The impact began after a lag of about five-days from the start of each of the three Super Radiance projects. The records also show a significant decline in fatalities and injuries due to terrorist activity during the 'intervention periods'. (See chart above)

Important points about the study:

Five factors in this study combine to reinforce the proposition that Super Radiance reduces terrorist activity.

1. Results predicted in advance
The hypothesis that Super Radiance would have a rapid and powerful influence on the level of international conflict was predicted in advance of

each of the separate projects. These predictions were communicated to the media and academic community. Even so the results evidently took world leaders and media observers by surprise and were clearly not anticipated by them.

2. No physical interaction was involved

The individual TM-Sidhas participating in these large groups were obviously unable to interact in any physical, social or diplomatic way with those pursuing terrorist acts thousands of miles away.

3. Effect replicated in multiple locations and at different times

From the onset of each of the three projects there was a simultaneous and dramatic change that occurred in multiple locations thousands of miles apart and thousands of miles away from the Super Radiance groups. Individual conflict zones as diverse as Latin America, the Middle East, Afghanistan, Pakistan and Southeast Asia were all affected.

4. Seasonal variations taken into account

Seasonal variations were accounted for in the study. For instance two of the projects took place over the new-year holiday period. So the question arose did the holiday period create a positive trend (Do terrorists go on holiday?). As a direct control, the researchers carried out a secondary time series analysis for each variable assessing its year-end behaviour in at least 5 previous years. The evidence showed no correlation between holiday periods and terrorist activity. In the case of international conflict generally however, there was a discernable trend and this was in the opposite direction towards more violence and conflict.

The researchers were also able to rule out the possibility that this reduction in terrorism was due to economic cycles, political trends, or drifts in the measures used.

5. The results are consistent with other smaller studies

The reduction in casualties and conflict during these three projects is entirely consistent with similar effects achieved by several other smaller Super Radiance groups effecting smaller populations in different parts of the world at different times over the last thirty years. As such this study adds further weight to the growing evidence that the Super radiance effect can quickly reverse negative trends in society and trigger a rapid reduction of violence, conflict and hostility.

Hope for the future

The small size of the groups needed to create the Super Radiance effect presents our society with an awesome possibility. The research tells us that we can create a positive influence of peace from any one place on earth, in any country. This can all be achieved:

- Without intruding in other nations' affairs,
- Without crossing ideological boundaries and religious divides,
- Without violating cherished rights and freedoms
- And at a tiny fraction of the cost of any single nation's defence budget.

Orme-Johnson DW, Dillbeck MC, Alexander CN; *Journal of Offender Rehabilitation* 36 (1-4): 283-302, 2003.

Research Summary 46

Alleviating political violence through reducing collective tension: Impact assessment analyses of the Lebanon war - Research abstract

This longitudinal social experiment replicates and extends an earlier study (Orme-Johnson, Alexander et al., 1988; 1990 research summary 34) in testing the proposal that political violence can be alleviated through reducing stress in the collective consciousness of a large population.

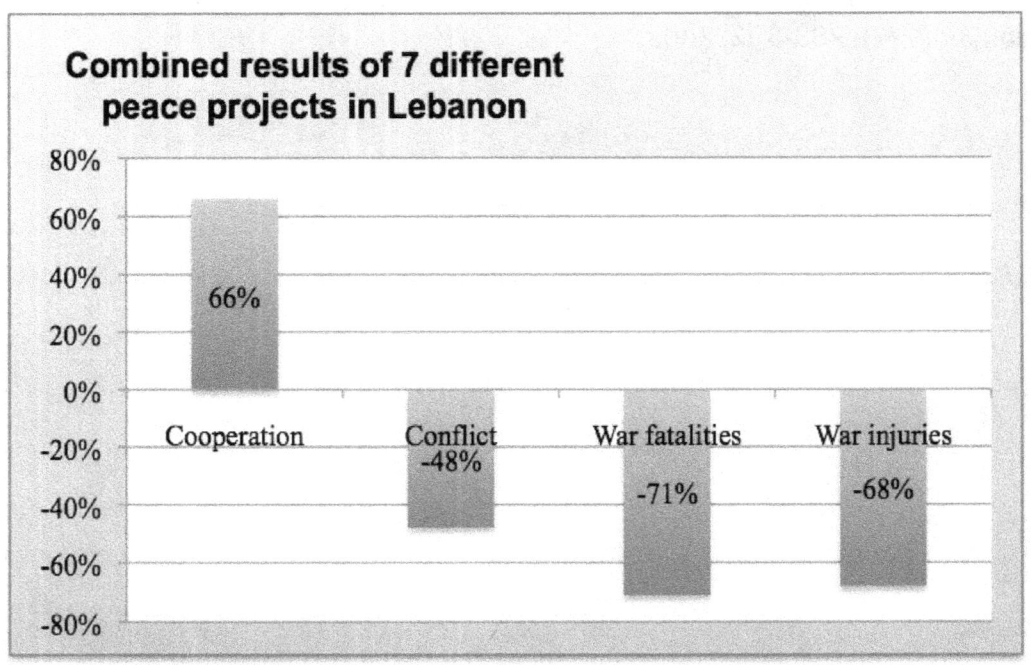

It was predicted that group practice of meditation techniques in a series of seven assemblies held within a two-and-a-quarter year period would reduce collective tension and violence and enhance cooperative behavior among antagonistic parties in the Lebanon War. Daily event-data were derived from nine international and regional news sources. An experienced Lebanese coder, blind to the hypothesis and techniques employed, scored levels of conflict, cooperation and casualties using Rasler's (1981) 16-point scales.

Box-Jenkins impact assessment analyses indicated that the assemblies had a highly significant impact in the predicted direction on all dependent variables, with an estimated

- 66% increase in cooperation
- 48% reductions in conflict,
- 71% reductions in war fatalities,
- 68% reductions in war injuries

($p < .00001$ for each variable).

Analysis of an index combining the dependent variables indicated that each of the seven assemblies also had a separate positive impact on the war ($p < .01$).

These results were robust across alternative models of the dependent series, and improvements could not be accounted for in terms of changes in temperature, holidays, weekends, or other forms of seasonality or trends in the dependent series, which were explicitly controlled for. Nor were results explicable in terms of "reverse causality" (assemblies being held in reaction to prior events in Lebanon), as experimental periods (assembly dates) were set months in advance and were statistically independent from prior levels of conflict.

JL Davies CN Alexander, *Journal of Social behavior and personality*, 2005, 285-338.

Research summary 47

Societal Violence and Collective Consciousness: Reduction of U.S. Homicide and Urban Violent Crime Rates

This long-term field study is one of a series of three, where the researchers seized a one-off chance to study the national impact of a four-year uplift in the size of a group of TM-Sidhas in the USA. This first in the series is a comprehensive, large-scale demonstration of the potential for Super Radiance to progressively reduce crime across a whole nation. The other two in the series look at the impact of Super Radiance on accidental deaths, (summary 48) infant mortality rates and drug related deaths (summary 49).

From past evidence the two researchers, Michael Dillbeck and Ken Cavanaugh, anticipated that as the group numbers grew to the Super Radiance threshold (the square root of 1% of the USA population), there would be a matching downward shift in crime trends. In other words the objective of this study was to confirm that the downward shift in crime levels had actually occurred as predicted.

As before, with previous Super Radiance studies, the two researchers conducted this new one on the premise that the enlarged Super Radiance group would improve **social coherence** through the medium of an underlying field of **pure consciousness**. These two terms may need clarification.

In this context, 'social coherence' is seen as spontaneously orderly and balanced thinking in society as a whole.

The term 'pure consciousness', sometimes referred to as the transcendence, is used to depict the unbounded and omnipresent field that connects individual human beings and indeed all energy and material elements, at the most fundamental level of existence.

According to Maharishi Mahesh Yogi, the founder of the Transcendental Meditation and the TM-Sidhi programme of meditation, pure consciousness is reflected at a social level by a 'collective consciousness'. Maharishi describes that each stratum of society has a corresponding 'collective consciousness' and this collective value applies whether it is for your family, local community, village, town, city, state, or nation or even the entire global population.

In effect, the collective consciousness derives from the combined consciousness of all the individuals in society. Importantly in the context of this major study, the quality of that collective consciousness, whether it is stressed, calm, orderly or violent, depends on the aggregate experience of all the 'component parts' in the system (i.e. people in the society being studied). This aggregate experience is influenced by the myriad day-today, week-to-week, month by month social interactions, life experiences, thoughts, desires and emotions that make up the general quality of the atmosphere.

Maharishi's theory goes on to predict that the group practice of the TM-Sidhi program, because it has the unique feature of enlivening the pure consciousness of the individual practitioners, it also has an enlivening effect on the collective consciousness of the host society. It is this enlivening effect on the collective consciousness that alleviates social stress and at the same time enhances social coherence.

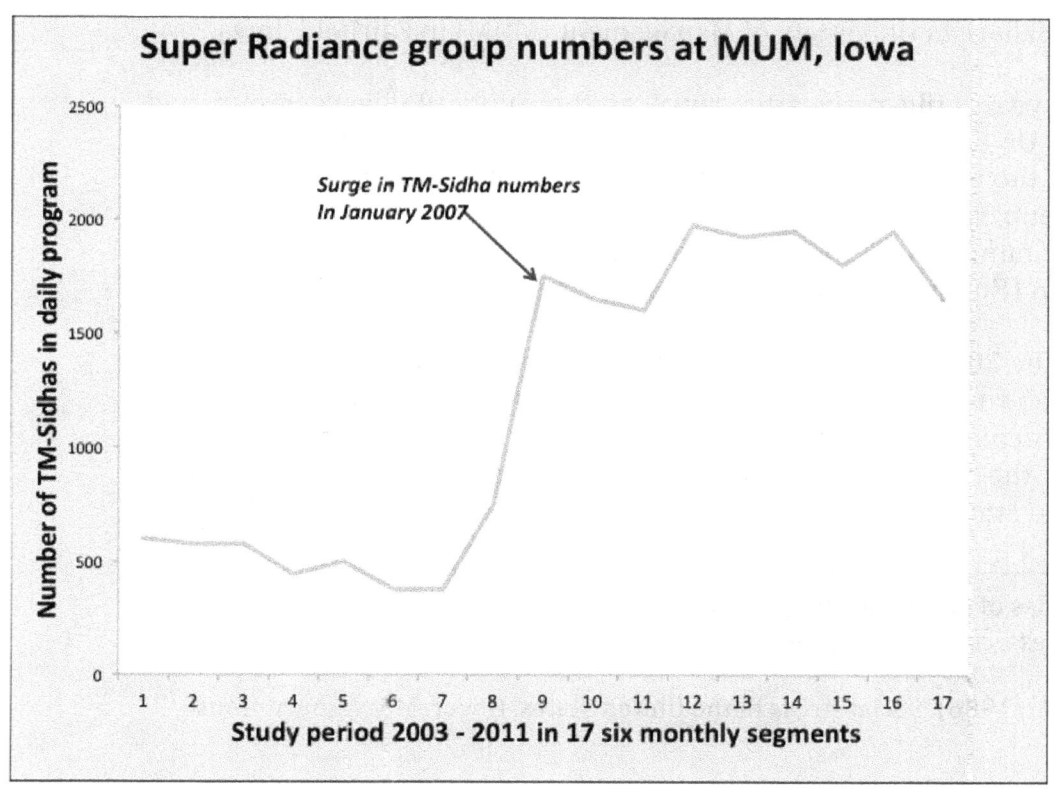

In turn, the reduced collective stress and enhanced collective coherence reduces stress and violence in individual thinking and activity. As a result, negative trends within society such as terrorism, crime, suicides, vandalism and antisocial behaviour tend to diminish. In other words, with Super Radiance, we find that spontaneously more people feel less inclined to go and do bad things to themselves or other people.

As we have already seen, the earlier research studies used crime statistics, to confirm that the improved brain-wave coherence emanating from a large TM-Sidha group would reduce stress in society. Even in mainstream academic circles it has become more recognised that crime in society is a manifestation of societal stress[6]. Crime figures in the USA are measured in a fairly uniform way across the whole country and are also publically available, so it makes sense to test the effectiveness of the Super Radiance effect by studying the available crime statistics.

Clear before and after effect

The opportunity for this long-term study arose, because of a sudden and dramatic upward shift in the numbers of the USA national Super Radiance group at Maharishi University of Management (MUM) in Fairfield, Iowa.

Over the years, the daily attendance at the Super Radiance group had dwindled. On occasions, as little as two or three hundred TM-Sidhas were practicing the twice-daily coherence-creating programme. The average size of the group was running at about 587 participants. This figure is well below the number of 1,792 required to achieve the Super Radiance effect for the USA (Roughly, the $\sqrt{}$ of 1% of the 297 million population).

However in 2006, the MUM University faculty resolved to improve the situation and made a determined effort to bring the numbers back up to 1,792. To achieve this would be no mean feat, but on this occasion help arrived in the form of a private donor who sponsored a cohort of Indian students to study at MUM. These students had already been trained as TM-

---

[6] As examples of academic thought see: Linsky, A. S., Bachman, R., & Straus, M. A. (1995). Stress, culture, & aggression. New Haven, CT: Yale University Press. Linsky, A. S., &
Straus, M. A. (1986). Social stress in the United States. Dover, MA: Auburn House.

Sidhas, and so were immediately able to add to the ranks of the Super Radiance group. As a result the university managed to accomplish their goal of an enlarged group of TM-Sidhas in early 2007. For the next four years the average daily size of the group was maintained at Super Radiance level or near to it.

This profound step-change in the Super Radiance condition and its maintenance over a four-year period offered a clear before and after effect for the empirical analysis of medium term crime trends. Basically, during the period before the enlarged Super Radiance group was in place, the researchers expected to see generally higher crime figures. After the establishment of the renewed group they expected a significant and positive shift in national crime trends.

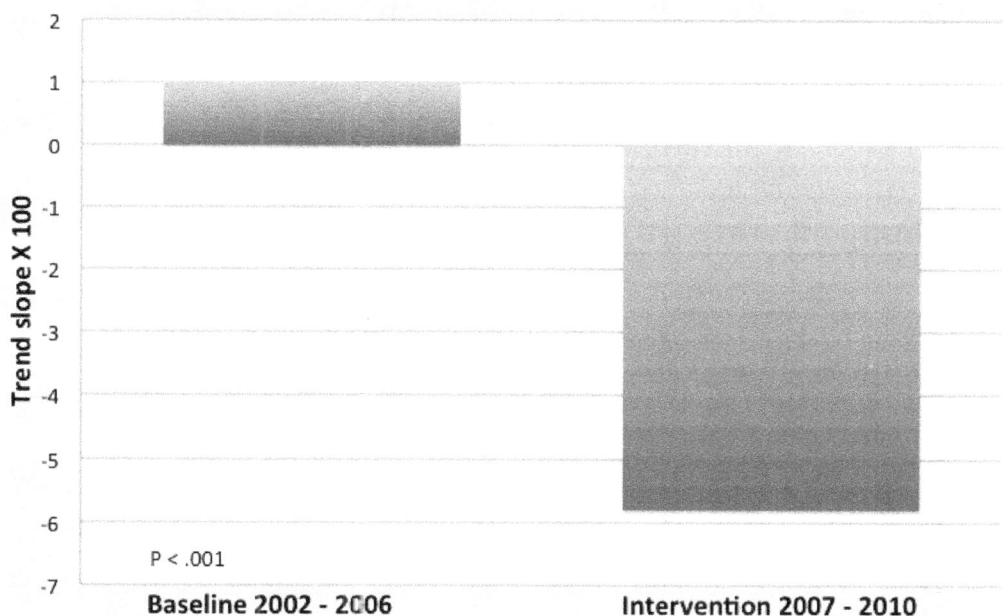

Extensive research base

To make the study as thorough as they could and to counter any bias from small samples, the researchers looked at crime figures from no less than

206 cities throughout the USA. They selected these cities on the twin criteria of each one being a minimum size of 100,000 people and also each one being able to provide crucially uninterrupted monthly crime statistics for the entire study period 2002 to 2011.

As this was a study of reasonably long-term trends, the researchers also wanted to take into account any population fluctuations during the period in case they might distort the findings. For this reason the figures were broken down to show the rate of homicide per 100 million population.

Crime measurements

The researchers used three main measures of crime each with a slightly different statistical base and method of extraction:

HOM = Higher homicide rate
VCR = Violent crime rate; measured as the monthly rate of violent crime, reported by the FBI Uniform Crime Report system as comprising murder and non-negligent manslaughter, forcible rape, aggravated assault, and robbery
MUR = FBI reported rate of murder with non-negligent manslaughter

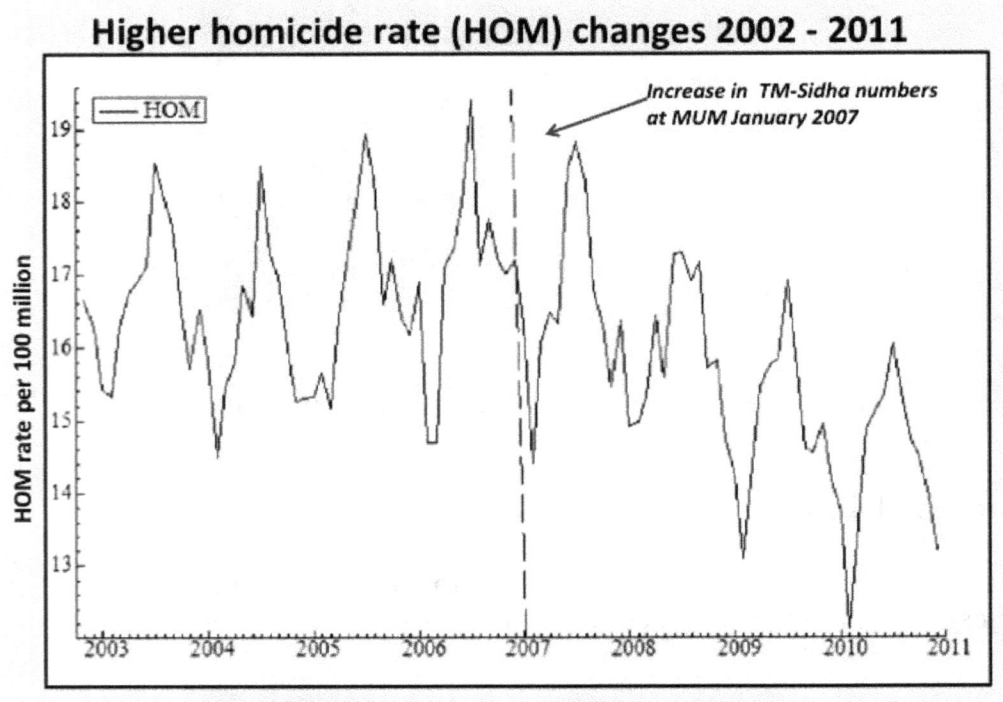

Study period dates showing seasonal fluctuations in homicide rates

Methods of analysis

Methods of analysis included intervention analysis or interrupted time series analysis. The statistical analysis of monthly data for 2002-2010 uses time series regression to estimate a broken-trend, or segmented-trend intervention model for each outcome variable.

Summary of findings – 186,774 less violent crimes

At the onset of the enlarged Super Radiance group from January 2007, (termed as the intervention period) all measures show a declining trend that continues through to the end of the study period (See seasonal charts).

You can see from the charts that there are strong seasonal fluctuations. Although these fluctuations show a reasonably flat but slightly overall upward trend in the period before the establishment of the Super Radiance group, there is a definite declining trend after 2007. The decline is measured at an overall 21.24% for the remainder of the study period compared with the mean pre-2007 rate of 16.6714 homicides per 100 million people.

This trend change is equivalent to an annual decline of 5.31% in HOM during the post 2007 period. The researchers calculated that the cumulative reduction in homicides per 100 million population translates to a total expected reduction of 8,157 homicides for the intervention period.

The VCR statistics showed a reduction of 18.54% compared with the rate of 22.43 per million people prior to the renewed Super Radiance group. This rate represents an annual decrease of 4.64%. In the 206 urban areas, the cumulative reduction in the daily rate of violent crime per million population translates to a total expected reduction of 186,774 violent crimes for 2007-2010.

There is an estimated trend shift in murder and non-negligent manslaughter (MUR) that implies a 28.40% total reduction (3,865 murders) for the 2007-2010 intervention period, or 7.10% annually, as compared to the pre-intervention trend.

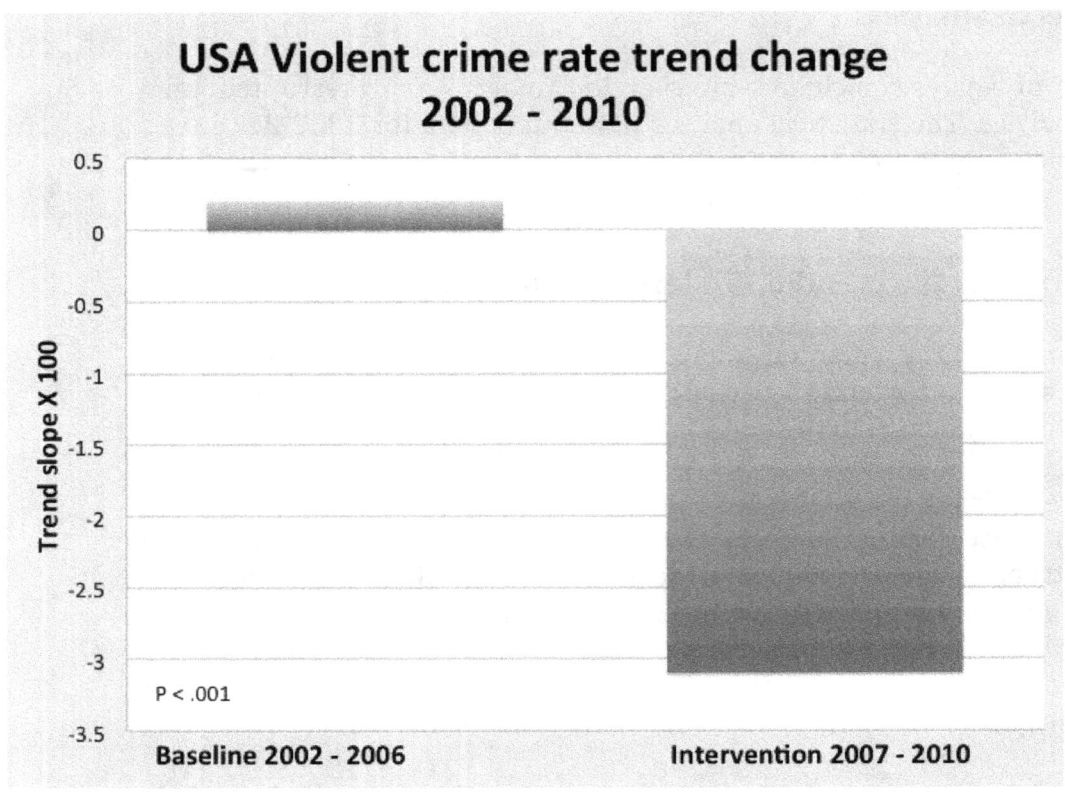

Were other factors at work influencing the reduction in violent crime and homicide?

A number of social and economic factors are understood to impact crime trends. So with this study, Dillbeck and Cavanaugh recognised it was important to see if any of these factors were contributing to the declining trends in crime. They analysed several possible alternatives to see if, at the time of the study, they were likely to be influencing the decline in crime rates.

Unemployment

Contrary to the consistent experience of previous recessions, the reduction in crime trends occurred during a significant increase in U.S. unemployment that began in 2008 with the onset of the recession.

Prison population

Another factor that is sometimes seen to help falling crime is increased incarceration rates. The theory being if you lock up more bad guys, they will not be out and about committing crime. The Super Radiance experience in this case seems to confound this theory, as during the study period prison admissions and prison releases converged from 2006 to 2009. The result was a slowing of the growth of the U.S. prison population. In 2010, prison releases exceeded prison admissions for the first time since records are available.

Demographic trends – youth population

Another usual predictor of rising violent crime is the rising proportion of youth aged 18 to 25 in the population. The proportion of people aged 18 – 25 in the overall population rose steadily through the 2000s thus eliminating another possible alternative cause to the steady decline in crime.

Climatic temperature

There is also an argument that rising temperatures can help increase interpersonal violence. In past studies, researchers have found an estimated 4% increase in violence for one standard deviation of warmer temperature. But in this study, we see cyclical warmer temperature having a slightly reduced impact on the crime rate every year. The charts show that the seasonal variations in violence associated with annual cycles of temperature still occur, but you can also see declining peaks and troughs once the Super Radiance effect is in place.

Policing methods

The researchers accepted that the introduction of more effective policing strategies would contribute to reduced rates of homicide and violent crime. However, it must be pointed out that more effective policing strategies would have to be implemented simultaneously across all 206 cities to have achieved the consistent effect observed by the research. No such nationally systemic improvement in policing was evident during the study period.

Surveillance technology

Increased surveillance technology may have a deterrent effect, particularly on property crime, but is less of a deterrent with violent crime and homicide. In the case of these more serious crimes, irrational impulsive thinking and behaviour and substance abuse usually influence the propensity to commit crime regardless of surveillance. In addition, there is also no evidence that there was a simultaneous implementation of increased surveillance across all of the 206 cities.

The inescapable conclusion is that there are no compelling alternative explanations for the sudden crime trend changes during the study period.

Implications for government crime prevention policy

It is clear from this and earlier studies that Super Radiance groups are a supremely practical means to achieve declining trends in crime and also to reduce other forms of destructive or anti-social behaviour including of course the modern scourge of terrorism.

The Super Radiance effect can be created by a proportionately minute number of the population, who can all be collected in one place and do not need to be dispersed among the communities they serve. There is no need for heavy equipment, extra infrastructure, bureaucratic state departments, public relations initiatives, or any other of the usual means of public policy deployment. This keeps the cost way below normal crime prevention or counter terrorism initiatives. Neither does the Super Radiance effect have the brutalising consequences of a militarised police force and the controversial privacy violations prevalent with the current counter terrorism strategies. The general population do not even have to know such a group exists.

All that seems to be lacking at the moment is the understanding among a sufficient number of government officials and politicians that Super Radiance works. And what seems to be getting in the way of this understanding is the existing beliefs, prejudices and conditioning that prevent people from seeing the obvious facts as they are and then acting upon them.

One way of overcoming any prejudice is to find out the truth for yourself by direct personal experience. In this context, this could mean an appropriate government agency taking on the responsibility of running a pilot project. Then government officials could monitor and evaluate the Super Radiance effect at first hand and would then be in a position to draw their own conclusions as to the feasibility of adopting the Super Radiance effect on a wider scale.

Dillbeck MC, Institute of Science, Technology and Public Policy at Maharishi University of Management; Cavanaugh KL Institute of Science, Technology and Public Policy at Maharishi University of Management

SAGE Open April-June 2016: 1–16 The Author(s) 2016 DOI: 10.1177/2158244016637891 sgo.sagepub.com

Research summary 48

The Contribution of Proposed Field Effects of Consciousness to the Prevention of US Accidental Fatalities: Theory and Empirical Tests

Summary 48, like summary 47, looks at the impact of the newly revived US Super Radiance group between 2007 and 2010. As such this summary is the second study in a series of three. Here the researchers focused on motor vehicle accident fatalities and other accidental fatalities. They found that during the study period there occurred a 20.6% reduction in US motor vehicle fatalities and a decline of 13.5% in all other accidental deaths.

As a direct result of these positive trends, the researchers estimate that Super Radiance averted 19,435 motor vehicle fatalities and 16,759 other accidental deaths across the USA during the four-year duration of the study.

As we have seen from summary 47, between the years 2007 – 2010 the size of the Super Radiance group of TM-Sidhas in the USA group in Iowa, reached 1,725 participants. This number is approximately the square root of 1% of the US population and the proportion required to create a positive shift on the quality of life in the US.

A brief explanation

It is already well understood by psychologists that the stress response can quickly restrict our awareness, impede our attention and focus, unbalance our rational judgment, weaken our decision-making ability, make us over-confident and reckless (or less confident and over cautious) and confuse us generally. As a result of this medley of hindrances, one harmful effect of the stressed mind is that it can make us accident-prone. From this understanding it is easy to imagine that if the whole population were suddenly to become slightly less stressed, then there would be a commensurate decline in unfortunate accidents.

Super Radiance, created by a sufficient sized group of TM-Sidhas, reduces stress across a whole society.

Conditioned as we are to rely on our sensory perception to make sense of the world, it is difficult to believe that people, sitting in a room in the middle of America can, simply by dint of their settled but lively state of being, reduce the stress levels of the 300 million other people in the country. The truth of this can only be realized when we reach beyond our reliance on our senses and take on board the scientific fact that at the most fundamental level of our existence we are pure energy.

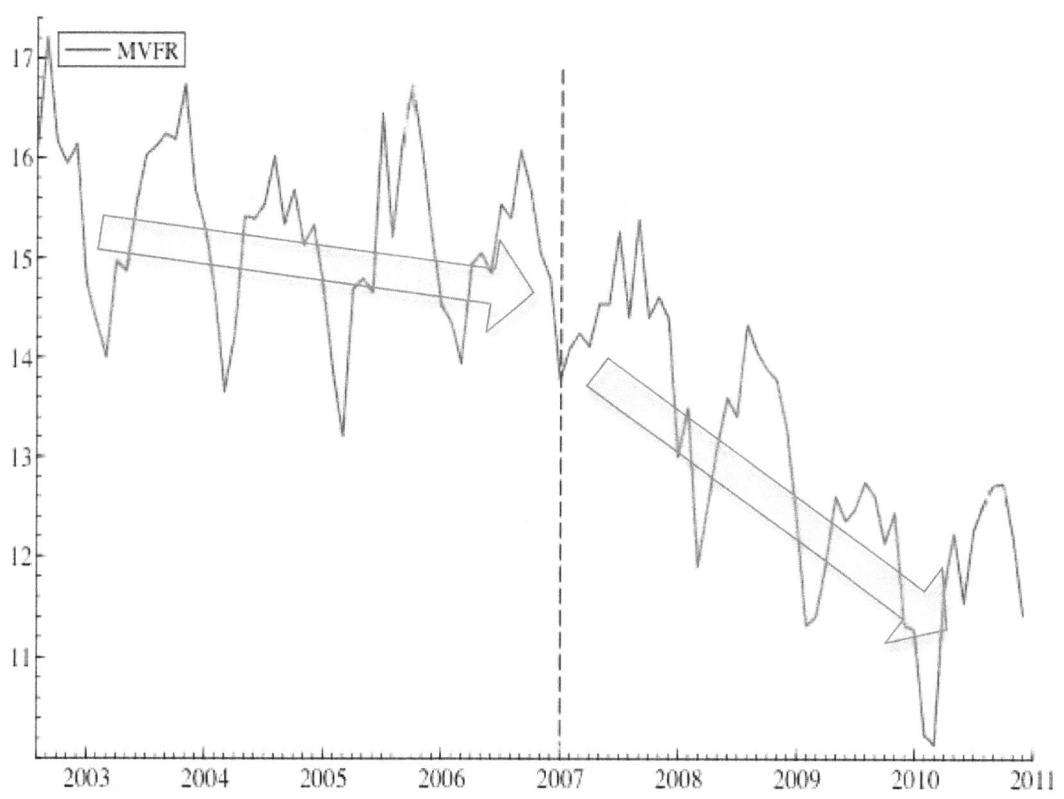

Figure 48.1 Motor vehicle fatality rate 2002-2010

Maharishi Mahesh Yogi, the original founder of the Super Radiance effect, explains that there is a universal energy field at the basis of the material universe and this of course naturally encompasses the basis of everyone's thinking, behaviour and activity. When practitioners of Transcendental Meditation experience 'pure consciousness' during their meditation, they are in effect experiencing this universal field as part of their own being (Please see chapter 5 for a fuller explanation). In other words they become more intimately connected with the rest of society at the most fundamental level of that society's existence.

In contrast to the stubborn beliefs generated by our senses, that trick our intellect into thinking otherwise, the reality of life is not that we are separated from one another in time and space, but that each one of us is an integral part of this universal energy field. It follows then that when a group of meditators experience pure consciousness they enliven this field of energy for everyone else around them. The more meditators there are, the wider this field effect is and the more people get bought into the embrace of this positive wave of energy. As a direct result, and through the medium of this field effect meditation positively influences the individual quality of consciousness of everyone else in the host population. And the benefits occur in much the same way as though the whole society was practicing meditation. The non-meditating members of the population start benefiting (albeit in diluted form) from the stress reducing qualities of Transcendental Meditation and the even more powerful stress reducing effects engendered by the TM-Sidhi program, even though they are not actively participating themselves. The net result is we find increased alertness, improved attention and less stress in the general population, and in turn this contributes to an overall reduction in accident rates.

In their analysis, the researchers first calculated a baseline trend for both types of accidental fatality rates during 2002–2006, then used time series intervention analysis to compare that baseline with the corresponding trend for the intervention period 2007–2010.

For example, they found that the slightly declining trend of vehicle fatality rates (MVFR) seen during the baseline period 2002–2006 accelerated significantly from January 2007 (vertical line) and this rate of decline continued during the intervention period 2007–2010 (see Figure 48.1). The irregular ups and downs of the fatality rate shown in the graph are largely due to seasonal fluctuations around the trend.

In the case of fatality rates for all other accidents (ACCFR), we see a highly significant shift from a rising trend in 2002–2006 to a substantially slower but positive trend in 2007–2010 (see Figure 48.2).

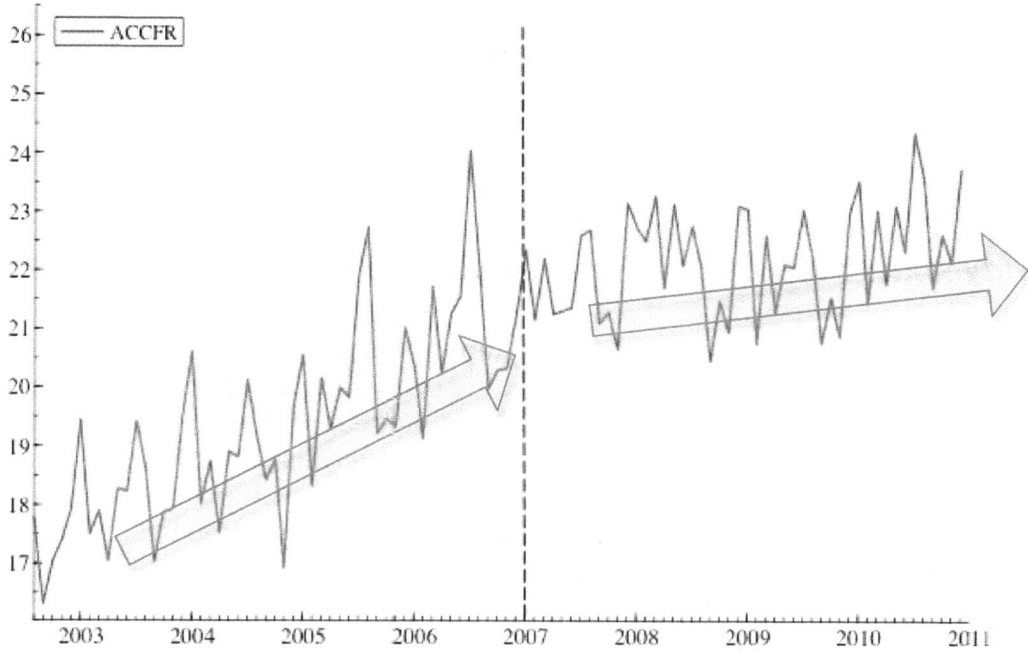

Figure 48.2 Fatality rate for other accidents 2002–2010.

The probability that the reduced trend for motor vehicle fatalities could simply be due to chance was reported to be 3.7 in 10 million million and for fatalities due to other accidents, less than 8.4 in 1 million.

The researchers noted that both reduced accident trends occurred at the predicted time and in the predicted direction, and neither reduction could be predicted from what was happening earlier (baseline trends) or seasonal cycles (seasonal temperatures, holidays and so on). After due investigation, the researchers also ruled out other alternative explanations for the shift. They were able to exclude any influence from a reduction in miles travelled, weather patterns, the proportion of young drivers on the road, improved vehicle safety features, improved roadway conditions, or alcohol consumption.

Dillbeck MC, Institute of Science, Technology and Public Policy at Maharishi University of Management; Cavanaugh KL Institute of Science, Technology and Public Policy at Maharishi University of Management; Journal of Consciousness Studies, February 2017.

Research summary 49

Group practice of the Transcendental Meditation and TM-Sidhi program and reductions in infant mortality and drug-related death: A quasi-experimental analysis

Major study shows 30% reduction in drug related deaths

In recent years, the USA has experienced a fairly unremitting surge in drug-related deaths that has been giving public health professionals cause for real concern. The surge began around 1990, and appeared fueled by skyrocketing rates of unintentional prescription drug overdoses, largely from painkillers and anxiety drugs. Prescription drug misuse has now become such a problem that in 2009 drug related deaths actually exceeded motor vehicle accidents as a cause of death. Typically more than 37,000 people die every year in the USA due to this type of drug misuse or overdose. It does not have to be that way. This study, the third in the series by Kenneth Cavenaugh and Michael Dillbeck shows how, from one central point, society can reverse the burgeoning crisis in health care, due to prescription drug-misuse.

As we have seen in summary 47, the USA enjoyed a prolonged period of Super Radiance between 2007 and 2010. Apart from crime, the researchers decided to look at other areas of society that might be benefiting from the improved social coherence and found that the upward trend in drug-related deaths was reversed with a substantial 30.4% reduction in drug-related fatalities. During the same period, the rate of infant mortalities declined by 12.5%.

As a result of this sudden trend reversal the researchers reckoned that there were 26,425 less drug-related fatalities and 992 less infant deaths.

Methodology

The researchers arrived at their conclusions by first calculating a baseline trend for monthly fatality rates during 2002–2006, for both categories. They then used a technique known as time series intervention analysis to compare this baseline with the subsequent trend experienced when the USA was benefiting from the Super Radiance effect (2007 – 2010 intervention period). What they found was that a rapidly rising trend in the drug-related fatality rate (see graph 49.1) during the baseline period leveled out and slowed significantly when the Super Radiance effect commenced during January 2007 (vertical dashed line). This flatter trend continued from 2007 through 2010. The irregular ups and downs of the fatality rate shown in the graph are largely due to seasonal fluctuations around the trend.

The probability that the reduced trend in rates of drug-related fatalities could simply be due to chance was reported to be 3.1 in 10 billion.

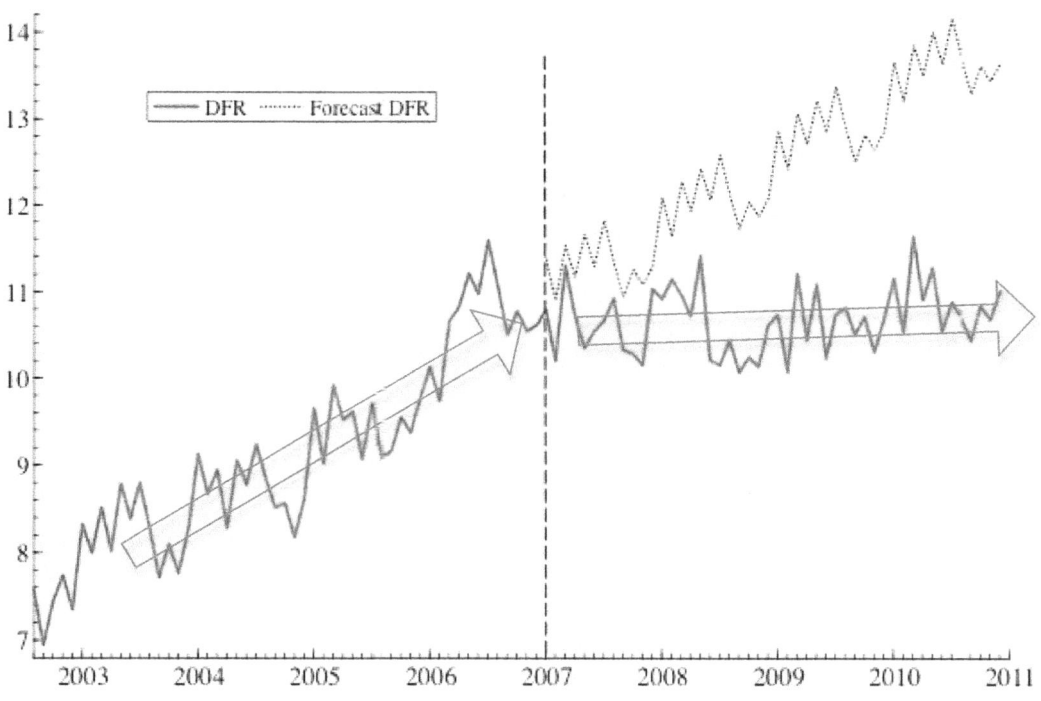

Graph 49.1 Drug-related fatality rate 2002-2010.
The graph depicts the monthly drug-related fatality rate (DFR) for 2002-2006 baseline and 2007-2010 intervention periods (solid line) with DFR forecast (dotted line) based on the baseline trend. Fluctuations around the trend are largely due to seasonal variation. Super Radiance commences 2007 depicted by vertical dotted line.

Yet again we see that intervention from the silent realm of pure consciousness has a spontaneous but profound impact on social trends and everyday living across a whole country, a country even the size of the USA.

In his own words, lead author, Professor Michael Dillbeck explains that "The practice of the Transcendental Meditation technique is said to enable individuals to effortlessly enjoy a state of restful alertness, increased brain integration, reduced individual stress, and enlivenment of one's inner potential. These benefits are the natural by-product of the experience during Transcendental Meditation practice of a silent, wakeful state of the mind known as 'pure consciousness'."

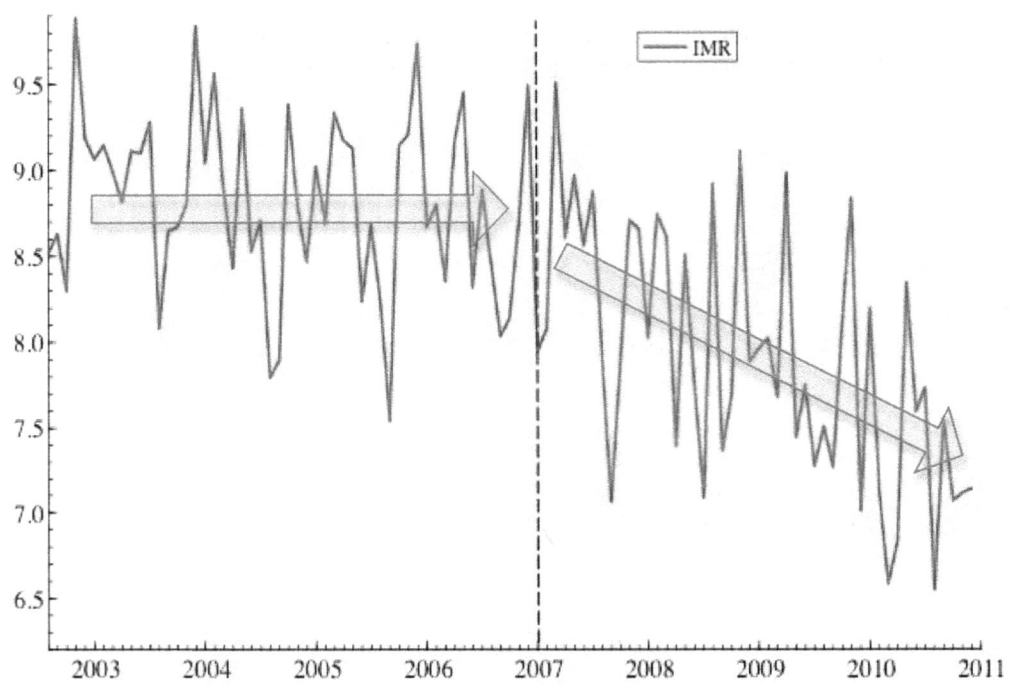

Graph 49.2 Infant mortality rate 2002-2010
The graph depicts the monthly infant mortality rate (IMR) (solid line) for 2002-2006 baseline and 2007-2010 intervention periods. Fluctuations around the trend are largely due to monthly seasonal variation. Super Radiance commences 2007 depicted by vertical dotted line.

Co-researcher Professor Kenneth Cavanaugh expands on this theme by saying that "The basis for the effect on society is that pure consciousness has a field-like character and is a universal field at the basis of everyone's thought and behavior. When the participants in a group equal or exceeding the square root of one percent of the entire population are experiencing pure consciousness during the group practice of the Transcendental Meditation and TM-Sidhi program, the field of pure consciousness is enlivened in the entire population. This field effect positively influences the quality of consciousness in the individuals in society in much the same direction as that experienced by those individuals practicing the Transcendental Meditation technique."

Michael Dillbeck further explained, "This research tests the hypothesis that practice of the Transcendental Meditation and TM-Sidhi program by a group of sufficient size will result in reduced stress and increased alertness in the individuals in society, thus contributing to reduced trends of these two stress-related public health indicators. Chronic stress contributes to increased likelihood of illness as well as to the use and abuse of illicit and prescribed drugs. Stress can reduce the degree of conscious alertness and vigilance necessary to avoid drug misuse, especially highly potent and potentially addictive narcotic painkillers."

This same field effect was also found to work in the case of infant mortality rates (IMR). The two researchers observed a highly significant shift from a flat or slightly declining trend in IMR during the period 2002–2006 to a substantially faster declining trend in 2007–2010 (see graph 49.2).

The probability that the reduced trend in rates of infant mortality is due to chance was reported to be less than 2.1 in 100,000.

It is important to note that the reductions in both the trends occurred at the predicted time and in the predicted direction, based on the Super Radiance hypothesis. On the other hand neither reduction could be predicted from baseline trends or seasonal cycles. The researchers also ruled out other alternative explanations such as a reduction in unemployment and other national economic conditions. At the time there was no increase in the public and professional medical awareness of the hazards of opioid painkillers, and sales of such painkillers that may have attributed to a reversal of the drug misuse trend.

Dillbeck MC, Institute of Science, Technology and Public Policy at Maharishi University of Management; Cavanaugh KL Institute of Science, Technology and Public Policy at Maharishi University of Management; March 2017, The social science journal, *SAGE Open*.

The Super Radiance effect

Chapter 2: Laboratory research

Research Summary 50

Can time series analysis of serotonin turnover test the theory that consciousness is a field?

The study suggests that stress indicators in the physiology of non-meditating subjects located in the vicinity of a meditation programme are reduced. During the study, as the numbers of a meditating group increased, there was a correlation between a decrease in a nearby subject group's cortisol levels (a hormone associated with stress) and an increase in their serotonin levels (a hormone associated with mental well-being).

"We have hypothesized that group practice of the TM-Sidhi program can affect society, and this study helps to understand the effect," Dr. Walton, one of the researchers conducting the study, is quoted as saying. "Group practice actually reduces the effects of stress, in those in the vicinity, in a manner similar to the reduction within the individual meditator when he practices the Transcendental Meditation programme."

Pugh ND, Walton KG, Cavanaugh KL, *Society for Neuroscience Abstracts* 14: 372, 1988.

Research Summary 51

Inter-subject EEG coherence: Is consciousness a field?

This fascinating study was intended to demonstrate that an individual's coherent brain waves influence other people at a distant and without any other physical interaction taking place. The theory is that consciousness is an underlying unbounded field that connects us all. If this hypothesis were true, then we would expect changes in individual consciousness to also affect the overall field. Positive findings from this study are important as it is this 'at a distance' or 'field' effect that enables Super Radiance to have its remarkable broadcast effect on society.

Super Radiance is achieved when only 1% of a given population practise Transcendental Meditation or the square root of 1% of a population practise the TM-Sidhi programme together in a group. When these numbers of meditators are established they not only create brainwave coherence for themselves but also create coherence in the collective consciousness of the whole population.

This coherence results in an immediate and significant drop in a range of negative and incoherent behaviour such as social disorder, warfare, crime, accidents and so on. At the same time there is a commensurate rise in more positive activity such as business start-ups, increased employment etc.

Researchers have observed that EEG is sensitive to changes in individual consciousness (EEG stands for electroencephalogram. Essentially an EEG is a recording of the 'brainwaves' or the electrical activity of the brain.). So, in this study, EEG readings were used to test the theory that, if consciousness were an unbounded field, then matching or similar fluctuations in this field would be detected by EEG readings among different individuals.

The speculation was that subjects under test might show synchronised rises and falls in EEGs in the same way as corks rise and fall together on the same wave.

The researchers carried out their experiment in 1979, during the Amherst study when 2,500 TM-Sidhas meditated together in one group (See research summary 9). The experiment was designed to see if individuals 1,170 miles away would register changes in their EEG readings at the same time the 2,500 TM-Sidhas were meditating.

Inter-subject EEG coherence was measured between three healthy individuals during six experimental periods. These experimental periods occurred during the exact time when the group in Amherst were carrying out the advanced TM-Sidhi programme of meditation. In addition, the researchers carried out the same measurements during six-control periods when the 2,500 group was not meditating. This was a blind study in that the subjects were unaware of the timing of the Amherst group's activities.

As predicted there was a significant increase in the level of inter-subject EEG coherence during the experimental periods in comparison with the control periods. In other words, the subjects' brainwave coherence was seen to increase considerably more on experimental days compared to control days. ($p = 0.02$)

Orme Johnson DW, Dillbeck MC, Wallace RK, 1982; *International Journal of Neuroscience 16: 203 – 209*

Collected papers v.3.222

Research Summary 52

Field model of consciousness: EEG coherence changes as indicators of field effects

Research abstract.

In this experiment the researchers looked at changes in EEG coherence patterns in different subjects to test the theory that there is a common field of "pure consciousness" that links all individuals. The logic being that if there is a common field, as predicted by quantum physics, then humans must also be part of that field and if humans are conscious, then as they are part of that field, the field must also be conscious.

In ten trials, EEG was concurrently measured from pairs of subjects, one practicing Transcendental Meditation (TM) and the TM-Sidhi technique of "Yogic Flying" (YFg) said to enliven the proposed field of consciousness. The other subjects performed a computer task.

Box-Jenkins ARIMA transfer function analysis indicated that coherence changes in the YF's 5.7-8.5 Hz band, the band sensitive to TM and YFg, consistently led to coherence changes in the other subject's 4.7-42.7 Hz band. In addition, a clear relationship was seen among subjective reports, coherence patterns, and strength of intervention effects. It was concluded that these data support a field model of consciousness. Alternate explanations are explored within the study and excluded.

Travis FT, DW Orme-Johnson DW; International Journal of Neuroscience 1989 December; 49(3-4)203-11.

Research Summary 53

Effect of group practice of the Transcendental Meditation program on biochemical indicators of stress in non-meditators: A prospective time series study – Research abstract

This study investigates a proposed psycho-neuroendocrine mechanism that may help to explain, at least in part, the observed reductions of behavioural indicators of social stress reported in other studies on the group practice of the TM and TM-Sidhi programme.

Dynamic regression analysis of time series observations over the experimental period (77 days) found that the daily change in the size of a TM group was a significant predictor of immediate subsequent mean (natural log) overnight excretion rates of

a) Cortisol and the main metabolite of serotonin (5-HIAA) and

b) The ratio of rates for 5-HIAA and cortisol.

An increase in the day to day size of the group for the afternoon session was a significant predictor of reduced cortisol excretion later that night in a group of 6 non-practitioners living and working up to 20 miles from the group ($p=.004$)

An increase in the daily change of group size also was a significant predictor of increases in both the excretion rate of 5-HIAA ($p=.03$) and the ratio of excretion rates of 5-HIAA to cortisol ($p<.0001$)

Walton KG, Cavanaugh KL, and Pugh ND; Journal of Social Behavior and Personality 2005;17(1):339-376.

The Super Radiance effect

Chapter 3: Is the research reliable?

"There is more evidence that the group practice of Transcendental Meditation can turn off war like a light switch than there is that aspirin reduces headache pain" John Hegelin

It is so easy to be sceptical about something new and extraordinary.

This is particularly so for something as extraordinary as the broadcast effect of Transcendental Meditation (TM) and the TM-Sidhi programme on social behaviour. For this reason, as the studies on the Super Radiance effect have accumulated, the researchers have become more and more rigorous in developing and organising their research protocols. The result of this rigorous attention to detail is that there is now a body of academic literature unique in the social sciences field for its clarity and unequivocal conclusions.

As John Hegelin, a leading quantum physicist and distinguished authority on the Super Radiance effect, says, "There is more evidence that the group practice of Transcendental Meditation can turn off war like a light switch than there is that aspirin reduces headache pain."

The vision of consistency

A large part of the success of the research into TM derives from the systematic way in which it is taught and practiced. As mentioned in the introduction, almost from the start of his life long mission to bring the benefits of Transcendental Meditation to the Western World, Maharishi realised the need for rigorous independent research to validate the claimed benefits of daily deep meditation.

Maharishi's vision was to use the searchlight of scientific enquiry and analysis to penetrate the fog of ignorance that pervades the West about the human mind and consciousness. To enable this scientific approach, ever since the 1960s Maharishi set about establishing meticulous standards of systematic teaching. Maharishi taught all the thousands of TM teachers around the world to teach their students in exactly the same way following a well-established seven-step procedure.

This systemisation has been invaluable for research purposes. The consistency of approach adopted by all accredited TM teachers ensure that, whenever scientists have to work with large groups of meditators, they can be completely confident of the consistent practice and consistent benefits being derived from the practice. The systematic nature of both the teaching and the benefits experienced have allowed for a high degree of replication in research activity with stunningly consistent results.

The six features that underpin the reliability of Super Radiance research

It is this consistency that provides such a strong foundation for research study into the Super Radiance effect. The reliability of teaching and consistency of results enable the research to benefit from six features. Together these six features produce a degree of credibility to the research findings almost unique in the social sciences field:

1. Repeated findings show a strong correlation
2. Publically available standardised evidence gives independent unarguable validation
3. Lead-lag analysis confirms the before, during and after effect
4. The unique precision in timing and numbers for many of the projects removes alternative explanations
5. Time series analysis creates a reliable gauge for comparison
6. Peer reviewed and published work show the methods are backed up by independent scientists

1. Repeated findings on peace projects

Peace creating groups of TM-Sidhas have been set-up on innumerable occasions over thirty-five years in about twenty-one countries. All of these groups have achieved what are now familiar results to both outside observers and the participants. The fifty one actual studies that have arisen from these many events provide a thoroughness of field-testing that is rare if not unique in the social sciences.

A number of studies are multiple studies within themselves with several groups of TM-Sidhas or several different communities of meditators being monitored.

Not least of which are the early studies carried out in the 1970s firstly on the 1% effect in eleven different US towns (summary 1), then ten or so suburbs in Cleveland (summary 2), then a further 48 towns across the USA (summary 4) and so on. The repetition of studies all yielding pretty much unfailing results demonstrate a strong correlation between the TM peace-creating activity and reductions in international hostility, war deaths, terrorist activity, violent crime and so on. This repetition reduces the probability that the results are achieved by random chance to effectively zero.

2. Publically available standardised evidence

One of the advantages that the TM peace researchers have is that they do not have to find or construct their own means to measure the results. The studies draw on publically available statistics to back up the research.

Developed nations, where many of the peace projects took place, all have various government departments and agencies collecting and collating data on factors ranging from fatal car accidents, homicides, suicides, terrorist activity, other violent crime as well as a range of economic statistics.

Even in chaotic war zones there are international agencies monitoring and publishing statistics on war deaths. Inter government activity and international relations are closely monitored by a number of different research organisations and think tanks that publish their results.

The public and independent nature of the statistics provides the opportunity for other researchers to check and even replicate a study and this provides a strong precaution against scientific bias or incompetence.

3. Lead-lag analysis

The precision of both the results gained and the timing of peace group activity mean that lead-lag analysis can be used to determine the causal factor. In other words, researchers can easily observe which moves first. Is it the initiation of the peace group or the initiation of the social change?

The lead-lag evidence indicates that the initiation of the peace group is the causal factor every time and this has been a winning argument in achieving publication of important studies. One excellent example that demonstrates the cause and effect factor is the Lebanon study, where war deaths fluctuated on a daily basis, over several weeks, in line with how many TM-Sidhas were attending the Super Radiance group (summary 19).

4. Precision in timing and numbers removes alternative explanations

All published studies involve careful research into the possibility that the social changes have not been caused by alternative factors.

So, studies look at various possible alternative factors such as police procedures, weather changes, seasonal differences, government initiatives and so on. The precision in the timing of both the start and finish of TM based peace projects helps rule out other possibilities as being alternative causal factors. Particularly good examples of this factor occur with the Washington study (summary 41) and the Rhode Island study (summary 7).

5. Time Series Analysis (TSA)

In a number of the studies you will see that the researchers have used time series analysis. This is especially the case in the published peace research studies.

TSA is a mathematical tool that helps clarify the confusing complexity of social interaction. TSA creates a statistical model that enables a reasonable prediction to be made as to what is likely to be happening in any given social situation. This prediction is carried out by factoring in known data on social, seasonal, weather and economic trends. If, when a Super Radiance intervention takes place, there is a sudden and dramatic change that contradicts the TSA prediction then it helps reinforce the argument that there is a new causal factor in play.

This tool was useful for the first global peace project that assessed the impact of a global coherence group on a wide range of QOL factors across the world.

6. Peer reviewed and published peace research projects

As a result of the five factors above, thirty-two research studies on TM based peace projects have now been published in peer reviewed scientific journals or have been presented to academic conferences.

To be published in academic journals or to be submitted to a conference debate means that the research has been read, analysed and accepted by panels of distinguished and independent experts in the relevant field of academic work. In other words, having a paper accepted for publication demonstrates that the research is judged by academic peers to be of sufficient professional quality to be worthy of attention by a wider community of academic experts.

What the scientists say

"I think the claim can be plausibly made that the potential impact of this research exceeds that of any other ongoing social or psychological research program. It has survived a broader array of statistical tests than most research in the field of conflict resolution. This work and the theory that informs it deserve the most serious consideration by academics and policy makers alike." Dr David Edwards Ph.D., Professor of Government, University of Texas at Austin

"Although I myself have not been directly involved in this research, from my perspective of almost 40 years of study of foreign policy, arms control, and theories of social change, I can say that this is extremely significant research. I have participated in urging members of Congress and other government leaders to try it. The cost of implementing a permanent coherence creating group in the world is less than a single B2 bomber." Dr. David Edwards.

"The hypothesis definitely raised some eyebrows among our reviewers. But the statistical work is sound. The numbers are there. When you can statistically control for as many variables as these studies do, it makes the results much more convincing. This evidence indicates that we now have a new technology

to generate peace in the world." Raymond Russ, editor of the Journal of Mind and Behaviour.

"I was initially sceptical, but having studied the research completed to date, I have concluded that these studies on the Maharishi Effect have subjected theory to proper empirical tests. They have shown sound results which demand serious interest." Ken Pease, Professor of Criminology at the University of Huddersfield, Chairman of the Belfast-based Centre for the Independent Research and Analysis of Crime, and Home Office adviser.

"In the studies that I have examined on the impact of the Maharishi Effect on conflict, I can find no methodological flaws, and the findings have been consistent across a large number of replications in many different geographical and conflictual situations. As unlikely as the premise may sound I think we have to take these studies seriously." Ted Robert Gurr PhD, Professor of Government and Politics, University of Maryland.

"I want to express my support for this research. What we are really looking at here, I think, is a new paradigm of viewing crime and violence; and the new paradigm says, look to the individual acting in concert with other individuals to reduce crime constructively.... Having worked extensively on social problems in the District of Columbia for some 24 years at the University of the District of Columbia ... I'd like to encourage taking this new idea very seriously ... I would like to recommend that this new model that is being offered and advanced here, after a number of exhaustive and very carefully controlled studies, be considered, and that we think about ways that it might be implemented in the inner city with youth and community people who live here." Anne Hughes, PhD, Professor of Sociology and Government, University of the District of Columbia.

"These studies provide a great hope for humanity, a breath of fresh air. We have repeatedly seen that international law, treaties, and even the United Nations cannot prevent war, or even contain it within certain rules such as the Geneva Convention. Can we afford to overlook this research? It breaks my heart that so many people are being killed every day, including many fine young Americans, when we haven't even tried this first." Professor Ved

Nanda, Director of International Legal Studies at the University of Denver College of Law.

The Super Radiance effect

Chapter 4: Published Super Radiance research

The body of research papers published in peer-reviewed journals or presented to academic conferences is growing and currently amounts to thirty-two studies as at 2017.

Collectively these studies present overwhelming proof of the power of the Super Radiance effect to impact open warfare, terrorism, political violence, social cohesiveness and economic prosperity.

Journal, conference etc	Research Title	Authors
Chapter 1		
SAGE Open April-June 2016: 1–16 The Author(s) 2016 DOI: 10.1177/2158244016637891 sgo.sagepub.com	Summary 49: Societal Violence and Collective Consciousness: Reduction of U.S. Homicide and Urban Violent Crime Rates	Dillbeck MC, Cavanaugh KL
Journal of Consciousness Studies, February 2017	Summary 48: The Contribution of Proposed Field Effects of Consciousness to the Prevention of US Accidental Fatalities: Theory and Empirical Tests	Dillbeck MC, Cavanaugh KL
The Social Science Journal, *SAGE Open* March 2017	Summary 47: Group practice of the Transcendental Meditation and TM-Sidhi program and reductions in infant mortality and drug-related death: A quasi-experimental analysis	Dillbeck MC, Cavanaugh KL
Journal of Social Behavior and	Summary 46: Alleviating political violence through	Davies JL, Alexander CN.

Journal, conference etc	Research Title	Authors
Personality, 2005, 285-338.	reducing collective tension: Impact assessment analyses of the Lebanon war	
Journal of Offender Rehabilitation 36 (1-4): 283-302, 2003.	Summary 45: Preventing terrorism and international conflict: Effects of large assemblies of participants in the Transcendental Meditation and TM-Sidhi programs.	Orme-Johnson DW, Dillbeck MC, Alexander CN.
Technology and Public Policy Technical Report 94:1, 1994. Social Indicators Research (47: 153201, 1999)	Summary 41: Results of the national demonstration project to reduce violent crime and improve governmental effectiveness in Washington, D.C.	Hagelin JS; Orme-Johnson DW; Rainforth M; Cavanaugh K; and Alexander CN Institute of Science.
Psychology, Crime and Law 1995 Also presented to the Annual Conference of the British Psychological Society on Criminal and Legal Psychology, 1-3 March, 1993, Harrogate, England.	Summary 40: The Maharishi Effect (Super Radiance effect): A model for social improvement: Time series analysis of a phase transition to reduce crime in Merseyside metropolitan area	Hatchard GD; Deans AJ; Cavanaugh KL; and Orme-Johnson DW.
Dissertation Abstracts International 51(12), 1991.	Summary 39: Improved quality of life in Iowa through the Maharishi Effect.	Reeks DL, Abstract of Doctoral Dissertation, Maharishi University of Management, U.S.A.
Journal of Conflict Resolution 34(2): 756-768, 1990.	Summary 38: The effects of the Maharishi Technology of the Unified Field: Reply to a methodological critique.	Orme-Johnson DW; Alexander CN; and Davies JL.
In Proceedings of the	Summary 37: The	Gelderloos P; Cavanaugh KL; and Davies JL

Journal, conference etc	Research Title	Authors
American Statistical Association, Social Statistics Section, Alexandria, VA 1990	dynamics of US-Soviet relations, 1979-1986: Effects of reducing social stress through the Transcendental Meditation and TM-Sidhi program.	
Psychological Reports 1995	Summary 36: Time series analysis of improved quality of life in Canada: Social change, collective consciousness, and the TM-Sidhi program.	Assimakis PD, and Dillbeck MC
Paper presented at the Annual Conference of the American Political Science Association, Atlanta, Georgia, USA, August 1989.	Summary 35: Time series impact assessment analysis of reduced international conflict and terrorism: Effects of large assemblies of participants in the Transcendental Meditation and TM-Sidhi program.	Orme-Johnson DW; Dillbeck MC; Alexander CN; Chandler HM; and Cranson RW;
Paper presented at the 85th Annual Meeting of the American Political Science Association, September 1989. (Refer also to Dissertation Abstracts International 49(8): 2381A, 1988.)	Summary 34: Alleviating political violence through enhancing coherence in collective consciousness: impact assessment analysis of the Lebanon war.	Davies JL, and Alexander CN
Social Science Perspectives Journal 2(4): 80-94, 1988.	Summary 33: Creating world peace through the collective practice of the Maharishi Technology of the Unified Field: improved U.S.-Soviet relations.	Gelderloos P; Frid MJ; Goddard PH; Xue X; and Löliger SA
Dissertation Abstracts International 50(5) Sec. B, p. 2203, November 1989.	Summary 32: Change in the quality of life in Canada: intervention studies of the effect of the	Assimakis PD;

Journal, conference etc	Research Title	Authors
	Transcendental Meditation and TM-Sidhi program.	
Social Indicators Research 22: 399-418, 1990	Summary 31: Test of a field theory of consciousness and social change: time series analysis of participation in the TM-Sidhi Programme and reduction of violent deaths in the USA.	Dillbeck MC
Revised paper presented at the Annual Meeting of the Midwest Management Society, Chicago, Illinois, March 1989, Also published in R.G. Greenwood (ed.), Proceedings of the Midwest Management Society (Chicago, Illinois: Midwest Management Society): 183-190, 1989.	Summary 30: Consciousness and the quality of economic life: empirical research on the macroeconomic effects of the collective practice of Maharishi's Transcendental Meditation and TM-Sidhi program.	Cavanaugh KL; King KD; and Titus BD
Paper presented at the Annual Meeting of the American Statistical Association, Washington, D.C., August 6-10, 1989. An abridged version of this paper appears in Proceedings of the American Statistical Association, Business and Economics Statistics Section (Alexandria, Virginia: American Statistical Association): 565-570, 1989.	Summary 29: A multiple-input transfer function model of Okun's misery index: an empirical test of the Maharishi Effect.	Cavanaugh KL; King KD; and Ertuna C,
Paper presented at the Annual Meeting of the American Statistical Association, New	Summary 28: Simultaneous transfer function analysis of Okun's	Cavanaugh KL; and King KD;

Journal, conference etc	Research Title	Authors
Orleans, Louisiana, August 22-25, 1988. An abridged version of this paper appeared in Proceedings of the American Statistical Association, Business and Economics Statistics Section: 491-496, 1988.	misery index: improvements in the economic quality of life through Maharishi's Vedic Science and technology of consciousness.	
Revised and updated version of a paper presented at the Annual Meeting of the American Statistical Association, San Francisco, California, August 17-20, 1987, Also proceedings of the American Statistical Association, Business and Economics Statistics Section (Alexandria, Virginia: American Statistical Association): 799-804, 1987.	Summary 27: Time series analysis of U.S. and Canadian inflation and unemployment: a test of a field-theoretic hypothesis.	Cavanaugh KL;
The Journal of Mind and Behavior 9(4): 457-486 1988.	Summary 26: Test of a field model of consciousness and social change: the Transcendental Meditation and TM-Sidhi Programme and decreased urban crime.	Dillbeck MC; Banus CB; Polanzi C; and Landrith III GS;
The Journal of Mind and Behavior 8(1): 67-104, 1987	Summary 25: Consciousness as a field: the Transcendental Meditation and TM-Sidhi Programme and changes in social indicators.	Dillbeck MC Cavanaugh KL Glenn T Orme-Johnson DW; and Mittlefehldt V;

Journal, conference etc	Research Title	Authors
Dissertation Abstracts International 45(10) 3206B, 1984	Summary 24: A comparative study of dimensions of healthy functioning between families practising the TM programme for five years or for less than a year.	Chen ME
Journal of Conflict Resolution, 32(4): 776-812, 1988; Journal of Conflict Resolution (34: 756768, 1990)	Summary 19: International peace project in the Middle East: The effect of the Maharishi Technology of the Unified Field.	Orme-Johnson DW; Alexander CN; Davies JL; Chandler HM; and Larimore WE;
Social Science Perspectives Journal, 2(4), 127-146, 1988.	Summary 18: The long terms effects of the Maharishi Technology of the Unified Field on the US Quality of Life (1960-1984)	Orme-Johnson DW; and Gelderloos P; and Dillbeck MC;
The Journal of Mind and Behavior 8: 67-103, 1987.	Summary 7: Consciousness as a field: The Transcendental Meditation and TM-Sidhi programme and changes in social indicators, (Rhode Island Study)	Dillbeck MC; Foss APO; and Zimmermann W J
Journal of Crime and Justice 4: 25-45, 1981.	Summary 4: The Transcendental Meditation Programme and crime rate change in a sample of forty-eight cities.	Dillbeck MC; Landrith III GS; and Orme-Johnson DW;

Chapter 2

Journal of Social Behavior and Personality 2005;17(1):339-376.	Summary 53: Effect of group practice of the Transcendental Meditation program on biochemical indicators of stress in non-meditators: A prospective time series study.	Walton KG, Cavanaugh KL, and Pugh ND.

Journal, conference etc	Research Title	Authors
International Journal of Neuroscience 1989; 49:203-211.	Summary 52: Field model of consciousness: EEG coherence changes as indicators of field effects.	Travis FT, DW Orme-Johnson DW;
International Journal of Neuroscience 16: 1982, pp 203 - 209	Summary 51: Inter-subject EEG coherence: Is consciousness a field?	Orme Johnson DW, Dillbeck MC, Wallace RK,
Society for Neuroscience Abstracts 14: 372, 1988.	Summary 50: Can time series analysis of serotonin turnover test the theory that consciousness is a field?	Pugh ND, Walton KG. Cavanaugh KL,

The Super Radiance effect

Chapter 5: What is Transcendental Meditation?

The background to Transcendental Meditation

Maharishi's Vedic Science contends that all the fragmented values of matter and energy and every aspect of nature and natural law is held within and is an integral part of an unmanifest **unified field** of pure intelligence. These complex and multifaceted values of matter and energy include of course the human nervous system, human society and the material world that supports us.

As the fundamental building block of the entire universe, the unified field is seen to have a number of innate properties including infinite correlation, infinite organising power, infinite interconnectivity, infinite dynamism, immortality, infinite creativity, and self-referral functioning. Essentially, this last phrase means that this unified field of pure intelligence is aware of itself.

This key property of self-awareness gives rise to the understanding that the unified field is also a field of pure consciousness. In other words pure consciousness is seen to be, at its deepest level, the core essence of both solid matter and energy as well as any other non-material aspects of creation.

Being part of the unified field, the human nervous system is able to experience pure consciousness. This is despite consciousness being beyond the intellect and common senses and even beyond time and space. Our direct experience of this unified field of existence occurs in what is termed as transcendental consciousness. Transcendental consciousness is described by Maharishi Vedic science as the fourth state of consciousness, the first three being waking, dreaming and sleeping.

The most easy and natural way for you to regularly attain and experience transcendental consciousness is through the practice of Transcendental Meditation (TM) a mental practice carried out in silence whilst sitting comfortably with your eyes shut.

When you practice the TM technique you naturally turn your attention inwards towards the subtler levels of thought until your mind transcends the experience of even the subtlest state of thinking and arrives at the source of thought itself – the infinitely dynamic, unmanifest, all powerful, eternal, self-referral field of pure consciousness, the unified field of pure intelligence. The experience of pure consciousness is one of blissful total rest, deep inner silence and yet at the same time full alertness.

How TM is taught

The practice of TM is taught over four consecutive days in a sequence of seven steps. The teaching methodology is always the same and can only be delivered by an accredited professional teacher of TM. It is important to note that to become a TM teacher first and foremost you have to be an experienced meditator and then undertake a rigorous teacher training. Teacher training extends over a minimum of three years before the candidates are accomplished enough to pass on this practical knowledge to others in a systematic and reliable way.

Maharishi has trained tens of thousands of teachers around the world. As a result over six million people have taken up this simple, natural and easy practice. Almost universally, people who have learned TM and practice regularly, report a life of greater creativity, higher productivity, improved health, greater happiness, more positive behaviour, and deeper and more rewarding relationships.

This multiplicity of benefits derives from the principle that the two basic steps of progress are rest and activity. The human physiology cannot go on and on without resting to refresh, replenish nourish and repair.

An alert and healthy mind and its physical counterpart the brain are the key to a balanced healthy life, daily successful problem solving, harmonious relationship building, necessary learning and fulfilment. Without restoring strength and vigour to our brain physiologies through the regular deep rest of Transcendental Meditation we are prone to accumulate stress, make mistakes, develop ill-health and fall prey to negative emotions and destructive activity.

Is Transcendental Meditation a religion?

TM is sometimes confused with religion or religious activity. Understandably, this confusion arises for two reasons.

Firstly, we see confusion arise because the regular experience of transcendental consciousness expands the conscious mind, into what are commonly considered the realms of the unconscious mind. This expansion of the mind invokes a more acute awareness of and reverence for nature and the deeper values of life. People who practice TM increasingly experience the oneness of creation in their everyday life and their everyday social interactions. For those who are already religious the experience of this oneness gives both a deeper and wider appreciation of the depth of their religion and incidentally of other religions as well. As such, understanding and tolerance of other faiths is cultivated naturally and spontaneously.

Although TM itself does not require any religious belief and does not involve any form of religious worship or devotion, the number of religious followers who practice TM is wide and varied. As examples a Roman Catholic priest, Father Mejia has been a driving force behind the Super Radiance groups in Columbia. Buddhist monks in Cambodia practice TM. Various orders of Christian monks have adopted TM as part of their monastic regime. Israeli Jews in Jerusalem formed the basis for a TM-Sidha group there. Mayan tribes people in Mexico are recent enthusiastic supporters of the practice and many traditional Brahmin families in India are adopting TM as a sound basis for their daily routine of meditation.

The second reason that TM is confused with religion is that TM is sometimes seen as derivative of Hinduism. It is nearer the truth that TM and Hinduism are derived from the same holy tradition of Vedic Seers and saints. The ancient Vedic philosophy of India is countless generations old and predates the Hindu faith by thousands of years. Veda means knowledge of the fundamental laws of nature and as such is more akin to a science or philosophy rather than a belief or mode of worship.

The Super Radiance effect

Chapter 6: Contrast in meditation techniques

The difference between TM and other forms of meditation

If you wish to learn Transcendental Meditation it is important to understand that it differs from other forms of meditation.

In essence all the innumerable other types of meditation that you find in different cultures fall into two broad categories. They are either a form of contemplation or concentration.

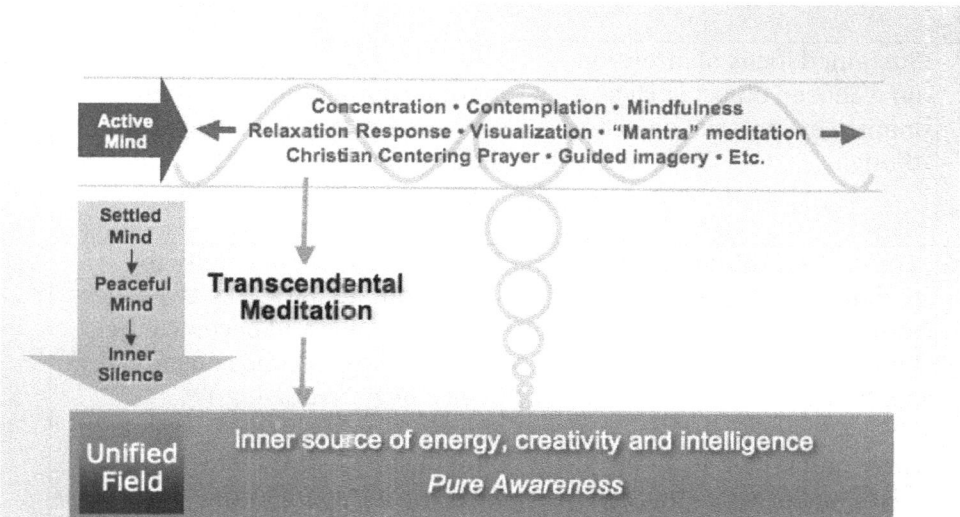

Whatever other merit these types of meditations provide, they suffer from the singular disadvantage that both types are apt to keep the mind functioning at the more superficial levels of experience. Contemplation and concentration tend to maintain the mind on the level of intellect and emotion. This constraint prevents the attention from transcending thought to arrive at the source of thought itself – to arrive at the realm of pure consciousness.

Only by slipping naturally and easily into transcendental consciousness do we experience the bliss of the infinite, self-referral realm of pure consciousness. And only when we have this regular experience does the mind and body accrue the sort of comprehensive benefits that are associated with Transcendental Meditation.

The table below outlines some of the contrast between Transcendental Meditation and the other forms of meditation such as mindfulness and other concentration techniques.

Technique	Mindfulness meditations/ Concentration techniques	Transcendental Meditation (TM)
Procedure	Sustained focus of attention on a chosen object such as a mantra or material object or thought.	The TM technique facilitates the natural inclination of the mind to settle down to quieter levels of thought until thought is spontaneously transcended.
Awareness	The various mindfulness techniques tend to keep the mind active, focused and localized on the object of meditation. After months or years of sustained practice this can result in the growing ability to experience periods of settled awareness with no explicit focus.	TM enables mental activity to subside immediately, as awareness itself broadens and becomes the primary state of consciousness. Even a beginner, using TM's effortless procedure, experiences a unique state of unbounded awareness known as the transcendental state of consciousness. It is this unique state of consciousness that gives the name to the Transcendental Meditation technique.
EEG signature	High frequency frontal gamma EEG readings, indicate controlled focus[2].	Widespread alpha coherence indicates relaxation and settled awareness[1].
Coherence	No increase in brainwave coherence observed.	Overall increase in brainwave coherence enabling enhanced interaction between different brain areas. Thalamus activity that processes sensory information

Technique	Mindfulness meditations/ Concentration techniques	Transcendental Meditation (TM)
		decreases, while frontal areas of the brain, associated with higher executive functions and moral reasoning, become more active.
Relaxation	No consistent evidence of deep relaxation being achieved other than would be expected from sitting quietly with the eyes closed for long periods.	Shown by research to provide physiological rest deeper than ordinary relaxation[3] and deeper than sleep, although, uniquely the meditator is still alert. The state is sometimes termed as restful alertness.
Anxiety	Techniques have been shown by research to moderately reduce anxiety[4].	TM is shown by research to significantly reduce anxiety[5].
Ease of use	It is accepted that mindfulness practices are relatively complex to master and are sometimes reported as tedious. Adherents often advise that success may take many years of perseverance. Observed benefits tend to have accrued to dedicated practitioners undertaking full-time residential courses that include intense and prolonged periods of meditation.	TM is renowned for being effortless to do, easy to learn and enjoyable to practice. Practitioners find they can quickly integrate TM's twice-daily twenty-minute sessions into everyday activity.

Even beginners tend to report benefits and fit the practice into a wide variety of lifestyles across all cultures and religions. |
| Learning | Most mindfulness practices take weeks or months of tuition with mastery alleged to take years. Most practitioners are reliant on ongoing input and guidance | TM is learned in one ninety-minute session with follow-up checking over three more sessions. These are run on consecutive days after the initial teaching. After then the practitioner is self-sufficient. |

Technique	Mindfulness meditations/ Concentration techniques	Transcendental Meditation (TM)
	from a teacher.	The ease of learning stems from the naturalness of the technique in that it enlivens the innate faculty of the mind to transcend thought and settle-down to a quiet state of settled alertness.
Enjoyment	Practitioners report varying degrees of enjoyment, monotony or tedium. Many become bored over time and as a result give up the practice.	The transcending experience is deeply satisfying. Many practitioners report a feeling of bliss and maintain a lifetime of practicing twice every day. Over time the bliss experienced during meditation permeates everyday activity outside of the meditation period.
Health benefits	Evidence of help with stress, memory, and verbal reasoning but mostly for practitioners who have undertaken lengthy training courses or have experienced extended residential retreats[6,7].	Practitioners experience health benefits early on after learning and these benefits improve and accumulate over time. Four decades of research studies, some 600 in number, show a range of health benefits. These include 87% reduction in cardiovascular disease and 55% in tumors[8], reversal of the ageing process[9], 50% reduction in personal health care costs[10], reduced PTSD[11], reduced drug and alcohol abuse[12] reduced blood pressure[13] etc.
Broadcast effect on society	No at-a-distance effect observed on non-meditators in the vicinity of meditators.	50 research studies testify to the broadcast effect of TM meditators on other people at a distance even across the globe. Unique research

Technique	Mindfulness meditations/ Concentration techniques	Transcendental Meditation (TM)
		into TM's social effect, especially the effect of group meditation has accumulated over twenty-years and documents drops in crime[14], violence[15], international hostility[16] terrorism[17] and even open warfare[18].

Research references

1. Consciousness and cognition, 8 302-318, 1999, Cognitive processing, 11, 1, 2010
2. Proceedings National Academy of Sciences, 101, 16369-73, 2004
3. American Psychologist [42] 879-81, 1987
4. Meditation programs for psychological stress and well-being. Comparative effectiveness
5. review 124; Agency for Healthcare Research and Quality, US Department of Health and Human Services; Goyal M, Singh Sonal et al; AHRQ Publication No. 13 (14)-EHC116-EF, January 2014.
6. Journal of clinical Psychology [45] 957-974, 1989
7. Jacobs TL et al, Health Psychology 2013 Oct; 32(10):1104-9. doi: 10.1037/a0031362. Epub 2013 Mar 25. Self-reported mindfulness and cortisol during a three month Shamatha meditation retreat.
8. Oman D et al; Meditation lowers stress and supports forgiveness among college students: a randomized controlled trial; Journal of American College of Health, 2008 Mar-Apr; 56(5): 569-78. doi: 10.3200/ JACH.56.5.569-578. Demonstrated improvements after 8 weeks of one 90-minute training session per week.
9. Medical care utilization and the Transcendental Meditation program, *Psychosomatic Medicine 1987, 49:493-507*. A retrospective study was published in *The American Journal of Managed Care Vol 3 No 1 January 1997*
10. The effects of the Transcendental Meditation and TM-Sidhi program on the ageing process; Wallace RK, Dillbeck M, Jacobe E, Harrington B; *International Journal of Neuroscience vol. 16, 1982, pp. 53 - 58*
11. The impact of Transcendental Meditation practice on Medical expenditure published in *Dissertation Abstracts International: Issue 12, Book A, Vol 53 - June 1993.*
12. Effects of Transcendental Meditation in Veterans of Operation Enduring Freedom and Operation Iraqi Freedom with Post traumatic Stress Disorder: A Pilot Study; Military Medicine, Volume 176, Number 6, June 2011; pp. 626-630(5)

13. Treating and preventing alcohol, nicotine, and drug abuse through Transcendental Meditation: A review and statistical meta-analysis, published in *Alcoholism Treatment Quarterly 11: 13-87, 1994.*
14. Blood pressure response to Transcendental Meditation: a meta-analysis; published by the *American Journal of Hypertension 2008 21:310-316*
15. Results of the national demonstration project to reduce violent crime and improve governmental effectiveness in Washington, D.C.; Hagelin JS; Orme-Johnson DW; Rainforth M; Cavanaugh K; and Alexander CN Institute of Science. Technology and Public Policy Technical Report 94:1, 1994; Social Indicators Research (47: 153-201, 1999)
16. Alleviating political violence through reducing collective tension: Impact assessment analyses of the Lebanon war; Davies JL, Alexander CN; Journal of Social Behavior and Personality, 2005, 285-338.
17. Creating world peace through the collective practice of the Maharishi Technology of the Unified Field: improved U.S.-Soviet relations; Gelderloos P; Frid MJ; Goddard PH; Xue X; and Löliger SA; Social Science Perspectives Journal 2(4): 80-94, 1988.
18. Preventing terrorism and international conflict: Effects of large assemblies of participants in the Transcendental Meditation and TM-Sidhi programs; Orme-Johnson DW, Dillbeck MC, Alexander CN; Journal of Offender Rehabilitation 36 (1-4): 283-302, 2003.
19. International peace project in the Middle East: The effect of the Maharishi Technology of the Unified Field; Orme-Johnson DW; Alexander CN; Davies JL; Chandler HM; and Larimore WE; Journal of Conflict Resolution (34: 756768, 1990)

"These days most people who come to us to learn TM have already tried one or two other techniques, such as mindfulness meditation" Ian Campbell accredited TM teacher in the UK.

The Super Radiance effect

The Super Radiance effect